KITCHEN
WISDOM

Pamela Cross

Camden House

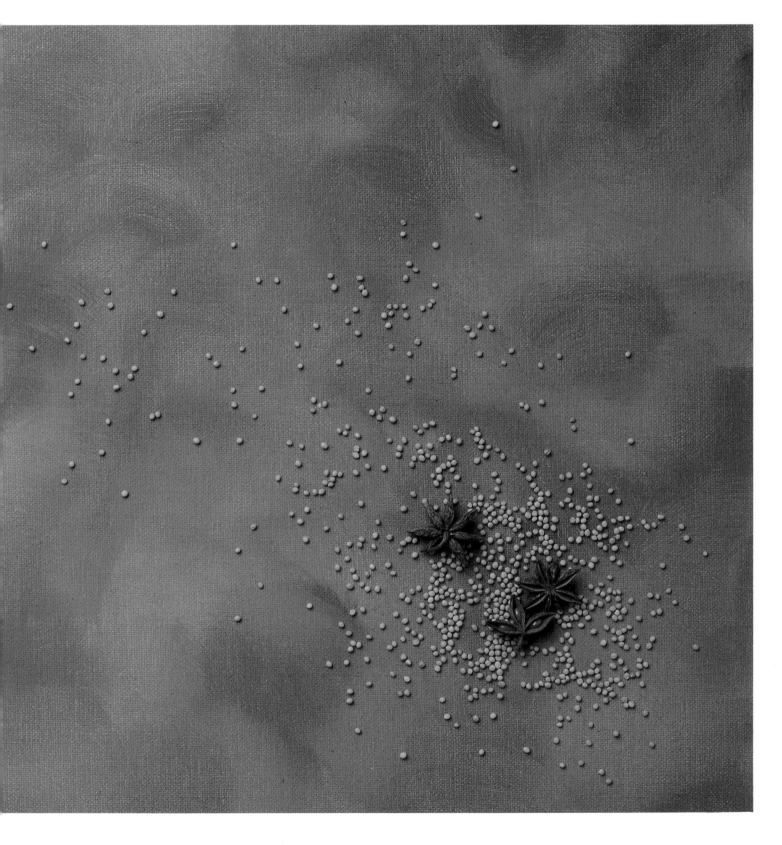

© Copyright 1991 by Camden House Publishing (a division of Telemedia Publishing
Inc.)

Canadian Cataloguing in Publication Data

Cross, Pamela
    Kitchen wisdom

Includes index.
ISBN 0-921820-37-2

1. Cookery, Canadian.   2. Cookery.   I. Title.

TX715.6.C76 1991   641.5   C91-094358-3

Trade distribution by
Firefly Books
250 Sparks Avenue
Willowdale, Ontario
Canada M2H 2S4

Printed and bound in Canada by
D.W. Friesen & Sons Ltd.
Altona, Manitoba, for
Camden House Publishing
(a division of Telemedia Publishing Inc.)
7 Queen Victoria Road
Camden East, Ontario
K0K 1J0

Design by
Linda J. Menyes

Cover photograph by
Ernie Sparks

Colour separations by
Hadwen Graphics
Ottawa, Ontario

Printed on acid-free paper

Acknowledgements

I would like to express my gratitude to former Camden House publisher Frank B. Edwards and editor Tracy C. Read for believing in this project, and to Laurel Aziz, who served a dual role as editor and food stylist, and assistant editor Mary Patton, both of whom spent hundreds of hours toiling over the manuscript. Thanks also to copy editors Laura Elston, Lois Casselman, Catherine DeLury, Charlotte DuChene, Christine Kulyk and Eileen Whitney for their painstaking efforts. A special thanks to art director Linda Menyes, typesetter Patricia Denard-Hinch, production manager Susan Dickinson and graphic designer Janice McLean. Finally, thanks to Jane Good, Steven Maynard and Jennifer Purvis for their help in the test kitchen.

CONTENTS

INTRODUCTION

Introduction

My mother was a remarkable 1950s' mother. She worked full-time in the home and divided her energies between housekeeping responsibilities and taxing her six children around to ballet and piano lessons, hockey games and skating competitions. Her mettle was further tested every night when she prepared a meal. She had trained as a nurse, and her professional conscience dictated fairly strict adherence to Canada's Food Guide, while financial constraints – my father was a junior university professor – restricted her to a limited budget. In addition, she faced the task of attempting to comply with the variety of individual likes and dislikes expressed by the offspring she found constantly underfoot. While we did not feast extravagantly, we did eat well.

As the eldest child in the family, I have vivid memories of mealtimes. The table was always neatly set, and despite my mother's valiant attempts to civilize us, our contained hysteria when we began to pass steaming dishes around the table would gradually build to an uncontrollable level and her pleas for us to take our time slipped by unheard and unheeded. Mealtime was loud and chaotic, with little limbs flailing across the table, and the food into which my mother had put so much effort would be consumed in minutes. But supper was also the focus for the family at the end of each day and the time when we recited the events of our active little lives to our father.

Young and energetic, my parents were generous with this time, and they were always willing to make room around the dinner table for any number of our friends. Since my mother did all the cooking, I can't say that I learned to cook under her guidance, but the experience of those years left a strong impression on my mind: I learned that food could bring people together and that both the preparation of a meal and the meal itself could be fun.

Today, I thrive on bringing a group of friends together almost every day at dinnertime. But while nothing gives me greater pleasure than spending all day in the kitchen and then presenting an impressive meal to a tableful of appreciative diners, my life style does not always allow me the luxury. I have found, however, that preparing a wholesome, simple meal – a tabouli salad and soup with whole-grain muffins and a fruit salad – can be as gratifying as assembling a multicourse dinner. And the pleasure that others derive from eating a meal I have prepared reflects the pleasure I take in creating it. I have also discovered that only a cook who is at ease in the kitchen can make his or her dinner guests feel comfortable.

Candlelight Dinners

I realize now that I took my mother's abilities for granted when I was growing up. Only after I was married at 19 and was confronted with the responsibility of feeding myself and my husband did I begin to appreciate the importance of basic cooking techniques and to realize the extent of my own inadequacies. Equipped with a copy of *The Penny-pincher's Guide to Cooking* (a wedding gift), four untried dessert recipes given to me by my grandmother and an electric frying pan, I set to work.

It is with a mixture of embarrassment and amusement that I think back to my early efforts in the kitchen. My previous cooking experience was restricted to rare excursions into the kitchen to make fudge, Rice Krispies squares and a sticky mess. While I cannot recall its euphemistic name, I remember distinctly the first recipe I prepared in my parents' kitchen: diced celery and green pepper suspended in rubbery lime gelatin topped with whipped cream – a finishing touch that always left a vague doubt in my mind as to whether my masterpiece was a salad or a dessert. Beyond toast, eggs, sandwiches, cookies and, for some inexplicable reason, sweet and sour chicken, my culinary repertoire when I set up my own home was extremely limited.

I will never forget my first solo trip to the grocery store after my marriage. Residual adolescent rebellion compelled me to purchase everything my mother had outlawed. Suddenly, I was that woman in the television advertisements for whom potato chips, cookies, soft drinks, Kraft Dinner, breaded fish sticks, Hamburger Helper and even a canned whole chicken were irresistibly tempting gourmet delights.

It was not long before our appetites reflected my culinary shortcomings. Rather than take on the task of learning to cook himself, my husband began suggesting with increasing frequency that we drop in on either of our nearby families for supper. Sensing failure, I began scouring homemakers' magazines, looking for suggestions that might transform me into a first-rate chef.

Never one to go halfway, I became a slave to the candlelight extravaganza. At home full-time to care for my newborn daughter, I would start to prepare some elaborate dinner for two: perhaps steak tartare, potatoes lyonnaise, green beans with almonds, glazed baby carrots, endive salad and chocolate mousse. These were not dishes I had ever eaten, let alone prepared, and I would set to work with only a glossy magazine photograph to remind me of my objective. Despite fastidious adherence to the instructions in each recipe, my efforts resulted in failure after spectacular failure: I could never get the timing right for finishing various dishes simultaneously; I was always having accidents – such as the time I set the kitchen curtains ablaze while making crêpes suzettes; I destroyed several cooking utensils; and once, I fused a cup of sugar to the bottom of an iron frying pan by heating it too quickly. I also wasted a lot of food,

Author Pamela Cross

including a bushel of apples that I did not peel or core before attempting to make into sauce. I lacked all of the most basic skills, and incentive and determination alone were not sufficient to make me a success.

Trial by Fire

In fact, I learned to cook only after a musician friend and I opened the Carden Street Café, a folk club that served ap-

ple cider, tea and baked goods. Soon after we began painting, renovating and furnishing the building, two things struck us: the first was that although we had only planned to be open in the evening, we were paying rent for 24 hours a day. Second, and perhaps more critical, a part of what we were paying for was a huge and reasonably well-equipped kitchen. I thought we should operate a restaurant. The idea captivated our imaginations, and we decided

to specialize in crêpes and become the only coffeehouse-crêperie in Guelph, Ontario.

A serious obstacle to realizing our dream was that neither of us knew how to make crêpes. For the entire week before the opening, I was up to my elbows in French-pancake batter. We experimented day and night with dozens of recipes, and we invented and tested every kind of filling imaginable. When we could not bear to eat another mouth-

Introduction

Stir-fry ingredients

cooking in the kitchen of the Carden Street Café than I have in any other period of my life. Experience taught me how to make soup stock; I discovered how a custard sets; I found out why mayonnaise curdles and how to make a mean pastry. Most importantly, I learned to be imaginative, to relax in the kitchen and to cook confidently without a recipe in front of me.

After a year of back-breaking work, I left Guelph and the café for Kingston, Ontario, where I began working as a part-time copy editor at *Harrowsmith* magazine. I was no longer cooking professionally, but I kept in practice by throwing elaborate dinner parties at home and catering for staff parties. When an editor was needed for the first volume of *The Harrowsmith Cookbook* — an anthology of recipes from the magazine's readers — the thought of once more cooking every day was so appealing that I was only too happy to volunteer.

While we had no idea of how our readers would respond to the invitation to "send us your favourite recipes," the privilege of testing the very best recipes from thousands of kitchens across North America was an opportunity of a lifetime. Nearly 10,000 recipes arrived in less than two months, and we spent hundreds of hours sorting, filing and cataloguing them. We weeded out duplicates and those that did not fit our criteria for food that was both attractive and delicious but without highly processed ingredients. We still had approximately 1,500 recipes to test by the time I began cooking. I cooked full-time in my home, and my family, friends and colleagues all indulged endlessly in the test recipes. While I still avoid baking bread and making gravy, those years of recipe testing turned me into a culinary adventurer — I somehow developed the kind of spirit crucial to a good cook. Although recklessness, which leads to the waste of good food, is unacceptable, a cook needs to feel a certain abandon to

ful, we recruited our friends as tasters. The restaurant opened on schedule, and people poured in. They came for the music initially, but they also ordered food: soup, salad, crêpes, quiche, the daily dinner special and an assortment of baked goods.

From Granola to Gâteau

Our customers enjoyed the food, and they kept coming back. The crêperie's

success arose from inspiration drawn from a variety of sources. I read every cookbook I could get my hands on, watched other cooks and ate at competing restaurants. I even invited the mothers of my friends to come into the kitchen as guest bakers.

We worked harder than we had ever worked in our lives. We made mistakes. We burned food. We created things that never left the kitchen. They were hard lessons, but I learned more essential combine chocolate and chicken or orange liqueur and hot peppers.

When I cook now, I work from my head. I use a cookbook only for baking because, there, accurate measurement is too important to be left to memory or to improvisation. Sitting in the living room late at night, I read, think and compare recipes, watching for the similarities and differences in various dishes and styles of cuisine. I am likely to jot down a number of meal ideas and a grocery list and will probably not refer to the cookbooks again. When I prepare the meal, I contribute my own ideas.

My cooking style has evolved through several stages. When I began working for *Harrowsmith,* I was a strict health-food cook. Sugar, bleached flour and white rice were nowhere to be found in my kitchen, having been supplanted by blackstrap molasses and whole grains. Eventually, I felt too restricted by this kind of cooking, and it was clear to me that there was not much value in preparing the healthiest foods in the world if no one enjoyed them. Now, I have found a comfortable compromise: I have learned to use wholesome, healthy ingredients to their greatest advantage. Whole wheat flour, for example, provides texture and flavour in heavier baked goods such as muffins and cookies, but white flour is better in delicate piecrusts.

I believe that North Americans need to kick the sugar habit, introduce more fibre into their diets, cut down on fat and generally eat less. Many of the nutrients our bodies require can come from food rather than from a pill bottle. But even though we need to learn to like brown rice, bran muffins and tofu, our digestive systems will not grind to a halt if we eat meat, and sugar in small quantities will not kill us. As with everything else, moderation is the key. From a very early age, our children are beguiled by images of teenagers with flawless complexions indulging in a diet inspired by

Vegetable stir-fry

random cravings. Fast, easy, convenient and ubiquitous, junk food is available within two blocks of every urban high school. It is not realistic for me to expect my children to prefer a carrot stick to a bag of potato chips, but I can live with it when they eat homemade cookies or muffins instead. Nutrition and pleasure in eating are not mutually exclusive, but effort, imagination and resourcefulness are needed to unite the two.

These days, I am most intrigued by Eastern styles of cooking, which contain less fat than Western cuisine does. And unlike Western cooking, in which the goal is to integrate flavours, the combinations of ingredients and seasonings of Asian cuisine create contrasts of pure, fresh, vibrant flavours: a searing Indian curry is perfectly complemented by a cool raita, while Chinese hot and sour soup embodies flavour contradictions unknown in Western kitchens.

Treading Lightly

Another factor that has shaped my cooking habits is an aspect of the North American life style. The inhabitants of the Western world, simply put, live and eat far too well, with little awareness of or consideration for the sources of our food. We allow ourselves to be manipulated into believing that we need strawberries in January even though they are picked prematurely by underpaid migrant workers and despite the fact that they are tasteless when they arrive. We complain about the high cost of domestic food without considering the demise of the small Canadian farm or the tightening stranglehold that agribusiness has on agriculture.

I believe it is possible, however, to eat well and at the same time tread lightly on the earth, its ecosystem and its peoples. A commitment to learning more about how to do this, along with a bit of extra effort with our shopping and cooking, is a beginning.

For some people, cooking is an annoying chore, deserving little effort and yielding equally little pleasure. Some people do not care what they eat as long as it relieves their hunger; others, who appreciate good food in the company of friends, imagine that they lack the ability to prepare a meal for themselves. But this is a book for everyone who passes through the kitchen door, whether reluctantly or compulsively. It is for everyone, regardless of level of skill, who likes to cook or who wants to like to cook. It is for those who would like to explore new avenues in food preparation and for those who want food to be fun. It describes the food and the tools and some simple but fundamental preparations and cooking techniques that can make that goal a reality. And it includes many recipes, the best of the best of their kind. If I fulfill my aim, experienced cooks will be inspired to create something they have never prepared before and timid novices will learn that every meal can be a joyous experience in which families and friends can share. Happy cooking!

PANTRY

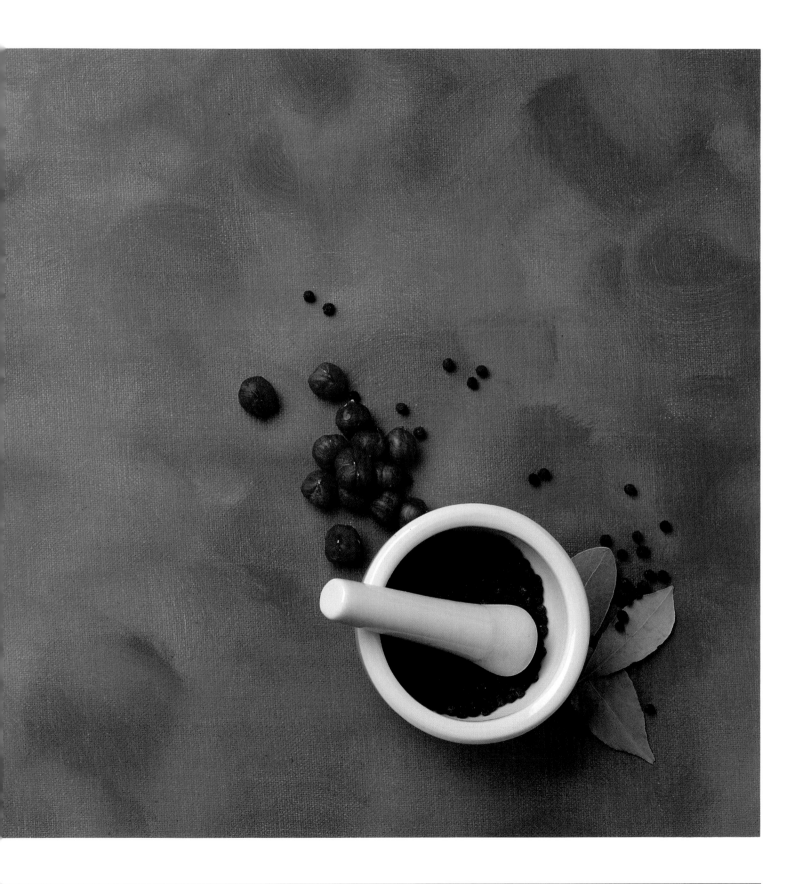

Pantry

I know that I have created a great meal if it inspires lively dinner conversation about food. As if to derive greater pleasure from contemplating aloud what is already tangible, we review the taste, aroma and texture of each delectable morsel and then move on to memories of other mouth-watering meals, further whetting culinary imaginations.

One of the most tantalizing East Indian spreads my taste buds have encountered prompted one such discussion. Under the spell of the smouldering flavours of potato samosas, vegetable pakoras, cubed lamb korma, chicken pieces prepared tandoori style, vegetable biryani, potato and cauliflower curry, hot buttery chapatis and ice-cold beer, my friends and I talked about great cooks we had known and what made them great. Perfecting a particular dish – the ultimate spaghetti sauce, for example – and mastering a specialty, such as the delicate art of pastry making, were suggested as evidence of accomplishment in the kitchen. But we eventually agreed that a true culinary virtuoso is someone who can create a delicious meal using only the supplies on hand without cheating: no emergency dashes to the corner store.

The ability to assemble a meal after a few quick trips to the refrigerator, pantry and freezer demonstrates both creativity and a broad understanding of food. Understanding and creativity, however, amount to little if the cupboard is bare. So a fast but good meal is also the sign of an organized cook, one who maintains a pantry containing a wide variety of basic ingredients, such as herbs, spices and dried goods and probably some specialty foods like purées, preserves and soup stocks. A well-stocked pantry is more important for the serious cook than the design of the kitchen, the quality and quantity of the tools in it or a repertoire of exotic recipes. This chapter is a comprehensive list of the basic ingredients that every cook should have on hand to make delicious meals. Only fresh foods – produce, meat and dairy products – need be added.

Great Beginnings

Maintenance of a well-stocked pantry requires a little effort, lots of common sense and regular trips to the grocer. Great meals start with good, fresh ingredients, and while most of the pantry items are relatively nonperishable, they will grow stale over time, deteriorating in both flavour and nutritive value. You can increase the little control you have over the freshness of a product by shopping at a store that brings the food from the producer to the shelf in the shortest time. Shopping at a neighbourhood natural-food store that stocks most pantry items in bulk will eliminate the delay, expense and excess packaging of individually wrapped items that have come through a distributor.

At home, you can monitor the freshness of your pantry stock by labelling all storage containers with the date of purchase. You can further maintain freshness by using the remnants of earlier purchases before adding new food to a container; otherwise, you may wind up with five-year-old baking soda in your tea biscuits. A couple of times a year, inspect all the containers for invasions of meal-eating wildlife, and test their contents for spoilage. When dried goods smell, they are probably rancid, so discard them and start fresh. For dry herbs and spices, the opposite is usually true: a washed-out colour and a diminished aroma indicate that the seasoning has lost its punch, and while not a threat to your health, it will be a disappointment the next time you try it in a recipe.

Storage Strategies

For both aesthetic and practical reasons, I suggest that you store pantry goods in airtight, wide-mouthed glass jars. These containers give easy access to pantry stock, and you can remove the exact amount you need with a measuring cup or scoop. Since you want to keep only a minimum amount of frequently used ingredients on the shelf, the transparent containers allow you to see at a glance what is available so that you can restock before you run out. To prevent mildew, thoroughly wash and dry empty pantry containers before refilling them; easy-to-clean glass is an advantage here. Only experience (usually bad experience) will show you how much to keep on hand in the pantry. (I cannot count the number of times I have reached for an empty flour canister after creaming together the butter and sugar for a cake.)

A freezer is useful for storing such infrequently used specialty items as besan (chickpea flour) or pine nuts. It is also a good place to keep an extra supply of foods consumed in large quantities – flour, grains, rice, dry beans and fresh herbs. As you remove the last package of one of these from the freezer, make a note of it on your grocery list.

Dried goods kept in the freezer, however, require special care. Aluminum foil is not airtight, and neither a single layer of plastic wrap nor lightweight plastic food bags will endure lengthy exposure to the frigid temperature. If you do use them, much of the food will eventually end up either frost-burned or bound to the freezer floor. Triple-bagging freezer items will protect them, but you then face the hassle of unwrapping and rewrapping a complicated package every time you need to use the contents. Rigid snap-top plastic containers and recycled margarine and yogurt tubs are by far the most durable, airtight and convenient for storing frozen food.

When retrieving freezer-stored foods, remember that they have undergone certain changes and require special han-

A well-stocked pantry: the cook's head start

dling. The cycle of freezing, thawing and refreezing destroys the natural texture of the food and encourages bacterial growth, so only remove from the freezer what you need at one time. Any excess should be stored in the refrigerator, not the pantry, and used soon afterward. Remember, too, that frozen goods, with the exception of herbs, cannot be added directly to a dish: the gluten in frozen flour for pasta or bread making is not easily stimulated, and icy

dried beans will not absorb water in the same amount of time as will beans at room temperature. Try to plan ahead, and remove food from the freezer the night before use, thawing it in the refrigerator and bringing it up to room temperature immediately before using it.

Essential Tastes

The single most important section in this chapter is the one on herbs and

spices: whether a tomato's destiny is to become part of a decadent Neapolitan pizza topping, a zesty Mexican salsa or the broth for a Mediterranean lamb stew depends on the richness of its seasoning. The distinction between spices and herbs—both derived from plants—is based largely on geographical origin and role in the kitchen. Herbs are defined botanically as nonwoody plants possessing special systems of vessels used for absorbing and circulating water and nutrients, a definition that does not do justice to a group of plants whose members are variously fragrant, medicinal, ornamental and edible. It is the leafy portions of the edible group (and the roots in a few outstanding examples such as horseradish, garlic and onions) that are known as potherbs: seasonings for food. These herbs can be cultivated in almost any warm, sunny patch of well-drained soil.

Spices—often more aromatic than herbs—are perhaps best described as the herbs' exotic cousins. The flavours imparted by some spices frequently evoke the cuisines of particular cultures. Spice plants are tropical and slow-growing, features that make them difficult to grow in temperate climates. The edible portion of a spice plant may be the bark, the root, the fruit, the bud, the blossoms or the seeds.

Because of the time involved in shipping them great distances and because they often require processing before they are ready for use—as is the case with peppercorns—spices are very rarely available fresh. They are sometimes sold whole in a dry form—seed, nut, flower or bark—but are most often available as a powder. While whole spices are preferred for their flavour, many of them are tough and woody and require heavy-duty equipment to grind them finely. Powdered spices are often the only genuinely practical choice. To guarantee the freshness of a spice, be sure to buy only what you can use in a few months, as the flavour of ground seasonings dissipates very rapidly. Store spices in a cool, dark place away from direct heat and light, and no matter how convenient it may seem, never store them directly over the stove, since regular exposure to heat accelerates the rate of flavour loss.

Herbs come in a range of forms that vary in flavour quality. In descending order, these forms are: fresh, dry whole, dry flaked, dry crushed and dry ground.

Fresh and dried herbs

When cut from the living plant immediately before use, herbs have a colour, texture and flavour not found in any of the other forms. Ideally, every chef should have his or her own herb garden, whether in a small plot in the backyard or in rows of clay pots on the windowsills. (A number of useful and beautiful books about herb gardening are available. *The Harrowsmith Illustrated Book of Herbs* by Patrick Lima is an outstanding example that provides all of the information necessary to design, plant and care for a garden containing the herbs on which cooks rely most often.)

If you do not grow your own herbs, buy them fresh whenever possible. Many fresh herbs freeze well for use in both cooked and uncooked dishes; their natural, rich colour and flavour are best preserved this way. To prepare them for the freezer, wash and dry the herbs thoroughly, chop them either by hand or in a food processor, and place them in an airtight container. Frozen herbs can be added directly to food.

Another method of freezing is to pack the herbs into ice cube trays after you chop them. Once they have frozen solid, store the cubes in a plastic container, and use them as required. Be sure to label the storage containers clearly and permanently: minced frozen herbs tend to look alike. Let them thaw first if the recipe calls for herbs to be sprinkled on top, but for cooking, just add the entire cube. This is a good way to prepare herb mixes. If you cook a lot of Italian food with a standard combination of basil, oregano, thyme and parsley, for example, you can freeze the herbs together in an ice cube tray. They will be measured and ready to use whenever you need them.

Dried herbs, which are available whole, flaked, crushed and ground, are always fresher and considerably less expensive when they are purchased loose rather than prepackaged in jars or cellophane. Dried herbs still on the branch are the most flavourful, and they should be rubbed gently between the palms of your hands before use. Flaked dry herbs, which are the most common, have a fair bit of flavour if purchased from a reliable grocer with a high turnover. Powdered herbs have no texture and very little flavour, and I use them only in the direst of emergencies.

Caveat Emptor

While adding fresh herbs is one of the easiest ways to make any meal taste as if it is in season no matter what the time of year, a similar use of fresh produce is next to impossible. For this reason, I will offer only a few general comments about purchasing fresh food. Whenever possible, buy locally grown produce. Make the effort to get to a farmers' market for the pencil-sized local asparagus in May; for the berries, cherries, corn and leafy green vegetables at the peak of summer; and for the cornucopia of tomatoes, apples and squash in late summer. Freeze, can, pickle or preserve local vegetables so that you can recapture summer freshness in cold February by making a strawberry mousse, a chowder with fresh corn or a pasta sauce with home-preserved tomatoes.

Buying local produce supports the area's economy, domestic agriculture and the North American family farm. In addition, when you buy from a local

Dried beans

farmer or market gardener, you increase your chances of getting chemical-free food. Unless otherwise stated by the chain-store supplier, you can assume that imported vegetables have been treated in the fields with pesticides, some of which have probably been banned in North America but which will nonetheless find their way to your table if you buy these foods. Imported foods are picked prematurely to arrest ripening, then treated with a combination of growth hormones and preservatives and left to mature in the back of a refrigerated rig that hauls them across the country. It seems hardly worth the trouble: winter produce is expensive, the tomatoes taste like wax, the broccoli is woody and the lettuce tough and bitter.

Kitchen Secrets

As you read this chapter, you will be opening the door of a cook's larder to discover the most basic secrets of the kitchen. Needless to say, what is included will not always meet with every-

one's approval. In compiling what I hope is a comprehensive list of entries, I began the research in my own home, where I considered the ingredients I find indispensable. I next surveyed other kitchens, and I concluded by wandering through specialty-food stores to recruit more exotic candidates. All entries conform to a single prerequisite: each one is a pure food, albeit sometimes preserved. Some items you use regularly may have been omitted, others may be unfamiliar to you, and a few might seem too specialized for inclusion in the pantry. For the benefit of novices, I have included recipes focusing on many of the unusual entries. (If you have trouble finding any item in the Pantry chapter, please refer to the book's index, which I hope will help to unravel any idiosyncratic cataloguing of the various ingredients. I have, for example, listed coconut under Grains, Beans & Things rather than under Baking because I use coconut most frequently in savoury cooking.)

I am unrepentant, however, about excluding highly processed items from the Pantry. I hope the cooks who use ketchup in the kitchen will be encouraged to switch to tomato paste or to the genuine article, tomato purée. And if you eat instant rice, I hope you will take a few extra minutes to cook the noninstant variety, whether brown, white, basmati or short- or long-grain. If you have always bought ground, prepackaged seasonings from a chain-store grocery, perhaps you will keep your eyes open for fresh herbs at the local market. Convenience-food junkies can reduce their dependency with a minimum of fuss and bother: I have included recipes for homemade pantry items that are delicious and easy to make. The best ingredients available should line your pantry shelves; assembling a well-stocked pantry is the first step in making your cooking the topic of pleasant dinner conversation.

Baking

Baking Powder

Until the creation of baking powder in the mid-19th century, cooks leavened foods using yeast, large numbers of whipped eggs, fermented products like beer and wine or long and strenuous mixing to introduce air into baked goods. By comparison, baking powder is an effortless way to leaven food.

A combination of ingredients, baking powder is made up of an alkaline constituent such as bicarbonate of soda, an acid such as cream of tartar and a starch such as rice flour, which absorbs any moisture the powder picks up from the air. The leavening effect of baking powder is based on a simple chemical reaction: when the alkaline and the acidic components are mixed with a liquid, a gas is produced that forms bubbles in the batter; the bubbles then expand when heated during cooking.

Originally, baking-powder ingredients were combined to produce a single-acting powder that reacted very quickly to contact with the liquid ingredients. If a baker failed to act equally quickly, the gas would be lost to the air and the baked goods would not rise.

It is quite simple to make a single-acting powder at home that is far more sensitive than the double-acting leavening agent. To make it, combine 2 teaspoons (10 mL) of cream of tartar with 1 teaspoon (5 mL) of baking soda. If you want to keep some on hand, add 1 teaspoon (5 mL) of cornstarch.

The introduction of double-acting leavening agents meant that split-second timing was no longer necessary. The alkaline and acidic ingredients leaven the food twice: first, when they are activated in the bowl by the liquid ingredients when cold, and again, when the batter is placed in the hot oven. Even with the increased convenience of double-acting powder, a cook should not become lazy – only mix dry and moist ingredients together when it is time to put the batter in the oven.

Baking powder is much less expensive when purchased in bulk from health-food stores than in the small containers available in supermarkets. To keep it fresh and to keep moisture out, store large quantities in an airtight container in the freezer. When you are baking, bring out small amounts as required, but be sure to warm it to room temperature before using it.

Although baking soda is an ingredient in some baking powders, the two are not used in the same way. Baking powder causes foods to rise vertically and so is best in rich, heavy batters such as those for muffins or those containing chocolate. Baking soda, on the other hand, causes food to expand horizontally and is thus an important ingredient in baked goods such as cakes. Nonetheless, baking soda and baking powder are often used in combination.

Baking Powder Biscuits

Although ¾ cup (175 mL) of milk or sour milk can be substituted for the yogurt in this recipe, yogurt adds to the richness and lightness of the biscuits.

2 cups	flour	500 mL
1 Tbsp.	baking powder	15 mL
1 tsp.	sugar	5 mL
½ tsp.	baking soda	2 mL
7 Tbsp.	butter	105 mL
½ cup	yogurt	125 mL
⅓ cup	milk	75 mL

Sift together flour, baking powder, sugar and baking soda. Cut in butter until crumbly. Combine yogurt and milk and stir into flour mixture. Mix until smooth, then knead gently for 1 minute.

Roll out dough to a ½-inch (1.25 cm) thickness, cut into circles and bake on ungreased cookie sheets for 10 minutes at 425 degrees F (220 °C).

Makes 18 to 20 2-inch (5 cm) biscuits.

Baking Soda

The effervescent quality of the mineral salt bicarbonate of soda, or baking soda, which has made it a common addition to carbonated beverages, artificial mineral water and pharmaceuticals, has also made it an effective leavening agent. At one time, baking soda was a coarse white crystal that could not be mixed directly with other ingredients. That is why old recipes may encourage you to dissolve baking soda in water rather than combining it with the dry ingredients. Now, it is a highly processed soluble powder, and dissolving the crystals ahead of time is no longer necessary.

As with baking powder, the leavening effect of the alkaline baking soda is based on a chemical reaction that takes place when it is combined with an acid and a liquid. In baked goods with an acidic ingredient such as lemon juice or buttermilk, baking soda will neutralize the acid and thereby improve the flavour of the final product. But don't be surprised if both baking soda and baking powder are called for in such recipes. The baking soda neutralizes the acidic ingredient, and the baking powder acts as the leavening agent.

Keep baking soda on hand for a wide variety of other uses. It can replace abrasive cleansers for scouring tasks, and it will remove stubborn stains when combined with a little vinegar. Opened boxes of baking soda in both the refrigerator and the freezer will absorb odours; a supply beside the stove can be used to quench a grease fire.

Carob

Carob is often thought of as the health-food fanatic's chocolate, an association that is unfair to both foods. Carob has shortcomings as a chocolate substitute, and chocolate deserves a place of its own. Think of carob as something else altogether, and you will find it to be most palatable. There are good reasons to eat carob – unlike chocolate, it has no caffeine and contains very little fat. Buy it in powder form, and use it in baking if, for dietary or other reasons, chocolate is forbidden to you. It will keep indefinitely on the pantry shelf if covered tightly.

Beware of candy bars made with carob – the value of carob is often lost entirely when manufacturers add large quantities of oil to turn the powder into liquid and large quantities of sweeteners in an attempt to mask carob's unchocolatey flavour.

Chocolate

I find it a little difficult to trust anyone who claims to not like chocolate. It is a food that understandably finds favour everywhere and can be prepared and served in any number of dishes from main courses to desserts. Some people may reject chocolate because it is not particularly healthy, and others may turn it down on political grounds (cacao is grown and processed by Third World peasants who own no land and have minuscule incomes), but they usually do so with a considerable sense of self-sacrifice, because chocolate, quite simply, is delicious.

Europeans had their first taste of chocolate when early explorers brought it back from their journeys to the Americas. The Aztecs made a bitter drink from cacao, or cocoa, beans that, refined and sweetened in Europe, endures to this day as hot chocolate. But it was not until the 19th century that the first chocolate bar was produced. While today a massive industry supplies us with every possible variety of the sweet, from gourmet chocolates to mass-produced candy bars (which actually contain very little pure chocolate), for a long time, the enjoyment of chocolate was restricted to the very rich.

Baking powder biscuits

Cacao trees grow only within 20 degrees of latitude of the equator. The beans develop in melonlike seedpods, which, once harvested, are split open to expose the beans to the air for about a week. This fermentation removes the raw taste and develops the oils. The beans are then dried before shipping. Once they arrive at the processing plant, they are husked, cleaned, roasted and cracked into small pieces. They are further processed to reduce their size and to liquefy the cocoa butter to a substance called cocoa liquor, which can be processed in one of three ways. Poured into moulds to cool and solidify, the cocoa liquor becomes baking chocolate. Pressed to separate much of the butter from the liquor, it leaves behind cocoa solids, which are pulverized into cocoa powder. Finally, it can be sweetened, a delicate process that needs to be done properly to achieve a smooth-tasting finished product.

Baking

True baking chocolate, which is always unsweetened, is pure chocolate liquor. Semisweet chocolate (also called bittersweet) is only 35 percent liquor, the remainder consisting almost entirely of sugar. Sweet chocolate contains only 15 percent liquor and 85 percent sugar. Milk replaces some of the chocolate liquor in milk chocolate, a sweeter and less chocolatey product. Dark chocolate has no milk in it. Cocoa powder (not to be confused with hot-chocolate powders) contains approximately 15 percent cacao fat. The deceptively named white chocolate consists of the cocoa butter left after the solids have been removed, plus sugar, milk and vanilla flavouring. Because it is called chocolate, many people think it tastes of chocolate; in fact, it has almost no chocolate flavour.

Chocolate should be stored at a constant temperature around 65 degrees F (18 °C). Wild fluctuations will make it tough. If frozen, it will develop an unappealing grey coating that does not affect the flavour. Well-wrapped chocolate will keep indefinitely as long as it is stored in a dark, dry place. Some people feel that its flavour improves with age, but I can never keep any around long enough to find out.

It is often possible to substitute one kind of chocolate for another in baking. To replace unsweetened chocolate with semisweet, use 2 ounces (60 g) of semisweet for every ounce (30 g) of unsweetened, and reduce the sugar in the recipe by 2 teaspoons (10 mL) for every 2 ounces (60 g) of chocolate. Three tablespoons (45 mL) of cocoa powder plus 1 tablespoon (15 mL) of butter will replace 1 ounce (30 g) of unsweetened chocolate.

Extracts

A number of extracts are commonly used in cooking to flavour foods. Vanilla is foremost, followed by lemon, almond and peppermint. All are available in natural and synthetic forms, the natural costing substantially more. I often use liqueurs in place of extracts. A teaspoon (5 mL) of chocolate-flavoured liqueur is wonderful in cookies and mousses, as are coffee liqueur, almond liqueur and a dozen others. I generally substitute with similar quantities.

Natural vanilla, despite the high price, is well worth buying. Since it is used in small amounts, it is not much of an indulgence to pay top dollar for good quality. Europeans first tasted vanilla in the 16th century, when Mexico was invaded by the Spanish. Its aroma and flavour were so irresistible that it was soon being consumed in vast quantities. Today, it is grown in many places around the world; Madagascar is the largest commercial supplier to North America. Anyone who has spent time in Mexico knows that it is readily available there at a fraction of its cost in Canada. If you buy it there, however, be sure that it does not contain coumarin – an active ingredient in rat poison that can be fa-

Baking Tips

- Always use fresh eggs.
- Eggs separate more easily if cold, but the whites whip better at room temperature. When a recipe calls for separated eggs, separate them as soon as you remove them from the refrigerator, but let them warm before whipping.
- Except when making pastry, all baking ingredients should be at room temperature.
- Use an oven thermometer to make certain that the heat is evenly distributed throughout the oven.
- Use an electric mixer for blending cake batter; it makes a smooth batter much more quickly and easily than does beating by hand.
- When a cake recipe instructs the cook to alternate dry and wet ingredients, always start and end the series with the dry and beat the mixture thoroughly after each addition.
- Unless a recipe states otherwise, always bake on a rack positioned in the centre of the oven.
- When baking, always measure ingredients precisely.
- Before baking a cake batter, grease the pan, using a pastry brush to spread shortening over its entire surface. For a floured cake pan, dust lightly and remove the excess flour by holding the pan upside down and shaking it before pouring in the batter.
- Cool a cake for 10 minutes in the pan on a cooling rack. Then remove the cake from the pan, and place it directly on the rack.
- Remove cookies from the hot baking sheet immediately after taking it out of the oven; cool the cookies on a baking rack. Allow the pans to cool before starting the next batch.
- Always use the size of pan specified in the recipe. For most cake recipes, the pan should be half to two-thirds full. If the pan is too full, the batter will spill over the edges while cooking and the cake will collapse. On the other hand, if the batter is less than an inch (2.5 cm) deep, the cake will not rise.
- While a cake is baking, open the oven door as seldom as possible, or the cake may not rise properly.
- A cake is done when its surface springs back from a light touch or when a wooden skewer or knife blade inserted into the centre emerges clean.
- Up to one-quarter of the batter can stick to the sides of a mixing bowl, so always scrape the sides thoroughly with a flexible spatula.

tal if consumed even in small amounts. Buy vanilla in bottles with the ingredients listed on the label, and you will have nothing to worry about.

The vanilla plant is a type of orchid, one that must be pollinated either by hand or by a bee native to Mexico. The vine grows on the trunks of large trees and produces beans that resemble string beans. Vanillin, the primary flavour component of vanilla, is extracted from beans picked when green, then dried and chopped. Alcohol and water are poured over them, the mixture is filtered, and a sweetening agent is added. The end product is vanilla extract – the strongest pure vanilla flavouring available to the consumer. Vanilla flavouring is also natural but has a less concentrated flavour. Imitation vanilla is made from a by-product of the paper industry and has a harsher flavour than true vanilla.

If stored tightly covered and in a dark, dry place, vanilla will keep indefinitely. It can only improve in flavour with the passage of time, so if you have the opportunity to buy a large quantity of pure vanilla, do not turn it down. Vanilla beans can also be purchased. Wrap them in plastic to store in the freezer, or break them into chunks and leave in a jar of sugar for instant vanilla sugar.

Flours

In this section, I will discuss a number of flours, some more commonly used than others, but it would be impossible to deal with every type that exists. Wheat flours (either whole or white) are generally the most familiar and most frequently used in everyday North American cooking, but corn, rice, rye and buckwheat flours also appear in many recipes – those for breads in particular. And many of us are beginning to use specialized flours, such as chickpea, for recipes from other parts of the world.

No matter what kind it is, flour should always be stored tightly covered. In fact, I keep my flours in the freezer and bring out only a few pounds at a time. That keeps them fresh, eliminates concern about rancidity and weevils and allows me to buy in bulk. Those without ample freezer space can drop a bay leaf into the flour container to prevent infestation by weevils.

Wheat Flours: Wheat, in the form of bread, is the primary food staple of 45 countries, including Canada and most of the Western world. The rest of the world relies on rice. Less and less wheat flour is used in family cooking, however, because fewer people are baking at home today than ever before.

Wheat can be milled in a number of ways, each of which produces its own kind of flour. When the bran, endosperm and germ components of the kernel are left intact, the result is whole wheat flour; when the bran and germ are eliminated, the end product is white flour. Whole wheat flour has a substantially higher nutritional value, as the bran contains most of the fibre and other nutrients.

After it is cleaned, washed and milled, wheat retains its yellowish colour; at this point, it has traditionally been stored for a few months to allow it to whiten and to develop the proteins in the flour. The proteins are necessary to produce gluten (which allows dough to rise) when the flour is mixed with a liquid. Because the process is time-consuming (and therefore expensive), a faster method, chlorine bleaching, has been developed. Milling and bleaching flour to the state of refinement that most North Americans have come to expect also, predictably, eliminates most of the nutrients, so it is now enriched by the addition of a variety of vitamins. Unbleached flour, which is still available in health-food stores, contains more naturally present vitamins than bleached, but whole wheat is the richest.

A number of varieties of wheat flour are available. They can be either hard or soft. Hard flour has more gluten and is thus the kind that should be used in yeast baking; soft flour is more appropriate for cookie, pie and cake baking. Durum, the hardest wheat of all, is used almost exclusively in pasta. Gluten is present only in wheat flours, so it is necessary to use at least some in food that is to rise.

All-purpose flour is excellent for nothing yet adequate for everything. It is the flour most commonly found in supermarkets, and it contains a middling amount of gluten. Thus, it can be used for yeast-bread making as well as more delicate baking. Cake flour, which imparts a drier, crumbly texture, is made from soft, very finely milled wheat mixed with cornstarch and has a low protein content. Pastry flour has a little more protein than cake flour and is not as heavily bleached. Bread flour has twice the protein of cake flour.

Whole wheat flour has less gluten than white because the bran and germ form part of its bulk. I generally mix whole wheat and unbleached white flours when cooking, as I find the taste and texture of whole wheat by itself to be too coarse and heavy. I thus add some nutrition without sacrificing the aesthetic quality of the end product. I must admit that I am not exactly a purist about nutrition, and when making fine cakes and crusts for pie or pizza, I always use white flour alone. For cookies, muffins and most quick breads, though, a half-and-half combination of the two is entirely acceptable.

Stone-ground flour is slightly more nutritious than that milled in the modern way, as the wheat is not heated as much in the process. It tends to be slightly coarser in texture. A health-food store is the most likely place to find stone-ground flours.

Rye Flours: Rye contains very little protein and consequently needs to be combined with a wheat flour in breads

Baking

Onion pakoras

that rise. Pumpernickel flour is rye that still contains the germ and bran, whereas rye has been milled to eliminate them.

Rice Flour: Although rice flour originated in the Far East, it is now used by many North American cooks. A very fine flour, it can be added to foods in which particularly delicate taste and texture are desired. Made from a variety of rices, rice flour is an excellent thickener, because it will not separate when cooked as may other thickeners.

Semolina: Made from the endosperm of durum wheat, semolina is available in a range of grinds from fine to coarse and is used primarily in pasta making. Semolina pasta is firmer and more golden in colour than that made from other wheat flours. Available in health-food stores and many supermarkets, semolina flour will keep indefinitely if stored in a cool place. Once again, I recommend freezer storage.

Chickpea Flour: Also known as besan, chickpea flour is very nutritious and high in protein. Its flavour is distinctive, so it should be used only where specif-

ically called for. The following recipe is for a common Indian appetizer consisting of vegetables dipped in a batter made with besan and then deep-fried.

Pakoras

2 cups	chickpea flour (besan)	500 mL
1½ tsp.	garam masala	7 mL
¾ tsp.	turmeric	3 mL
¾ tsp.	ground chilies	3 mL
2 tsp.	salt	10 mL
1	clove garlic, mashed	1
6 cups	chopped mixed vegetables (cauliflower, broccoli, onions, potatoes) oil for deep-frying	1.5 L

Stir together chickpea flour, garam masala, turmeric, chilies and salt. Gradually work in 1 cup (250 mL) water, stirring to make a thick batter. Stir in garlic and beat well, then let stand for half an hour. Beat again.

Stir vegetables into batter to coat thoroughly. Heat oil in wok, then fry pakoras a few at a time, turning, until golden all over. Drain. Just before serving, reheat oil and refry briefly until golden brown. Drain on paper and serve.

Serves 6 as part of an appetizer tray.

Buckwheat Flour: The plant from which buckwheat is obtained is native to the Soviet Union, and its seed is available as flour, groats or grits. The flour has a very nutty flavour and is usually used in North America in buckwheat pancakes. In eastern Europe, that use is expanded to include blini and varenyky.

Corn Flour and Cornmeal: Corn flour is milled more finely than cornmeal but has the same taste. It can be substituted for part of the wheat flour in a recipe if a corn flavour or a smooth rather than a grainy texture is desired.

A number of forms of cornmeal are available. Yellow is more nutritious than white, and stone-ground is more so than roller-ground. All cornmeals can

be used interchangeably, but do not confuse cornmeal with either corn flour or masa harina. I recently used blue cornmeal in a corn muffin recipe. Taste and texture remained the same, but the muffins were a distinctive, somewhat startling, shade of blue. The following recipe is for a corn bread that is light, tender and redolent of corn in both flavour and texture.

Masa harina, a flour made from specially prepared corn, is used in a dough similar to the Mexican masa, which is used to make tortillas. It can also be employed as a thickener. Do not substitute masa harina for corn flour or vice versa. Masa harina is available in packaged form in some supermarkets and specialty-food stores.

Corn Bread

1 cup	flour	250 mL
1 cup	coarsely ground cornmeal	250 mL
3 Tbsp.	sugar	45 mL
2 Tbsp.	baking powder	30 mL
1	egg	1
1 cup	yogurt	250 mL
3 Tbsp.	melted butter	45 mL

Combine dry ingredients. Beat together egg, yogurt and butter, then stir into dry ingredients. Mix well, then spoon into greased 9" x 9" (2.5 L) cake pan. Bake at 350 degrees F (180°C) for 30 minutes. (To make a more liquid batter suitable for corn bread moulds, substitute milk for yogurt.)

Honey

More than 30 types of honey are recognized commercially, two of the most common being clover and buckwheat. Many other kinds are derived from wildflowers as well as from mixed nectars. Honey aficionados will understand how different all these kinds of honey are. The flavour can vary from season to season, from location to location and

Corn bread

from one source of nectar to another. Once you find a honey you like, it is worthwhile to continue purchasing from the same producer to ensure consistent flavour.

Honey is much "sweeter" than sugar; if substituting in a recipe, use only half as much honey. In some recipes – such as those for light cakes and pastries – honey does not work as a substitute because of its heavy, liquid form. Honey is, however, a healthier sweetener than sugar because it undergoes less processing and refinement and contains more complex carbohydrates. Honey should be stored in the pantry, away from direct heat and light. If it solidifies or crystallizes, heat it gently over hot water.

Beeswax skin cream, a by-product of the honey industry, is wonderful for dry skin and has the same scent as the nectar that was used in the honey. Honeycomb is also a real treat that can be found at many open-air markets.

Molasses

Molasses is the brown syrup that remains after sugar crystals have been extracted from sugarcane. The earlier in the extraction process the molasses is removed, the lighter it is. It becomes increasingly strong and bitter in flavour with each stage of extraction. Blackstrap molasses is the strongest. Most types have had cane syrup added to moderate their flavour. The product sold in

Baking

Chocolate chip oatmeal cookies

health-food stores is generally free of this additive, so you should test its flavour before using it in a recipe.

Molasses adds colour and softness to foods. It can be substituted for half the sugar in a recipe, but many recipes call for it specifically. It will keep for several months in a dark, cool place. If it crystallizes, heat it gently.

Oat Bran

Oat bran is a recent addition to the list of foods for health-conscious consumers, and consequently, it is hard to know how long the infatuation will last. A soluble fibre that apparently soaks up excess cholesterol and removes it from the body, oat bran, in quantities of ½ to 1 cup (125 to 250 mL) a day is said to lead to cholesterol-level reductions of 20 to 30 percent. The bran tastes good and is easy to use in baking and other cooking. You can replace one-sixth of the flour in a recipe with oat bran – it has no gluten, so it cannot entirely replace wheat flour in baking.

Oat bran can be made into a tasty breakfast cereal as well. Mix ⅓ cup (75 mL) of oat bran with ⅓ cup (75 mL) of skim milk powder, 1 cup (250 mL) of water and ⅛ teaspoon (0.5 mL) of salt and cook for 15 minutes or until thick. Cinnamon or chopped dried fruits such as dates, raisins, apricots or apples may also be added for more flavour.

Store oat bran in the refrigerator to prevent rancidity.

Oat Flakes

Both oatmeal and rolled oats are included under this heading, although they are quite different and should not be confused. Rolled oats are individual flakes formed when the hulled groats are rolled and then steamed. The thinner oats are called "quick-cooking" and the thicker ones "regular." I prefer quick-cooking oats for most baking purposes because they blend more readily into the batter or dough.

As with most other dried goods, it is best to buy oat products in bulk from a shop that has a rapid turnover. Store them tightly wrapped in the freezer, taking out only enough for current purposes and allowing sufficient time to reach room temperature before using.

The following cookie recipe is a favourite with *Harrowsmith* staff. Make lots, because they won't last long.

Chocolate Chip Oatmeal Cookies

1 cup	butter	250 mL
½ cup	white sugar	125 mL
1 cup	brown sugar	250 mL
1	egg	1
1 tsp.	vanilla	5 mL
1½ cups	flour	375 mL
1½ cups	rolled oats	375 mL
¾ cup	coconut	175 mL
1 tsp.	baking soda	5 mL
1 tsp.	baking powder	5 mL
⅛ tsp.	salt	0.5 mL
1 cup	chocolate chips	250 mL

Cream butter, then add sugars and mix thoroughly. Stir in egg and vanilla. Combine dry ingredients and add to creamed ingredients. Mix thoroughly, then stir in chocolate chips.

Drop by spoonfuls onto greased cookie sheet and bake at 375 degrees F (190°C) for 10 to 12 minutes.

Makes 5 dozen cookies.

Granola

There must be as many versions of granola as there are leftover hippies. By steering away from the packaged, highly sweetened commercial brands, one can be reasonably sure of purchasing a product made with whole grains and fruits that is relatively free of refined sugars. Read all labels, though, so you know what you are buying. Many bulk granolas are available in health-food stores, usually at moderate prices, so it is easy to get away with not making your own. I always keep it on hand—it can be used as a quick topping for a fruit crisp, as a treat in a school lunch and, of course, as a delicious, nutritious quick breakfast. It will keep indefinitely on the pantry shelf if stored in jars with tight-fitting lids.

Granola is simple to make and fills the house with a delicious aroma while baking, so you may want to give it a try. The following is a good basic granola to which many other ingredients can be added.

½ cup	honey	125 mL
⅓ cup	oil	75 mL
1 Tbsp.	vanilla	15 mL
⅓ cup	sunflower seeds	75 mL
⅓ cup	sesame seeds	75 mL
½ cup	wheat germ	125 mL
2 cups	coconut	500 mL
6 cups	rolled oats	1.5 L
½ cup	oat bran	125 mL
1 cup	slivered almonds	250 mL
½ cup	chopped dried apricots	125 mL

Heat honey, oil and vanilla until well combined and thin. Remove from heat, and stir in all remaining ingredients except apricots. Mix well (you will probably have to use your hands) and half fill baking dishes that are 2″ to 3″ (5 to 7.5 cm) deep. Bake at 350 degrees F (180°C), stirring every 5 minutes, for 35 to 45 minutes, or until golden brown and slightly crispy. Cool, stir in apricots, then store.

Sugars

One-quarter of the calories each of us consumes daily consists of sweetening agents—a significant part of our diet, especially when we choose to eat commercially prepared foods. It is important to remember that almost everything, from fast-food hamburgers to take-out doughnuts, contains sugar of one kind or another. As a result, most of us have become sugar-dependent, even if we try to keep sugars to a minimum in our own cooking. But although everyone needs to be concerned to some degree with the long- and short-term health effects of dietary sugar, it does not mean we should never eat anything sweet. I recently attended a potluck supper populated with back-to-the-land natural-food fanatics—people whose children had apparently never tasted evils like sugar or refined flour. One of the desserts was a carrot cake made with almost no sweetener and covered in icing to match. Kids and adults alike rejected it. Just as, for me, the thought of a piecrust made from 100 percent whole-grain flour is completely unappealing, a diet entirely free of sugars would prolong a life not worth living.

That said, there are more and less healthy ways to consume sugar. Commercially prepared foods contribute about 80 percent of our sugar intake. I would far rather eliminate many of these "hidden" sugars from my diet—things like ketchup, sweet mustard, sweetened fruit juices and so on—and concentrate instead on eating sugar where I can actively enjoy it—in a chocolate mousse, for instance.

Sugar can be bought in a number of forms—white, brown, caster, demerara, raw and icing. Not all of these are available to the consumer; raw sugar, for instance, may not be sold at the retail level because it has not been through a cleaning or purifying process. Years ago, when I knew considerably less about food than I do now, I co-owned and operated a small restaurant with a natural-foods philosophy and decided to work only with raw sugar. I figured that raw must be better than processed, but it was useless—hard, coarse, lumpy, almost impossible to dissolve and very dirty. It ended up in the garbage.

Sugar is derived from both sugar beets and sugarcane; cane supplies about 60 percent of the world's sugar. Granulated, or white, sugar—which most of us have on our tables and use in baking—is almost entirely sucrose, which consists of fructose and dextrose. It can be made from either beets or cane. Caster, or extra-fine, sugar is granulated sugar that has been ground even more finely. It dissolves very quickly, making it

Baking

the sugar of choice for many professional bakers.

Confectioners', powdered or icing sugar is granulated sugar that has been ground to a powder and sifted. The designation of, for instance, 3X or 10X on a package indicates how many times it has been sifted. The higher the number, the finer the sugar – and the more expensive. Confectioners' sugar generally contains cornstarch to help keep it from caking.

Brown sugar can be made in any number of ways. In the traditional method, the sugar is removed from processing with some molasses still in it (white sugar is processed until all of the molasses is removed). The resulting brown sugar is less refined than white and retains the flavour of the molasses. The more molasses, the darker the sugar, and brown sugar will often be marked as light, dark or very dark. Because of its higher moisture content, brown sugar lumps more readily than does white. To prevent this, store a slice of apple with it in the jar.

Brown sugar can also be made by adding molasses or a synthetic caramel colouring to refined white sugar. The labelling does not always indicate which is which, so if you are concerned, shop at a reputable health-food store where you know the owner will check on the processing method.

Demerara sugar has been partially refined and consists of fairly large crystals that are light brown in colour (unless the crystals have been dyed) and dissolve quickly, making it popular for sweetening coffee.

Turbinaro sugar is another partially refined sugar, but it has smaller crystals than does demerara. Because it dissolves very quickly, it is the sugar of choice for such techniques as combining sugar with egg whites.

Fructose – one of the two simple sugars that make up table sugar – is the one that occurs naturally in fruits. It can also be manufactured from cornstarch. It is 70 percent sweeter than table sugar but has the same number of calories.

Corn syrup and maple syrup are two other commonly used sweeteners. Corn syrup is manufactured from cornstarch and water and consists mostly of dextrose. It is available in both light and dark forms. Light corn syrup is mildly flavoured, whereas the dark has a much stronger flavour and also contains caramel colouring.

A true luxury even for those of us who live in syrup country and an almost-unheard-of delicacy for those who do not, maple syrup can vary in colour and flavour from very clear and mild to dark, thick and strong. The differences are due to the amount of processing to which the sap is subjected. It is not a sweetener to use indiscriminately, because it is costly and because it has a very distinctive flavour of its own. I keep maple syrup for pouring over pancakes or French toast, for adding to fruit drinks (especially if I am trying to mask the flavour of brewer's yeast) or for beating into whipping cream to top a dessert.

Maple syrup, if bought in bulk, should be stored in the freezer to prevent a breakdown in flavour and consistency. The dry sugars, on the other hand, have a long shelf life if kept in tightly covered containers.

Yeast, Baker's

Yeasts are living organisms. Combining them with warm water and sugars activates them, and they begin to produce carbon dioxide. Subsequent combination with glutenous flours continues the process, which results in leavened foods. Thousands of natural, or "wild," yeasts abound in the air – these are the ones used to produce sourdough, a slow and not altogether reliable process. Consequently, most sourdough is now started with baker's yeast or a small piece of leftover dough.

Dry yeast is available in bulk, in 1-tablespoon (15 mL) packages and in compressed form. Predictably, the bulk form is the least expensive. Bulk dry yeast will remain potent for several months if stored in a tightly capped glass jar in a cool place. Allow it to return to room temperature before working with it. Compressed yeast, which comes as a moist cake, has a shorter shelf life. Store it in the refrigerator, where it will stay fresh for two weeks. Frozen, it will last for up to two months.

Cinnamon Buns

Dough:		
½ cup	warm water	125 mL
¼ cup	granulated sugar	50 mL
1 Tbsp.	dry yeast	15 mL
½ cup	milk	125 mL
¼ cup	butter	50 mL
1 tsp.	salt	5 mL
2	eggs, beaten	2
4 cups	all-purpose flour	1 L
Filling:		
¼ cup	butter	50 mL
¾ cup	packed brown sugar	175 mL
½ cup	coarsely chopped pecans	125 mL
1 Tbsp.	cinnamon	15 mL
Glaze:		
¾ cup	butter	175 mL
¾ cup	packed brown sugar	175 mL

In warm water, dissolve 1 teaspoon (5 mL) of the sugar, and sprinkle in the yeast. Let it stand for 10 minutes or until frothy, then stir. In a small saucepan, combine milk, remaining sugar, butter and salt and heat until the butter melts. Set aside and cool to lukewarm. In a large bowl, combine eggs with milk and yeast mixtures.

With an electric mixer, gradually beat in 1½ cups (375 mL) of the flour, mixing for a few minutes or until smooth. Stirring with a wooden spoon, gradually add the remaining flour to make a soft, slightly sticky dough that comes away from the sides of the bowl. On a lightly floured counter or cutting board,

Cinnamon buns

knead the dough for 10 minutes until it is smooth and elastic.

Place the dough in a large bowl that has been greased with shortening, turning to grease all over. Cover with plastic wrap (or greased wax paper and dampened tea towel). Let rise in a warm place for 1 to 1½ hours or until doubled in size. Punch dough down, and on a lightly floured surface, roll it out into an 18-by-14-inch (46 by 36 cm) rectangle.

Now make the filling: Melt butter in a small saucepan, and brush half of it over the dough, leaving a ½-inch (1 cm) border uncovered. Combine brown sugar, pecans and cinnamon and sprinkle over the buttered area. Starting at one of the long sides, tightly roll up the dough, pinching seam to seal. Brush the roll with remaining butter. Using a serrated knife, cut into a dozen slices and place, loosely spaced, on a greased pan or a floured board. Cover the slices with a dampened tea towel and let them rise for 1 hour or until doubled, then place the buns in well-greased, lightly floured muffin tins and bake at 375 degrees F (190 °C) for about 15 to 20 minutes.

For the glaze, melt butter and sugar together over medium heat, whisking until smooth. Brush it over the tops of the buns 10 minutes before the end of the baking time. Return the tins to the oven and bake for an additional 10 minutes, or until the buns are golden brown.

Remove from oven and allow to cool for 5 minutes before removing from tins. Brush any remaining glaze on buns when reheating before serving.

Grains, Beans & Things

Arrowroot

Although North America's indigenous peoples once used arrowroot to draw poison from arrow wounds, the world's largest supplier of arrowroot today is St. Vincent in the Caribbean. There, in its unprocessed form, the narrow, six-inch-long (15 cm) tuber is eaten as a vegetable: In powdered form, arrowroot acts as a thickening agent. When used this way, it has the advantage of being almost neutral in taste, and it provides sauces with a particularly beautiful glaze. Arrowroot is also the easiest to digest of all the starches.

To use as a thickener, substitute 1 teaspoon (5 mL) arrowroot for every 1½ teaspoons (7 mL) cornstarch. Combine with cold water first to make a paste, then stir slowly into boiling liquid and continue mixing. Once the sauce or soup has thickened, reduce the heat immediately, or the arrowroot's thickening properties will be lost.

Arrowroot powder is available in health-food stores, Asian and Caribbean specialty stores and many supermarkets. However, I recommend that you purchase it loose at a specialty store: when it is prepackaged, the price is highly inflated.

Arrowroot will keep indefinitely on the pantry shelf as long as it is packaged tightly to seal out moisture. It can also be stored in the freezer and brought out in small amounts for immediate use.

Barley

One of the oldest cultivated grains, today barley is used mostly by the brewing industry, although it has considerable value as a food. Because of its mild flavour and soft texture, barley is often found in soups and baby foods. Pearl barley can be purchased in supermarkets and health-food shops and will store indefinitely on the pantry shelf.

Scotch Broth

Scotch Broth is a classic barley soup that many of us recall from childhood lunches. It is a perfect soup to make with the leftover lamb or mutton from a Sunday dinner, although a leg of mutton can be purchased especially for it.

1	leg mutton	1
3 Tbsp.	oil	45 mL
1	onion, chopped	1
3	carrots, sliced	3
2	stalks celery, chopped	2
1	small turnip, sliced & boiled until almost tender	1
1 cup	barley salt & pepper thyme	250 mL

Cover mutton with water and cook for 3 to 4 hours to make a rich stock. Meanwhile, heat oil in heavy skillet, and sauté onion, carrots, celery, turnip and barley. Season to taste with salt and pepper and thyme.

Strain stock, and cut the meat from the bone. Add meat, vegetables and barley to stock and bring to a boil. Reduce heat, then cover and simmer until vegetables are tender and barley is cooked—40 to 60 minutes.

Serves 6.

Beans

Beans have historically constituted a large part of the cuisine of almost every culture in the world. Today, only modern North American cooking does not rely heavily on beans as a source of protein. There are simply too many kinds of beans to describe here (in fact, a number of them cannot be purchased in any form in North America). Instead, I will give specific information about only those beans most commonly used on this continent and offer some general information about purchasing, storing and cooking them.

Dried beans can be stored for a year if they are kept away from dampness and light. But be forewarned: the older the beans, the longer they take to cook. It is impossible to know how long the beans have been stored at their point of origin, so the best you can do is buy them from a shop with a rapid turnover.

Beans almost always taste better if they are cooked a day ahead of time, then refrigerated and reheated before serving. You can store cooked beans for a week in the refrigerator. To keep them longer, boil them for 10 minutes every few days and return them to the refrigerator. Cooked beans may also be fro-

The Basics of Beans

- Always use clean, clear water for soaking beans, and change it frequently.
- Salt inhibits the absorption of water through the beans' skins. Do not add it to the soaking or cooking water unless the beans are already tender.
- Simmer beans at a moderate temperature rather than boiling them.
- Make certain that the beans remain moistened throughout the cooking time by replacing any evaporated water.

- Most beans double in weight after they are soaked and cooked. Eight ounces (250 g) dry beans yields 1 to 1¼ pounds (500 to 625 g) cooked beans.
- Most beans double in volume after they are soaked and cooked. One cup (250 mL) dry beans yields 2 to 2¼ cups (500 to 550 mL) cooked beans.
- Acidic foods, such as lemon and tomato juice, toughen bean skins, so add only to fully cooked beans.

zen for more than a year. Drain the cooking liquid off first, and freeze them in small quantities so that you can remove only the amount you need for adding to stews and soups. Puréed beans also freeze well.

Cooking times and techniques vary from one kind of bean to another, but a few basic procedures are common to all of them. Wash beans thoroughly in cold water before soaking or cooking. Be sure to check carefully for small stones at this point because most batches will contain a few; it can be very painful – and damaging – to bite down on a pebble in a mouthful of cooked beans.

Soaking dried beans softens the outer layer and allows them to cook more quickly, thus retaining nutrients otherwise lost by excessive heating. Some people cook beans in their soaking liquid to avoid losing nutrients that leach out during soaking. On the other hand, nutrient loss through soaking is likely minimal, and beans are easier to digest if cooked in clean water. To soak beans, cover them with three times as much water as there are beans, changing their water three or four times during soaking. Or place beans in the same amount of cold water, bring them to a boil, turn off the heat, and soak for one hour. Only a few beans, such as the tough-skinned fava and soy, require overnight soaking.

To cook the beans, drain them and place them in a large, heavy pot, adding enough cold, fresh water to generously cover the beans. Do not add salt until the last half-hour of the cooking time because it will toughen the beans. Bring the liquid to a boil, skim the scum from the top, reduce the heat to maintain a slow simmer, partially cover, and cook until tender. See page 126 for cooking times for different beans.

The quickest and easiest way to prepare beans – and the method that leaves the most nutrients intact – is pressure-cooking. Rinse the beans, checking for pebbles, then follow the instructions for

Scotch broth

your pressure cooker. The beans will cook in a matter of minutes. The only problem I had when first using my pressure cooker for beans was that I consistently overcooked them. But with a bit of practice, it is possible to produce tender, firm beans in a very short time.

Adzuki Beans: Most commonly used in Chinese cooking, adzuki beans are small, dark red and almost shiny in appearance. Their flavour is quite sweet when they are cooked, and they are readily available in health-food shops and Chinese specialty stores.

Black Beans: Also known as turtle beans and Mexican black beans, black beans are tiny, flat and dusty black with a small white spot. They are the most popular cooking bean in Mexico and the Caribbean, where they are used in a wide variety of dishes. They work wonderfully in soups. Sherry is a particularly effective taste enhancer in black bean dishes.

One of my favourite black bean recipes is a very simple one: Soak 2 cups (500 mL) of beans overnight in cold water. Drain, and add water to cover. Cook approximately two hours, until almost tender. Meanwhile, chop 1 large onion, 5 cloves garlic and 2 green peppers, and sauté in 4 tablespoons (60 mL) of olive oil. Stir in chopped, seeded jalapeño peppers to taste (for mild seasoning, 3 peppers), as well as a little tomato paste and a bit of cumin. Add mixture to

Grains, Beans & Things

Hummus

Cannellini Beans: Also called white kidney beans, cannellini are grown and widely used in Italy. The dried or canned beans available in North American supermarkets are imported from Italy. Navy beans and great northern beans can be substituted for them quite successfully, but I have never had trouble finding cannellini (usually tinned). If you are using tinned beans, rinse them thoroughly before starting to cook.

Cooked cannellini are very tasty when marinated in a tart vinaigrette sauce overnight and served cold. They are also a flavourful addition to hearty tomato-based soups.

Chili Beans: Most commonly used in refried beans (*frijoles refritos*), these are also called pink beans. They look very much like pinto beans, and the two can be used interchangeably. They are available either dried or tinned.

Fava Beans: The fresh, dried and canned forms of this dark brown or white bean are quite different in flavour and cannot be used interchangeably. Although the dried form is the one with which North Americans are most familiar, I will make one comment about fresh fava beans: never serve them in their pods, because some people have a very strong allergy to the pod lining. Peel dried beans after soaking and before cooking; otherwise, the cooking technique is the same as for fresh beans in general.

Garbanzo Beans: Garbanzo beans, also called chickpeas, are very popular with North Americans, especially those who enjoy Middle Eastern food. Cooking time, after soaking, is relatively short—45 to 60 minutes. They are delicious in soups, stews and salads, with their crunchy texture and mild, nutty flavour. They form the base of felafel, a tangy, tasty deep-fried fritter usually served in pita and topped with garlic-yogurt mayonnaise. Cooked chickpeas freeze well, and their cooking liquid is particularly flavourful in soup stocks.

beans and continue cooking for half an hour. Serve with sour cream, salsa and grated cheese.

This tangy bean dish is quick and easy to prepare (it tastes even better reheated the next day) and is also delicious served cold as a dip or a spread.

Black-Eyed Peas: A staple of western African cooking, black-eyed peas are widely grown in other parts of the world as well. Generally available both dried and canned in supermarkets, they can occasionally be found fresh in the summer. Very small, they are an off-white colour and have a black spot on the inner curve—hence their name. In the southern United States, they are often combined with pork hocks or salt pork and served with corn bread. Cooking time for black-eyed peas is 1½ hours after soaking. One pound (500 g) of the dried beans will serve six people. Yellow-eyed peas, which differ only in colour, can be cooked the same way.

Hummus

Hummus is a delicious chickpea dip that can be served with vegetables or pita triangles. Vary the quantity of garlic to suit personal taste—I like it very strong, and this recipe reflects it.

5	large cloves garlic, minced	5
¾ cup	tahini	175 mL
⅔ cup	lemon juice	150 mL
	salt	
2 cups	cooked chickpeas	500 mL

Mash 2 cloves garlic to a paste, then stir in tahini. Slowly add ½ cup (125 mL) water and ⅓ cup (75 mL) lemon juice, beating well. Add more water—up to ½ cup (125 mL)—a little at a time, until sauce is thick. Stir in salt to taste. Set aside.

In a separate bowl, mash remaining garlic. Add chickpeas and ½ cup (125 mL) water and mash until smooth. Beat in remaining lemon juice by tablespoons. Add garlic-tahini sauce in a thin, steady stream, beating continuously until incorporated.

Makes 2 to 3 cups (500 to 750 mL).

Great Northern Beans: One of the most readily procurable white beans, great northerns can be used interchangeably with navy beans, although they are somewhat larger. They are very tasty in baked bean recipes and delicious in cassoulet, a French casserole of beans, sausage and preserved duck. They can even be cooked, puréed and served as a side dish.

Kidney Beans: Red kidney beans are among the most popular in Canada. All too often, though, they show up in oversalted, oversugared and overcooked canned versions in which they might as well be cardboard for all the flavour and nutrition they contribute. They are the main ingredient in chili con carne and appear in many versions of baked beans and bean salads.

Chili con carne

Chili Con Carne

2 lbs.	stewing beef	1 kg
6 Tbsp.	oil	90 mL
2 cups	chopped onion	500 mL
3	large cloves garlic, minced	3
3 Tbsp.	chili powder	45 mL
6 oz.	tomato paste	175 g
2 cups	stewed tomatoes	500 mL
3 cups	beef stock	750 mL
	salt & pepper	
2 cups	cooked kidney beans	500 mL

Cut beef into ½-inch (1.25 cm) cubes. Heat 3 tablespoons (45 mL) oil in heavy skillet, add meat and cook, stirring, until browned. Place in large, heavy pot.

Heat remaining oil in skillet, and sauté onion and garlic until golden—5 minutes. Remove from heat, add chili powder, then tomato paste. Mix well, then add stewed tomatoes, beef stock and salt and pepper. Place the mixture in pot with meat, mix well and bring to a boil. Reduce heat, cover and simmer for 1½ hours. Add beans and cook for another 20 minutes.

Serves 6.

Lentils: Lentils are one of the beans that do not require soaking before cooking, and their cooking time is short: 20 minutes should be sufficient once the water has come to a full boil. Both brown and orange lentils, which have similar flavour and nutritional value, are available. I generally use the brown because the colour is less obtrusive.

Mung Beans: Mung beans are most commonly used for sprouts. Although many kinds of beans and seeds can be sprouted, mung bean sprouts are the ones generally found in supermarkets. Their delicate flavour and crispy texture hold up well in stir-fried dishes.

Green- or black-skinned mung beans will cook in less than an hour after a four-to-six-hour soaking. The uncooked beans can be stored in a dry place for several months.

Navy Beans: Navy beans, small, oval and white, are much like great northern beans and cannellini, so refer to those sections for details. Navy is the bean of choice for baked beans but is also delicious in soups or stews or marinated and served as a salad.

Grains, Beans & Things

Marinated White Bean Salad

2 cups	uncooked navy beans	500 mL
¾ cup	sugar	175 mL
1 tsp.	salt	5 mL
½ tsp.	pepper	2 mL
⅔ cup	vinegar	150 mL
1 cup	oil	250 mL
1	green pepper, chopped	1
1	onion, chopped	1
½ cup	chopped parsley	125 mL

Soak beans in water overnight. Add water to cover and cook until tender. Cool. Combine remaining ingredients. Pour over cooled beans and marinate overnight.

Pinto Beans: Pale pink and speckled with brown spots, these medium-sized beans can be used interchangeably with chili beans, described earlier.

Soybeans: Easily the world's most important bean, the soybean is loaded with protein. Grown throughout the world, it provides primary nutrition for millions of people. Although this bean originated in the Far East, the United States is now the world's largest producer.

Soybeans appear in many forms — whole and dried for cooking, hulled and roughly ground as soy grits, fermented into miso, turned into bean curd (tofu) and, of course, made into soy sauce. See the appropriate entries for information on miso, tofu and soy sauce.

Dried soybeans are readily available and very inexpensive. They can be stored indefinitely if kept dry. They require a long cooking time, so a pressure cooker is especially handy. Otherwise, soak them overnight, then cook them in simmering water for 2½ to 3 hours. Soybeans can be sprouted, although the taste is rather strong for most people.

Although the soybeans we usually see are white, there are also black types, generally carried only by health-food and Chinese-grocery stores. These

Marinated white bean salad

beans are also available fermented, which results in a very strong salty taste. The fermented black beans can be added to many Chinese dishes, particularly Cantonese style, and are usually cooked with garlic. Be sure to rinse them thoroughly before using. Fermented black beans are the base of

black bean sauce, which even though it is readily available commercially, can be made easily at home.

Split Peas: Both green and yellow split peas are available, the two forms tasting much alike. They cook quickly and do not require soaking. Their most common use is in split pea soup, where they are often combined with a ham bone for a hearty, tasty midwinter soup.

Split Pea Soup

4	cloves garlic	4
½ tsp.	cumin powder	2 mL
1 tsp.	peppercorns	5 mL
2 Tbsp.	oil	30 mL
1 Tbsp.	black mustard seeds	15 mL
1 tsp.	cumin seeds	5 mL
8	tomatoes	8
1 cup	water	250 mL
1 tsp.	turmeric	5 mL
1 tsp.	salt	5 mL
	lemon juice	
3 cups	cooked split peas	750 mL

Mash garlic, cumin powder and peppercorns with mortar and pestle, leaving some texture.

Heat oil in heavy skillet. Add mustard seeds and cook until they pop. Add cumin seeds and cook for 1 minute, then add mashed spices, tomatoes, water, turmeric and salt. Bring to a boil, then add lemon juice and peas. Simmer for 10 minutes. Garnish with fresh coriander.

Serves 4.

Bulgur

Cracked wheat that has been partially cooked and roasted, bulgur is the main grain product used in the Middle East and in Mediterranean Europe. It can be purchased in health-food shops and should be stored in the refrigerator. Tabouli, a salad made with bulgur, makes a light, tasty summer lunch.

Tabouli

1 cup	dry bulgur	250 mL
2	bunches parsley	2
6	tomatoes	6
2	onions	2
2	cucumbers	2
	juice of 2 lemons	
¾ cup	olive oil	175 mL
	salt & pepper	

Split pea soup

Cover bulgur with boiling water and soak until it is softened—about 15 minutes. Drain and rinse under cold water. Chop the vegetables, and combine them with softened bulgur, then toss the mixture with lemon juice and olive oil. Season to taste with salt and pepper. Chill well before serving.

Serves 8.

Coconut

In North American cooking, coconut is most often used in its dried, shredded form in cakes, cookies and muffins. Much of the rest of the world, however, has more varied uses for coconut—both fresh and dried—in stews, curries and

Grains, Beans & Things

other main-course dishes, as well as in beverages and desserts.

When buying a fresh coconut, shake it to make sure that it sounds as if it is full of liquid. When you get it home, poke holes through two of the three "eyes" on the end of the coconut, and pour out the liquid, which you can drink as is or add to other beverages for a sweetener. Crack the coconut with a hammer until the hard outer layer can be pulled off, and peel away the inner brown skin with a sharp knife. The coconut can then be eaten as is or chopped and shredded for use in cooking.

Dried coconut works well as a substitute for fresh in cooking. Store it tightly packaged on the shelf or in the freezer. Buy only unsweetened coconut, especially if it is for main-course dishes.

To make coconut milk (when a recipe calls for coconut milk, it does not mean the liquid inside the coconut), place 1 cup (250 mL) of shredded coconut (fresh or dried) in a blender, add 1 cup (250 mL) of boiling water or milk, and blend for a few minutes. Let it stand for 30 minutes, then strain, pushing it through the strainer with a wooden spoon to remove as much of the liquid as possible. Use the coconut with fresh liquid two or three more times before discarding it.

Cornstarch

The flavour of cornstarch when used as a thickener in sauces and soups is less noticeable than that of flour but more so than that of most other starches (arrowroot, for instance, which has practically no flavour at all). It dissolves readily and is inexpensive, so it is handy to keep around. Dissolve it first in a bit of cold water before adding it to the liquid to be thickened, which should be at a rolling boil. Stir in, and continue stirring until the liquid has thickened, then reduce the heat immediately. Serve as soon as possible, because the starch will soon begin to break down.

Gelatin

Gelatin is a carbohydrate derived from animal bones. Nonanimal gelatins, chiefly the vegetable gum agar, provide a viable alternative for vegetarians. Plain gelatin can be found in powdered form either in small envelopes or in bulk. It lasts indefinitely if kept absolutely dry, and I prefer to buy it in bulk to save money and packaging. I have kept some on my pantry shelf in a tightly covered glass jar for two years without any noticeable deterioration.

Use gelatin to set mousses and other chilled desserts. A gelatin-and-fruit-juice jelly is much better than a highly sweetened commercial mix. Work carefully, however, to avoid lumpiness. First, soften the gelatin in a bit of cold water, then add boiling water to dissolve it completely. Do not use too much, or the result will be gluey and rubbery. One tablespoon (15 mL) of gelatin thickens 2 cups (500 mL) of liquid, but soften and dissolve it first in 3 tablespoons (45 mL) each of cold and boiling water. When the gelatin is completely dissolved, add it to the liquid to be thickened. Stir thoroughly to prevent lumping. Clear liquids with gelatin added will need only about two hours of refrigeration to set, but if solids are mixed in, allow four hours or more.

Milk, Powdered

No pantry should be without a supply of powdered milk. Not only is it handy if you run out of liquid milk in the midst of preparing a dish, but small amounts also help to raise the protein level of muffins, quick breads and other foods. Both instant and noninstant powdered milk are available. The instant, found in most supermarkets, can be mixed into a liquid very quickly with no concern about lumping. The noninstant variety, which is often found only in health-food stores, must be mixed vigorously either by hand or in a blender, but it has the advantage of containing substantially more nutrients. Keep powdered milk tightly covered in the freezer, and bring it out as required. It can be mixed up straight from the freezer.

Millet

Although most commonly used in North America as birdseed, millet is a staple grain for many people in the world. It can be prepared as a breakfast cereal or cooked like rice, as described below.

Use 4 cups (1 L) of water for each cup (250 mL) of millet. Bring the water to a boil, and stir in the millet; lower the heat and simmer, covered, for 30 to 40 minutes, or until the water is absorbed. For a nuttier flavour, briefly sauté millet in oil before adding it to the boiling water. As with rice, sautéed vegetables can be added to the millet to produce a sort of pilaf.

Millet can be purchased at health-food stores and will keep indefinitely on the pantry shelf if tightly covered.

Nuts

Whether in the form of chopped walnuts in a fruit bread, whole almonds in a stir-fry, a garnish on a cake or pastry or an integral part of a main dish, nuts are used throughout the world in cooking of all kinds. Some cuisines rely heavily on nuts as a primary protein source; others use them as additions to dishes. Some nuts, such as walnuts and pecans, are seeds, others are fruits, and still others are tubers (peanuts). They all contain high amounts of protein and fat, and most have very little starch.

Nuts are available whole, chopped, sliced, ground, in butters, blanched, raw, roasted, salted and unsalted. My kitchen is never without a good supply of several kinds in various forms. Nuts

Tabouli

store best in their shells, but shelled nuts will keep as long as a year if frozen.

To blanch nuts, first shell them, then pour boiling water over them. Let them stand very briefly – one minute will be sufficient – drain, rinse with cold water, and drain again. The thin skin on the nut can then easily be popped or rubbed off. Nuts can be roasted to enhance their flavour in a moderate oven – 300 degrees F (150 °C). Turn them frequently so that they do not burn.

Buy nuts from a store that you know has a rapid turnover. You can keep them fresh once you buy them, but if they have been sitting on a shelf in a shop for a long time, there isn't much you can do. Buying nuts from a health-food store, where you can serve yourself and avoid overpackaging, is also more economical.

Almonds: Almonds are favourites both for cooking and for eating from the hand. Several varieties of roasted almonds are marketed these days, and if you stay away from the heavily salted ones, you can enjoy a quick, easy and relatively nutritious snack. For cooking, almonds are commonly available whole (blanched and unblanched), sliced, slivered, ground and in marzipan, a wonderful concoction of almond paste and confectioners' sugar that can be used in cake icings, candies and chocolates. Almond butter, although more expensive than peanut butter, is delicious as an oc-

Grains, Beans & Things

Gâteau Marguerite

casional treat and is the best nut butter for those with allergies to peanut moulds. Almonds are relatively low in fats and can be added to stir-fries, salads, chicken dressings and many other dishes without undue concern about calories.

Brazil Nuts: Brazil nuts are among the most difficult to shell, so unless they are for a nut bowl and accompanied by a very good nutcracker, it is best to buy them already shelled. The Brazil nuts imported to North America are those sturdy enough to withstand shipping and long storage. They have a coarser flavour than the delicate nuts that remain in Brazil, where their oil is used in cooking as we use olive oil. Simmer Brazil nuts for a few minutes in boiling water to soften them sufficiently for slicing. They benefit from a gentle roasting.

Cashew Nuts: Cashews are cultivated in Brazil, India and the West Indies, where the nut grows from the bottom of a pear-shaped fruit. Roasted and salted, cashews are very popular for eating, but they are among the richest and highest in fat content of all the nuts. The skin is highly toxic, although as cashews are generally available here only in blanched form, that is not a big concern. Cashews, particularly roasted and unsalted, are delicious in stir-fries, curries and soups.

Chestnuts: Still available hot and roasted from street vendors in many large cities, chestnuts have a strong flavour that takes some getting used to. Some varieties of chestnuts are native to North America, although many are imported from Europe, mostly from Italy. Chestnuts can be chopped and added to poultry stuffings and are also commonly mixed with red cabbage.

Many desserts include chestnut purée. To make it, cover shelled and skinned nuts with boiling water, and simmer for 25 minutes or until tender. Once soft, purée in a food processor or blender, or push through a strainer.

Filberts: Although the words filbert and hazelnut are often used to describe the same nut, they actually refer to two different kinds. Filberts are European nuts with a taste similar to but slightly more delicate than that of North American hazelnuts, and both resemble that of the more richly flavoured pecan.

An all-time favourite cake recipe that emerged during testing for the third volume of *The Harrowsmith Cookbook* makes a rich, dense cake loaded with hazelnuts that will leave everyone asking for more. Credit for the recipe goes to Trudi Keillor of Berwyn, Alberta.

Gâteau Marguerite

1 cup	butter	250 mL
1¼ cups	sugar	300 mL
¼ tsp.	salt	1 mL
	juice of 1 lemon	
4-5	eggs, separated	4-5
3 cups	flour	750 mL
1 Tbsp.	baking powder	15 mL
8 oz.	semisweet chocolate, chopped	240 g
2 cups	ground hazelnuts	500 mL

Beat together butter, sugar, salt, lemon juice and egg yolks until creamy. Stir in flour, baking powder, chocolate and nuts. Beat egg whites until stiff, then gently fold into batter. Spoon into a well-greased and floured 9½'' (2.75 L) springform pan. Bake at 350 degrees F (180 °C) for 1 to 1½ hours, or until a toothpick inserted in the middle comes out clean.

Peanuts: Surely the most popular nut in the world, peanuts—also known as groundnuts or goobers—make up an integral part of the diet in Africa, although they are native to Brazil. They were introduced to the African continent by the Portuguese and are now grown in several other parts of the world as well.

Almost every North American child (and many adults) considers peanut butter a daily staple. We could do much worse: peanuts contain large quantities of protein and relatively little fat. Eaten from the shell and without salt, they make a delicious and nutritious snack or a great addition to a bagged lunch. Raw peanuts do not have a long shelf life, so if you do not have a freezer, it is advisable to roast them before storing. Place peanuts on a cookie sheet in an oven set at 250 degrees F (120 °C) for 40 minutes, stirring frequently to ensure even roasting. Cool thoroughly before storing.

Groundnut stew is one of my favourite dishes. In its traditional African form, it consists of chicken, ground peanuts, tomatoes, chilies and hard-cooked eggs. My version is slightly different, although equally spicy.

Groundnut Stew

This spicy western African stew calls for chicken pieces, but it can be made equally well with strips of beef. If the stew base becomes too thick, dilute it with stock or water.

8 lbs.	chicken pieces	3.5 kg
	salt & pepper	
3 Tbsp.	oil	45 mL
2 Tbsp.	butter	30 mL
2	onions, chopped	2
4	cloves garlic, minced	4
1 Tbsp.	minced fresh ginger	15 mL
3	carrots, chopped	3
3	potatoes, peeled & cubed	3
3	sweet potatoes, peeled & cubed	3
8	tomatoes, chopped	8
1 tsp.	thyme	5 mL
2 tsp.	cumin	10 mL
1 Tbsp.	crushed dry red chili peppers	15 mL
1⅓ cups	peanut butter	325 mL

Sprinkle the chicken with salt and pepper. Heat oil and butter in a large, heavy pot. Brown the chicken lightly, then add onions and garlic and cook until both are translucent. Add the ginger and continue to sauté for 1 minute. Add carrots, potatoes and sweet potatoes and cook for 2 to 3 minutes over medium-high heat. Add tomatoes, thyme, cumin and chilies, then cover and simmer for 20 minutes. Stir in the peanut butter, mix well and heat thoroughly over very low heat. Serve over basmati rice.

Makes 8 to 10 servings.

Pecans: Oblong with a reddish shell, pecans are the most fat-laden of the nuts grown in North America. The deliciously rich nut meats are curly, irregular halves covered with a thin skin. Available whole in the shell, as unshelled halves and in pieces of various sizes, these nuts are used in such decadent treats as pecan pie and in sweet loaves, such as cinnamon and Chelsea buns, and they can be served with ice cream or coated with a sugary glaze.

Pine Nuts: Two varieties of pine nuts are commonly available—Portuguese, which are long and slender, and Chinese, which are rounder. Both can be found in health-food stores and Asian and Mediterranean shops. The Portuguese nuts are the more delicate in flavour and are considerably more expensive. Both kinds must be stored in the refrigerator, as they are very oily and go rancid quickly. They can be frozen, but their texture deteriorates slightly. Their most common use is in pesto, for which a recipe follows, but they can also be added to stuffings, many vegetable dishes, spaghetti sauce, pizza topping, paellas and pilafs.

Grains, Beans & Things

Pesto

Serve pesto over hot, buttered spaghetti, or add a couple of tablespoons (about 30 mL) to a vegetable soup to enrich the flavour. Pesto can be frozen easily and thawed for nearly instant use. I freeze it in ice cube trays, then bag the cubes so that I can take out small amounts at a time.

2 cups	fresh basil	500 mL
2	cloves garlic	2
½ tsp.	salt	2 mL
⅓-½ cup	olive oil	75-125 mL
¼ cup	Parmesan cheese	50 mL
3 Tbsp.	pine nuts	45 mL

Place basil, garlic, salt and ⅓ cup (75 mL) oil in blender or food processor. Process to a smooth paste, adding more oil if necessary. Add cheese and nuts and blend for a few more seconds, leaving the nuts in tiny chunks to provide some texture.

Makes 1 cup (250 mL).

Walnuts: Walnuts are highly polyunsaturated, so they are good nuts for those who must watch their intake of saturated fats. Their slightly bitter taste can be eliminated by blanching and then roasting.

Pasta

North Americans' enthusiasm for pasta, which began several years ago, shows no signs of waning: new pasta restaurants are springing up, delicatessens offer a wide variety of fresh pasta and specialty sauces, and an array of machines and gizmos is available for making and cooking pasta at home.

Pasta is a healthy food relatively low in calories and carbohydrates, so there is every reason to be encouraged by the trend. If dressed lightly in a sauce not laced with red meat, oil or dairy products, a pasta meal can be filling and satisfying without being heavy.

Groundnut stew

Dried commercial pasta will keep indefinitely if stored in an airtight container. Once the package has been opened, however, put the pasta in a glass jar or metal tin; if it absorbs any moisture, it will not cook properly.

Light sauces should accompany thin, flat noodles. Creamy sauces are best with tubular pasta such as elbow macaroni. Thick, chunky sauces go well with pasta that has holes (such as shell pasta) to catch the chunks.

For more information on pasta, see *The Harrowsmith Pasta Cookbook*.

Popcorn

No house should be without an ample supply of popcorn. It provides a healthy, relatively low-calorie (control the melted butter) late-night snack, and in a pinch, it can also serve as an emergency supper. We usually have our popcorn topped with melted butter, good-tasting yeast and a sprinkle of soy sauce.

Although many varieties of gourmet popcorn are on the market, the standard popcorn available in bulk at health-food stores is quite adequate.

To pop it successfully, use a heavy pot with a lid. Cover bottom of pan with oil, and heat before adding the popcorn. Place one kernel in the pot, and wait until it pops before adding the rest. Cover the bottom of the pot with a single layer of kernels – if you use more than that, you will end up with a lot of unpopped corn. Cover the pot, but leave a space between the lid and the pot for steam to escape. Lower the heat slightly, and shake the pot steadily until all popping has stopped. Pour the popped corn out of the pot as soon as it is finished.

Popcorn will keep indefinitely on the pantry shelf; it can also be frozen, although it must be at room temperature for use.

Rice

Rice, a staple food of most of the world's population, has been cultivated for more than 4,000 years. In the East, it is often a symbol for food itself and has considerable ceremonial importance. Rice did not appear in Europe until nearly 1000 A.D., and it arrived in North America only 400 years ago. Although North Americans are eating more and more rice, our consumption does not come close to that of the Chinese and Japanese, who daily eat between half a pound (250 g) and a pound (500 g) – far more than our annual 10 pounds (4.5 kg) per person.

Rice can be found in any part of a meal, up to and including dessert. While we are familiar with the ubiquitous rice pudding, far nobler rice desserts based on sweet rice have come to us from the East.

Rice comes in a variety of forms, the most common being brown, white, long-grain, short-grain and basmati.

Linguine with pesto

Wild rice, which is not rice at all but another kind of grain, is included in this section, as it is usually thought of as rice.

While different kinds of rice have varying climatic requirements, they all need vast amounts of water to grow. Once harvested, the rice is milled to remove its inedible hull, a process that produces brown rice. White rice is the result of further processing – removal of the bran.

Brown rice, with its nutty flavour and chewy texture, is heavier and less delicate than white but considerably more nutritious. Because it still contains the bran – the seed husks – it will go rancid fairly quickly (usually within several months), so buy it in small quantities or keep it in the refrigerator or freezer.

White rice has a rather neutral flavour and is best used as a cushion for more flavourful foods. It can be stored indefinitely on the pantry shelf if kept dry.

Parboiled, or converted, rice has been steamed while still in the hull, which drives the vitamins into the centre of the grain. The process was first developed to combat beriberi by retaining the vitamin B in the rice. Converted rice takes longer to cook than regular rice, and it is less sticky.

Instant rice is highly processed: it is cooked and then dehydrated. It need only be reconstituted in boiling water.

The kernels of long-grain rice, four times as long as they are wide, remain

Grains, Beans & Things

Chicken biryani

Because it is very expensive, it is often sold mixed with other rices, to which it adds its strong nutty flavour and chewy texture. It quadruples in volume when cooked. Rinse it first with cold water, then place it in a heavy saucepan and cover with three times as much water as rice. Bring it to a boil, cover, and reduce the heat. Simmer for 30 minutes without removing the lid. Remove from heat, and let stand for 10 minutes before serving.

We should use rice more often than we do – it is fairly inexpensive, easy to cook and full of nutrition. Rice is so versatile that you can serve it several times a week without people feeling they are eating the same thing day after day.

Even when rice is simply boiled (as described on page 102), the flavour can be enhanced and altered in several ways. Sauté some garlic and onion in the oil before adding the rice, or add a bit of soy sauce to the water. Cook it in stock instead of water. Add vegetables or finely diced cooked meat or seafood for the last few minutes of cooking. Use it in poultry stuffing instead of bread. Add it to soups: cook the rice first, separately, and add it to the soup only long enough before serving to heat it through; otherwise, the rice will absorb much of the liquid in the soup and become gummy.

Chicken Biryani

Biryani is a rich pilaf that is traditionally made with lamb, although chicken, beef or vegetables can be substituted. This recipe calls for chicken, but an equal amount of lamb could be used instead.

Chicken Filling:

3 Tbsp.	ghee (see page 94)	45 mL
2	onions, sliced	2
4	cloves garlic, crushed	4
1 Tbsp.	dried ginger	15 mL
4 Tbsp.	curry paste (see page 95)	60 mL
2 tsp.	salt	10 mL

separate in the fluffy food they constitute when cooked.

Basmati is an aromatic long-grain rice. Either brown or white, it is my choice for any situation, as it always cooks well (see page 102 for cooking instructions) and has a delicate yet distinctive flavour. Although it is more expensive than plain white rice, the cost is worth it.

Short-grain rice kernels are almost as wide as they are long. They cook into a creamy food rather than one in which the kernels retain individual integrity.

Sticky, or sweet, rice is a short-grain rice that should be used only when a recipe calls for it – it has a taste of its own. To cook sweet rice, rinse and drain it well. Soak for two hours in hot water or for eight hours in cold, then drain and rinse again. Steam, covered, over boiling water for 20 minutes.

Wild rice is the seed of a water grass that grows in the northern United States and around the Great Lakes in Canada.

2 Tbsp.	lemon juice	30 mL
2 lbs.	chicken breasts, skinned, boned & cubed	1 kg
1 tsp.	garam masala	5 mL
1 tsp.	cardamom	5 mL
1	red chili	1
Pilaf:		
2 cups	uncooked basmati rice	500 mL
5 Tbsp.	ghee	75 mL
1	large onion, chopped	1
2	cloves garlic, crushed	2
1 tsp.	grated ginger	5 mL
4 cups	hot chicken stock	1 L
½ tsp.	garam masala	2 mL
½ tsp.	cardamom	2 mL
¼ cup	toasted slivered almonds	50 mL

Chinese dumplings, chilled shrimp and Vietnamese chili sauce

To make chicken filling, heat ghee in a heavy pot and sauté onions, garlic and ginger until soft. Stir in curry paste, sauté for 1 minute, then add salt, lemon juice and chicken and sauté until chicken is coated with spice mixture. Add garam masala, cardamom and whole chili. Cover and simmer for 1 hour, stirring occasionally.

Meanwhile, prepare pilaf. Wash rice and drain. Heat ghee, and sauté onion until soft. Add garlic and ginger and cook, stirring, for 1 minute. Add rice and cook, stirring, until coated with ghee. Add stock, garam masala and cardamom. Stir, cover and cook over low heat for 15 minutes. Fluff rice and stir in almonds.

Grease a shallow casserole dish, then layer biryani—first half the pilaf, then the chicken filling and finally the remaining pilaf. Cover and bake at 325 degrees F (160 °C) for 20 minutes.

Serves 6.

Rice Paper

Such delicacies as Vietnamese spring rolls come wrapped in rice paper—a thin, translucent, dried dough made from rice flour and other starches. When dry, it is very much like paper and will break easily if handled roughly. It can be found in most Asian grocery stores and will keep indefinitely on the pantry shelf when tightly wrapped. Before using, soften the paper by dampening it with cold water and letting it sit for a few minutes. Once it is pliable, fill it and seal by moistening the edges with water and pressing them together. Let it rest briefly, then cook. Dishes made with rice paper may be boiled, deep-fried or baked.

The following recipe is for a hot dumpling that is delicious but somewhat time-consuming to prepare. The dumplings can be made early in the day and refrigerated until cooking time.

Chinese Dumplings

These dumplings can be filled with almost anything—ground pork, beef, minced chicken, vegetables or shrimp—and the seasoning can range from hot to mild. The dumplings can also be steamed or deep-fried. This recipe is for very spicy pork-filled dumplings. Make the dumplings small so that the meat will cook thoroughly before the rice paper burns.

1 lb.	ground pork	500 g
4	cloves garlic, crushed	4
1 Tbsp.	finely diced ginger	15 mL
1 tsp.	five-spice powder (see page 53)	5 mL
3 Tbsp.	Vietnamese chili sauce	45 mL
1	package rice paper, prepared as described above	1
1	egg	1

Combine pork, garlic, ginger, five-spice powder and chili sauce and mix thoroughly.

Cut prepared rice paper into 4-inch (10 cm) circles. Place a tablespoon (15 mL) of filling on one half of each piece of rice paper, and fold the other half over. Beat egg with ½ cup (125 mL) water. Moisten the edges of the paper with the egg-water mixture, and seal them together.

The dumplings may be steamed gently for 20 minutes or deep-fried in hot oil for 7 minutes or until the paper is golden brown and the filling cooked. Serve with a mild dipping sauce such as plum sauce.

Serves 8 as an appetizer. Makes approximately 32.

Grains, Beans & Things

Yogurt energy drink

Salt

Most of us unknowingly consume a lot of salt. Even the cook who never salts food while preparing it and does not provide a salt shaker at the table is protecting diners from only a small percentage of their daily salt intake.

Salt comes from three sources in North America: it is mined from underground salt beds; it is extracted from salt water (the water is captured in shallow ponds to evaporate, leaving the salt behind); and a more modern method, known as vacuum panning, involves pumping water through an underground salt deposit. The water is then pumped back to the surface and boiled until the salt in it forms little cubes.

Regardless of the method, the result is the same – almost pure sodium chloride. Iodine has been added to most salt since the beginning of this century, when it was discovered that it helps prevent a thyroid disease called goitre. Those who consume iodine from other sources need not be concerned about the presence of iodine in salt. Others, however, should be sure to use iodized salt. Magnesium carbonate is added to some salt to prevent it from sticking together in hot, humid weather. Even so, it is often necessary to add a few grains of rice to the salt shaker to keep it flowing smoothly.

Table salt is the most common form of salt available. Sea salt is derived from seawater, but so is much table salt. Its popularity can be attributed in significant measure to the food industry, which decided some time ago to make it a trendy food.

Coarse salt, also known as kosher salt, is not as strong as table salt but can be used in the same way. Because it contains no additives, it will lump in humid weather. The grains are large and unevenly shaped. Rock salt, which must, like peppercorns, be ground before use, is now carried by many gourmet food stores. Pickling salt is a pure, coarsely ground salt used in pickle brines and as a garnish for pretzels, rolls and bread.

All salts will keep indefinitely if they are completely dry. Although a slip of the hand that results in an extra bit of salt can ruin a soup, there are recipes that call for meats to be cooked on a bed of salt without making the meat taste salty at all.

Tapioca

Tapioca is used as a thickening agent and as the primary ingredient in tapioca pudding. It is derived from the cassava plant and is available both ground and in tiny white balls known as pearl tapioca. Because regular tapioca has to be soaked overnight before it can be used, quick-cooking tapioca is very handy. It will keep for several months on the pantry shelf if stored in an airtight container. Tapioca pudding seems to have lost its appeal for many; perhaps the following recipe will help to dispel its bad reputation.

Tapioca Pudding

4 Tbsp.	quick-cooking tapioca	60 mL
1/3 cup	honey	75 mL
2	eggs, beaten	2
2 cups	cream	500 mL
1/2 tsp.	orange-flavoured liqueur	2 mL
1 tsp.	grated orange rind	5 mL
1/2 cup	toasted slivered almonds	125 mL

Combine tapioca, honey, eggs and cream in the top of double boiler and cook, without stirring, over boiling water for 8 minutes. Stir and cook for another 5 minutes. Remove from heat, then stir in liqueur and orange rind. Refrigerate to allow pudding to thicken. Top with almonds when ready to serve.

Serves 4.

Tapioca pudding

Yeast, Nutritional

Yeasts are very high in vitamin B and so should be an important part of our diet, particularly for those who lead high-stress lives or consume large quantities of alcohol or sugar-laden foods. These life-style and dietary patterns deplete the B vitamins in the body; replenishing them promotes good mental health, efficient metabolism and the proper functioning of the nervous system. Since heat destroys the nutritive value of yeast, we cannot rely on baker's yeast as a vitamin B source. We also consume some nutritive yeasts in fruits and vegetables but not nearly enough for a

healthy diet. Several kinds of nutritional yeasts are available.

Brewer's yeast is the highest in nutritional value but also the worst-tasting, although the recipe that follows does a good job of masking its flavour. Torula yeast is also very bitter and is digested slowly. Engevita yeast is quite tasty and easily digested, but it is difficult to dissolve. Good-tasting yeast, not surprisingly, tastes good, is digested easily and dissolves instantly. It is my favourite yeast, and I throw a bit of it into almost everything I make, from soups and stews to muffins. It also tops every bowl of homemade popcorn. All of the above yeasts are available at health-food stores and should be kept in the refrigerator.

Yogurt Energy Drink

1 cup	yogurt	250 mL
2	eggs	2
2 Tbsp.	maple syrup	30 mL
2	bananas	2
1 cup	apple cider or other unsweetened fruit juice	250 mL
1 tsp.	vanilla	5 mL
1/2 tsp.	cinnamon	2 mL
1/2 cup	strawberries	125 mL
3 Tbsp.	brewer's yeast	45 mL

Combine all ingredients in blender and blend well. Chill thoroughly before drinking or serve over ice.

Makes 3 10-oz. (280 g) glasses.

Herbs & Spices

Allspice

With a name suggestive of more than one spice and a flavour reminiscent of cloves, cinnamon and nutmeg combined, allspice is actually the berry of a 40-foot member of the myrtle family native to the West Indies but now grown in Central America and India as well. Once it matures – a seven-year process – a tree will produce its tiny berries for more than 50 years.

The slightly musty-tasting allspice commonly appears in desserts, pastries and cookies. A little sprinkled over a fresh fruit salad is delicious. Pickles, curry powders and red cabbage also benefit from allspice, and its scent is recognizable in sachets and potpourris.

Anise

Anise originated in Egypt, and its popularity quickly spread through the Middle East and Mediterranean Europe to the rest of the world. The Romans and Greeks attributed a wide variety of healing qualities to this carrot-family member, and today, its medicinal and culinary purposes still overlap. An excellent digestive aid, anise can be brewed into a soothing tea or roasted whole with other seeds, such as cumin, fennel and coconut, for a pleasant after-dinner snack. In Holland, the seeds are traditionally steeped in hot milk to create a sedative drink. Anise's powerful licorice flavour makes it a valuable additive in commercial cough syrups because it masks the unpleasant flavour of other ingredients and has a penetrating, chest-warming effect.

In cooking, anise is used whole and ground, alone and in combination with other herbs and spices, particularly in India, Morocco and Arab countries. Its seeds often appear in recipes for heavy rye breads, and chopped fresh anise leaves enliven salads. Two of the plant's more festive applications are in anise cookies, a popular Scandinavian delicacy at Christmas, and anisette, a licorice-flavoured liqueur made of anise, fennel, coriander and sweetened vodka.

Anise Cookies

1¼ tsp.	anise seeds	6 mL
¼ cup	soft butter	50 mL
1½ cups	white sugar	375 mL
3	eggs	3
1 tsp.	anise-flavoured liqueur or vanilla	5 mL
3 cups	flour	750 mL

Crush anise seeds with a rolling pin or grind with a mortar and pestle and set aside. Cream butter, then gradually add sugar, mixing well. Add eggs one at a time, beating each time. Add liqueur. Stir in anise seeds, and gradually add flour, stirring sufficiently to mix. Chill the dough for 2 hours.

Remove dough from the refrigerator and knead lightly on a floured pastry board. Using a floured rolling pin, roll the dough out to ½-inch (1.25 cm) thickness. Cut the cookies with a 2-inch (5 cm) round cutter, place on a greased cookie sheet and bake at 350 degrees F (180 °C) for 18 to 20 minutes or until dough starts to firm.

Makes approximately 4 dozen cookies.

Asafetida

The hardened sap of giant Oriental fennel plants, asafetida was greatly valued in bygone days – the Persians called it a food of the gods, and the Romans depicted it on coins. It has an extremely powerful odour and a garlicky flavour. Used in very small quantities in much Asian-style cooking, it not only changes the flavour slightly but also aids digestion, particularly in bean dishes. Most commonly found in powdered form in health- or Asian-food stores, asafetida can also be purchased in blocks. It will store indefinitely if tightly packaged. If asafetida is not available, it may be omitted from a recipe without significantly affecting the outcome.

Basil

Basil has a long and interesting history. In Italy, it is credited with certain romantic qualities: a pot of basil in a woman's window is said to be an invitation to her lover to visit her. The Hindus wash their dead with basil water and place a leaf of basil with the body for its journey. Basil is grown near almost every Indian temple and dwelling because of its spiritual value.

More than a hundred varieties of the herb exist, and they range from the strictly ornamental to the fragrant and edible. Ruffled purple basil, tall lettuce-leaf basil, the neat little bush basil 'Spicy Globe,' lemon basil and the common cultivar, sweet basil, can all grace our gardens and our windowsills.

A member of the mint family, basil can be used in many different ways. Medicinally, it is a digestive aid and a mild sedative. In the kitchen, it is a common addition, along with oregano, to tomato sauces, and it is tasty cooked with eggs, vegetables, meat and fish. The sweet-clove flavour of basil intensifies with cooking, so start with a small amount and add more later if you want a stronger flavour.

Fresh, whole basil leaves are good in salads, and chopped basil in salad dressings and wine vinegars produces a pleasant flavour. Basil is also the main ingredient in pesto sauce, in which the fresh, whole leaves are blended with plenty of garlic, olive oil and pine nuts to make a delicious topping for hot buttered noodles or other pasta.

Keep basil tasting and looking fresh by storing it in the freezer. Wash and thoroughly dry the leaves, then chop them finely by hand or in a food processor and store frozen in an airtight bag. Small pieces can be cut off as needed for cooking in soups and stews.

Bay

The Latin name for the bay plant, *Laurus nobilis*, means "renowned bay tree." When the Greek sun god Apollo was smitten with the nymph Daphne, her father turned her into a laurel tree to protect her. In Daphne's honour, Apollo wore a wreath of laurel leaves forever after. Over the centuries, the laurel tree has been held in high regard as a sign of glory and accomplishment. Originally cultivated in the Mediterranean, bay is now grown commercially in Central America and the southern United States.

Today, bay has both medicinal and culinary uses. Bay oil can be rubbed into rheumatic joints for pain relief; in the pantry, a bay leaf in the flour canister discourages pests; and almost any dish – soup, stew or sauce – benefits from the addition of a leaf during cooking. Remember that a little goes a long way: one medium-sized leaf is plenty in a soup for eight people. Remove it before the dish is served: the sharp edge of a hidden leaf in a mouthful of food can be an unpleasant surprise.

Bergamot

Bergamot, or bee balm, is native to North America, where it was first cultivated and used by the Oswego Indians of upstate New York. During the Boston Tea Party, the 1773 American boycott of British tea, expatriate Britons drank bergamot tea as a substitute for their usual beverage. Bergamot's vivid red flowers, which attract hummingbirds, make it a valued ornamental plant, but it is also a colourful herb for cooking. Its mint-flavoured blooms are edible and can be added whole to salads or brewed with the leaves to make a soothing tea. The delicate flavour of the chopped leaves can find a place in everything from curry to fruit salad.

Anise cookies

Some hot varieties are useful in seasoning salsas and chili sauces.

Borage

Historically, borage had a reputation for inspiring courage in those who consumed it, but since it was primarily taken in wine, it is difficult to know which substance actually produced the courage.

Borage grows profusely in the wild. Fresh leaves taste like cucumber and are good sautéed in the style of spinach or beet greens. For either a hot or a cold drink, steep the leaves in boiling water, and add lemon and sugar. Peeled borage stems can be eaten raw, and its pink or blue star-shaped flowers are good in salads. Although the leaves are tasteless when dry, the flowers can be candied and used to decorate cakes and pastries.

Caraway

Indigenous to Europe, the Orient and northern Asia, caraway is also easy to grow in North America. The plant, which is easy to propagate from seed, looks much like dill and fennel but should not, in fact, be grown close to either, as they will suffer for it.

While caraway is an excellent digestive aid – its seeds can be chewed or steeped briefly in boiling water to make a tea – it appears most commonly in rye

Herbs & Spices

Cardamom bread

enough to do, since it is the second most expensive spice in the world, surpassed only by saffron.

Cardamom Bread

Traditionally a Swedish holiday food, cardamom bread has many variations. It is a relatively easy bread to make, with chopped fruit and nuts sprinkled on top. More ambitious bread makers may wish to braid the dough or shape it into a wreath and make a fruit-and-nut filling.

2 Tbsp.	dry yeast	30 mL
2 cups	milk	500 mL
⅔ cup	butter	150 mL
2	eggs	2
⅓ cup	honey	75 mL
1 tsp.	ground cardamom	5 mL
6-7 cups	flour	1.5-1.75 L
	chopped apricots	
	slivered almonds	

Dissolve yeast in ½ cup (125 mL) warm water and set aside. Scald milk, stir in butter and remove from heat.

Combine eggs, honey and cardamom, beating to mix well. Pour milk-butter mixture over this and mix well. Add 2 cups (500 mL) of the flour, mix to incorporate, then allow to cool to lukewarm.

Add dissolved yeast and enough flour—3 to 4 cups (750 mL to 1L)—to make a workable dough. Knead on floured board until elastic, adding flour as needed. Place dough in greased bowl, cover and let rise in a warm place until doubled in size—about 1 hour.

Punch dough down, knead again briefly, then let rise until doubled again.

Punch dough down one more time, divide in half, and shape each half into a loaf. Place in greased loaf pans, cover and let rise for 30 minutes. Sprinkle with apricots and almonds.

Bake at 375 degrees F (190°C) for 20 to 30 minutes, or until pans sound hollow when knocked on the bottom and a toothpick inserted into bread comes out clean. Remove from pans and allow to cool slightly. Serve.

Makes 2 loaves.

breads, where it adds a slightly acrid flavour and a crunchy texture. There are few foods that do not benefit from being combined with caraway—the nutty herb enhances cheese, eggs, vegetables and many other foods. I sauté a handful of seeds in butter, then toss them with boiled cabbage. The seeds can also be used in stews such as goulash. And those who really like the flavour of caraway can serve the root as a vegetable. It is delicious when peeled and sautéed in butter with sesame seeds or steamed plain and puréed. Caraway also appears in liqueurs, most notably aquavit.

Cardamom

Cardamom, a member of the ginger family, grew in the Hanging Gardens of Babylon and was used for its reputed aphrodisiac qualities. A woody perennial that takes three years to produce seeds, it can be purchased in pods, as seeds or ground. The seedpods are white, green or black, depending on the drying method: white pods have been bleached, green ones dried in an oven

and black ones dried in the sun.

Although it is a laborious task to remove the seeds from the pods, the effort is well rewarded; cardamom's delicate cinnamonlike flavour is best preserved in the whole form, so the spice will always be fresher and taste stronger if you buy pods and remove the seeds as needed. The easiest way to extract the seeds is to crush the pods with a rolling pin and pick the seeds from the shells. If making a simmered meal such as a rice dish or stew, you can use the entire pod for flavour, but remember to remove it before serving the meal.

The ground form of cardamom is used in both savoury and sweet dishes. It plays a key role in curry and is an ingredient in garam masala, a mixture of ground spices. In Sweden, cardamom is used in cakes, pies, cookies and breads. Swedish meatballs and sauerbraten also benefit from its flavour. Cardamom can be purchased ground, or it can be powdered by hand before being added to sweet dishes. Because it loses its flavour very quickly, keep ground cardamom only in small quantities. That is easy

Cabbage salad

Cayenne

I nearly sent my dinner guests home in tears one night by grinding my own cayenne pepper. I put some dried cayenne peppers into a blender to powder them, and when I innocently removed the lid, thousands of tiny but pungent particles charged the air. One of the hottest spices, cayenne is aptly named from the Greek word for "to bite." A member of the genus *Capsicum*, its active ingredient is capsaicin, which causes eyes to burn and noses to run. If you decide to grind cayenne from dried pods, be very careful not to inhale the dust – an uncontrollable sneezing jag or serious burns to your nostrils can result.

Use cayenne in cooking whenever you want a real bite of hotness, but do so with caution: different types vary in hotness, and people vary in their tolerance to it. Start with a bit, and add more if needed, bearing in mind that cayenne gets hotter the longer it cooks. A dish that is cooked, cooled and reheated also tends to be hotter than expected.

Oddly enough, cayenne provides relief from indigestion. It is high in vitamin C as well as in niacin, potassium and iron. I mix cayenne with boiling water, freshly squeezed lemon juice and maple syrup or honey for very effective cold and fever relief. Use as much cayenne as your body can stand to help sweat out a fever.

Today, cayenne is grown in eastern Africa, Japan, India, Mexico and the United States. The powdered form is a mixture of cayenne from these countries.

Celery Seed

Celery seed, from a wild variety native to southern Europe, should be added to food lightly since it has a rather bitter flavour. Most commonly used in pickling, it is also delicious added to melted butter and poured over cooked vegetables or brushed onto bread before baking. I generally add a sprinkling of celery seed to the mayonnaise dressing for coleslaw, and many of us are familiar with its role in Bloody Marys.

Celery seed can be bought dried and whole, dried and ground, ground with salt or ground with other herbs in a mixture known as celery seasoning. The following recipe is for a marinated cabbage salad with a celery-seed crunch.

Cabbage Salad

The longer it marinates, the better this cabbage salad tastes. You can add more cabbage, onion and green pepper to any dressing that is left over after the initial vegetables have been eaten.

1	cabbage	1
1	Spanish onion	1
1	green pepper	1
1 tsp.	celery seed	5 mL
1 tsp.	mustard seed	5 mL
1 tsp.	salt	5 mL
1 cup	white vinegar	250 mL
1 cup	sugar	250 mL
½ cup	oil	125 mL

Shred cabbage, slice onion into rings, and chop green pepper. Place in a large bowl. Combine remaining ingredients and mix well. Pour over vegetables and stir to combine thoroughly. Let stand at least overnight, stir and serve.

Serves 12 generously as a side salad.

Herbs & Spices

Dill pickles

Chervil

Since almost all of the flavour of chervil is lost in the drying process, it is only worth using when it is fresh. Chervil, native to all of the Eurasian continent, is a very delicate herb with a flavour somewhat reminiscent of tarragon. It is one of the ingredients of fines herbes (along with parsley, thyme and tarragon), a classic French herb blend for stews, fish and many other dishes. The plant itself bears a strong resemblance to flat-leaved parsley, and although parsley has a stronger flavour, it can be substituted for chervil when necessary. The main trick to cooking with chervil is to add it at the end of the cooking time to prevent it from becoming bitter.

Chives

Do not let these slender, hollow shoots deceive you. Added by a steady hand, chives give a delicate onion flavour to salads, soups and egg dishes (especially omelettes). Blend with butter or cream cheese, and serve over baked potatoes. As tiny as they are, chives left too long in a mild sauce or mixed with a soft cheese pack a potent onion punch.

Cinnamon

In North America, cinnamon is synonymous with treats: hot, buttery toast, apple pie with ice cream and the spicy, sweet aroma of mulled wine stirred gently with a cinnamon stick. But the spice's versatility is also expressed in such savoury delights as Malaysian rice dishes, Middle Eastern lamb casseroles and stews and Greek pastitsio and Moroccan chicken, in which its fresh, tingly taste mingles with tomatoes.

Cinnamon in stick form is the delicate bark of a tropical evergreen tree native to Sri Lanka. North Americans often purchase cassia, the inferior-tasting bark of a cinnamon-tree relative. The true spice has a subtle, sweet flavour, while that of cassia bark is stronger and sometimes bitter. Pure cinnamon comes only from Sri Lanka and India, although cassia is grown in many other parts of the world. The two are easily distinguished: cinnamon is always rolled, and cassia bark is flat and often chipped.

Many recipes call for cinnamon or cassia in powder form; unless you can achieve the necessary fine consistency with a spice grinder, it is best to buy the spices preground. As with many fragrant spices, the intense aroma of cinnamon is released when it is ground. Luckily, the flavour remains, so there is no compromise in quality when you buy it this way. However, for simmering in chutney and other exotic pickles and relishes, powder cannot replace chunks of whole cinnamon.

Cloves

An ancient spice, cloves are the flower buds of the evergreen clove trees native to the West Indies, southern Asia and Africa. Introduced to Europe in the Middle Ages, when they were used in pomanders and as an antiseptic, cloves today evoke in many North Americans memories of the aroma of a roasting clove-studded ham.

Equally at home in savoury or sweet dishes, cloves should nonetheless be used sparingly. I toss a few into the pot whenever I make soup stock. One or two cloves stuck into an onion can flavour roasting meat or a stew.

An essential ingredient in mulled wine, ground cloves are also frequently added to gingerbread, fruitcake, mince pies and cookies. Since ground cloves quickly take on a musty taste, it is better to buy them whole and grind them with a mortar and pestle as needed.

Oil of cloves has long been a home remedy for a throbbing tooth. I remember my mother using oil of cloves as a remedy for toothaches. The smell was overpowering, but the treatment always seemed to do the trick.

Coriander

The Chinese have been using coriander since 5000 B.C., and its frequent mention in the Bible caused its popularity to spread far and wide. In the form of fresh leaves, the herb is now used in all cultures, appearing as cilantro in Mexican cooking, as Italian parsley in some European cuisines and as coriander in many Indian and Chinese dishes.

The taste of coriander has been compared to that of soap, but I find it irresistible and can only describe it as green. When I bite into a fresh coriander leaf, I can smell, feel, taste and see the rich green of a meadow or a garden in full bloom. Fresh coriander leaves add a wonderful flavour to soups, salads and chutneys. It will keep for up to a week if the stems are placed in a jug of water and the leaves covered with plastic. Do not try to freeze it, because its flavour is too delicate to survive.

The greyish round seeds of the coriander plant are a fragrant, lemon-scented spice available either whole or ground. Their flavour is nothing like that of the leaves, and unlike many other herbs, the two forms cannot be used interchangeably. Coriander seeds have a place in many curries and in other Asian and Middle Eastern dishes.

Cumin

Cumin, the fruit of a member of the parsley family, is native to the Mediterranean and northern Africa, where it is used widely in food preparation; it also appears in Indian, Spanish and Portuguese cuisine. The dried seeds look much like those of caraway, dill and fennel, so take care in labelling the jars of spices. (It should also be noted that while white and brown cumin seeds are interchangeable, black cumin seeds are different – they are much less common, have a more powerful flavour and should be used only when specified.)

Cumin tastes best freshly ground, which is easy to do at home: roast the dried seeds gently in a heavy skillet, stirring over medium heat until they darken, then crush them with a mortar and pestle, or grind them in a blender.

Cumin appears in curries, curry powders, curry pastes, couscous and yogurt dishes and is added to drinks.

Dandelion

Instead of cursing the dandelion as an unbecoming weed, enjoy it not only for the colourful enhancement of your lawn but also for its culinary value. But be sure you know the origin of the dandelions you cook with, and never use them if there is any chance that they have been exposed to pesticides.

There is more nutritive value in dandelion greens than in spinach, and the fresh leaves can be added to salads, or like other greens, they can be sautéed and served as a vegetable accompaniment to any meal. A quick, easy and tasty salad can be made by tearing tender dandelion leaves into small pieces (cut out the central core if the leaves are old) and tossing them with crumbled, crisply fried bacon and garlic croutons. Dress with salt, pepper, olive oil and red-wine vinegar.

Herbs & Spices

Tomato dill soup

Dill Pickles

6-quart	basket cucumbers	6-L
1 cup	noniodized salt	250 mL
3¾ cups	vinegar	925 mL
2 Tbsp.	sugar	30 mL
1 Tbsp.	whole pickling spice	15 mL
¼ tsp.	mustard seeds per jar	1 mL
3	heads dill blossoms per jar	3
3-4	cloves garlic per jar, whole & peeled	3-4

Wash cucumbers thoroughly. Cover with cold brine made from 3 quarts plus 1 cup water (3.5 L) and ¾ cup (175 mL) of the salt. Be sure cucumbers are completely covered, and do not use a metal container. Leave cucumbers in brine overnight, then drain.

Combine vinegar, remaining ¼ cup (50 mL) salt, sugar and 6¾ cups (1.7 L) water in large saucepan. Add pickling spice tied in cheesecloth bag. Bring to a boil.

Meanwhile, pack cucumbers upright in clean jars, adding mustard seed, dill blossoms and garlic to each. Cover with boiling liquid to within ½ inch (1.25 cm) of top of jar. Seal, then process in boiling-water bath for 20 minutes.

Makes approximately 6 quarts (6.5 L).

Dill

One of the most delicious fresh herbs, dill can be added to a wide variety of foods – fish, soups, salads – and it always lends a fresh, crisp flavour. Readily available year-round in fresh form, chopped dill is a welcome antidote to midwinter doldrums. It is also available as dried leaves or whole seeds.

The fresh leaves, or dill weed, play a role in traditional Russian and Scandinavian cooking, and the seeds are commonly used in Asian cooking. Dill weed and dill seeds have quite different flavours and should not be used interchangeably. Fresh dill should be stored in damp paper towels wrapped in plastic in the crisper of the refrigerator, where it will keep for several days. It may be frozen for up to six months, but that should not be necessary, since fresh dill can usually be found. Dried dill weed manages to retain its flavour remarkably well and is a good substitute when the fresh form is unavailable.

Dill seed has a much stronger flavour than the leaves. Roast before using, and add small quantities to curries and other Asian dishes. Of course, dill seed is also used in making dill pickles.

The recipe on this page for tomato dill soup is an all-time favourite, particularly for deepest, darkest winter, when a touch of fresh dill can almost evoke the sun itself.

Tomato Dill Soup

When first tested for the second volume of *The Harrowsmith Cookbook*, this recipe was clearly a winner. The soup is a wonderful midwinter pick-me-up even if it must be made with frozen or canned tomatoes, because fresh dill gives it a taste as vibrant as spring. Credit goes to Ingrid Birker of Montreal for the recipe.

10	large ripe tomatoes	10
1	large onion	1
3 Tbsp.	butter	45 mL
2	cloves garlic, minced	2
5 Tbsp.	flour	75 mL
2 tsp.	tomato paste	10 mL

Five-spice chicken

5 cups	chicken stock	1.25 L
1 cup	whipping cream	250 mL
4 Tbsp.	chopped fresh dill weed	60 mL
	salt & pepper	

Coarsely chop 8 tomatoes without removing skins. Chop onion, and sauté it in butter with garlic and half of the chopped tomatoes for 3 minutes. Remove from heat. Blend in flour, tomato paste and stock, return to heat and bring to a boil. Lower heat, add remaining chopped tomatoes and simmer for 15 minutes. Add cream.

Peel and chop remaining 2 tomatoes and add to soup with dill and salt and pepper. Heat through gradually, stirring well so that cream does not curdle.

Serves 8.

Fennel

A beautiful plant originating in the Mediterranean region but now grown all over the world, fennel has feathery leaves and a celerylike bulb topped by a flower and seed head that resemble dill. The flavour of fennel is quite lic-oricey; you can, in fact, substitute anise for fennel in a pinch, but remember to use smaller quantities.

All parts of this plant can be used in cooking – leaves, stalk, seeds and bulb. The leaves and stalk are considered to be a herb, the seeds are a spice, and the bulb a vegetable. Use the leaves in salads and soups or as a garnish. Eat the stalks as you would celery, and use the bulb, sliced and sautéed, to make soup.

Dried fennel seeds, whole or ground, are found in northern European pickles and Malaysian curries. When lightly roasted, whole fennel seeds can be chewed as a breath freshener. The seeds are also sometimes an ingredient in Chinese five-spice powder.

Medicinally, fennel is still used to treat sore and inflamed eyes.

Fenugreek

Historically, fenugreek's primary place in the Western world was as animal fodder – in fact, its name is derived from the Latin for "Greek hay." It is also used medicinally in the treatment of diabetes and to lower blood pressure. Since fresh fenugreek leaves do not have a role in North American cooking, only the dried seeds are available here, and they can be purchased either whole or ground.

Fenugreek seeds are small, square and yellow-orange, and their flavour is strongest when they are roasted and ground as needed. Do not overheat them when they are roasting, or they will become bitter.

Fenugreek is used in many Indian curries, and it is also an ingredient in halvah.

Five-Spice Powder

Available in Asian-food shops and health-food stores, five-spice powder is also easy to make at home. Although the ingredients can vary from cook to cook and region to region, five-spice powder is generally a blend of anise seed, star anise, cinnamon, cloves and Szechuan peppercorns ground and combined in equal proportions.

Five-spice powder imparts a delicate yet slightly pungent flavour to meat in much Chinese-style cooking. I add it to tofu and meat marinades and sprinkle it into miso soup; for stir-fry sauces, I combine it with garlic, ginger, onion, peanut butter, soy sauce, oyster sauce, pepper, turmeric and cumin.

Five-Spice Chicken

6	whole chicken breasts, skinned & boned	6
2"	fresh gingerroot, cut into julienne strips	5 cm
5	large cloves garlic, crushed	5
4	Szechuan peppers, crumbled	4
2 tsp.	cumin	10 mL
1 Tbsp.	five-spice powder	15 mL
6 Tbsp.	oyster sauce	90 mL
½ cup	black bean sauce	125 mL
1 tsp.	hot Szechuan sauce	5 mL
½ cup	light soy sauce	125 mL
2 Tbsp.	honey	30 mL
½ cup	oil	125 mL
	black pepper	
	sesame oil	

Rinse and towel-dry chicken breasts and place in greased 9" x 13"(3.5 L) pans in a single layer.

Combine remaining ingredients and mix thoroughly. Pour over chicken, making sure that all breasts are covered with marinade and that some has seeped under the breasts as well. Marinate for 2 to 8 hours in the refrigerator, turning breasts at least twice.

Bake at 350 degrees F (180°C) for 25 to 30 minutes, or until chicken is cooked thoroughly but is still moist and tender.

To serve, pour sauce over chicken and accompany with rice or noodles.

Serves 6.

Herbs & Spices

Garam Masala

Used commonly in Indian cooking, garam masala's basic ingredients include cinnamon, cumin, cloves, coriander and black pepper. Although these spices can be combined in varying proportions, garam masala is not usually hot.

The flavour of this delicate spice powder is easily lost when it sits on the shelf, so although powdered garam masala is available in health- and Indian-food stores, it is best when freshly ground and mixed as needed. For proper effect, add garam masala just before the dish is served so that the heat of cooking will not destroy its flavour.

Garam Masala Recipe

There are many varieties of garam masala. The one offered here is spicy, but for a more fragrant effect, simply eliminate the black pepper and cumin.

5 Tbsp.	coriander seeds	75 mL
3 Tbsp.	cumin seeds	45 mL
1½ Tbsp.	black peppercorns	22 mL
1 Tbsp.	green cardamom seeds	15 mL
3	cinnamon sticks	3
1 tsp.	cloves	5 mL
1	nutmeg, grated	1

Roast the coriander, cumin, peppercorns, cardamom, cinnamon and cloves separately in a small, heavy frying pan. Place on a plate to cool thoroughly, then grind, using mortar and pestle or electric blender. Mix in grated nutmeg. Bottle.

Makes approximately 1 cup (250 mL).

Garlic

Pressed and tossed into a smoking wok or minced and stirred into a potato purée, garlic is an irresistible herb. But when its full, firm heads are roasted soft and sweet and spread on bread, garlic is a food. I find it almost impossible to imagine a meal, let alone a kitchen, that does not need garlic.

The whole garlic bulb is called the head, or bud, and each section is called a clove. To peel a clove, lay it on a chopping board; turn a broad knife on its side, place it on the clove, and hit the flat of the blade firmly with your hand. This will split the papery skin, making the clove easier to peel. Depending on the recipe, you can crush the garlic, chop it or press it through a commercial hand press. If you use a lot of garlic in cooking, you can save time by chopping several buds at a time, grinding them in a blender and then refrigerating the paste covered with olive oil in a tightly lidded glass jar. When cooking, substitute ½ teaspoon (2 mL) of garlic paste for every clove called for in the recipe.

Aficionados and unconverted alike will love the smooth texture and the rich, almost sweet taste of roasted garlic. Whole heads or individual unskinned cloves can be roasted in olive oil or placed around a chicken or a roast of beef for the last 30 minutes of cooking time. The garlic cooks as it absorbs the oil or meat drippings and is ready when soft. To eat a clove, simply pinch one end, and the garlic slips from the papery cover; it is heavenly when spread on bread and cheese or served with the main-course meat dish.

When buying garlic, squeeze the cloves all around the bud to make certain that they are all firm. If a clove collapses beneath your touch, the bud is probably old, dry and flavourless.

Like onions and leeks, garlic belongs to the lily family and shares with other members similarities of taste and usage, as well as a tendency to sprout green roots when stored in the refrigerator. To prolong its freshness, store garlic in a dry, dark place.

I do not use dried garlic, garlic powder or garlic salt, as I find the taste of fresh garlic so superior that the extra preparation is more than worth it. If you seldom use garlic, however, one of the dried forms may suit you well. I recommend dried chopped garlic as a first choice, garlic powder as a second. Try to avoid garlic salt, which is a combination of garlic and salt – none of us need yet another source of salt.

Ginger

Do not confuse fresh, or green, ginger with the powdered form. While the powder is a ground version of the same part of the plant – the root – the drying and grinding processes significantly reduce the intensity of ginger's flavour. While you can (in fact, should) use powdered ginger in desserts such as gingerbread, do not substitute it for fresh ginger in savoury dishes. Fresh ginger is an important ingredient in all Asian cooking. Combined with garlic, it is used in almost all Chinese cooking. It is often added to oil in stir-fries, briefly cooked and removed before the other ingredients are added.

When buying fresh ginger, look for a root that is plump, firm and unwrinkled. Most ginger sold in North America comes from Jamaica and has a strong flavour and a thick skin, which should be removed. Use a vegetable peeler, taking care to remove as thin a layer as possible: the freshest part of the root lies right under the skin. A fresh spring ginger from China does not require any peeling, but it is relatively hard to find in North America.

Store fresh ginger wrapped in plastic in the freezer, where it will keep for several months. Unwrapped and at room temperature, it will remain fairly fresh for a few weeks, but be selective when peeling and chopping it. Ginger that has been peeled and chopped can be stored in the refrigerator covered with lemon juice or sherry.

Ginger also comes in preserved and crystallized forms. Both are often ingredients in cooking and baking and will keep indefinitely in airtight containers. In my house, however, they barely get through the door before being devoured as snacks. Ginger can be purchased in whole, dried form, in which case it should be stored away from sunlight and beaten before use to loosen the fibres. This form of ginger is generally used to make ginger beer because it is easily discarded once its flavour has seeped into the liquid. Dried ground ginger is readily available, but whole ginger can be ground at home for a fresher taste. Use a spice mill (or a coffee grinder) to grind dried ginger to the desired consistency, then sieve to eliminate fibres.

Gingerbread

½ cup	shortening	125 mL
1	egg	1
⅓ cup	sugar	75 mL
2½ cups	flour	625 mL
1½ tsp.	baking soda	7 mL
¾ tsp.	cinnamon	3 mL
½ tsp.	cloves	2 mL
¼ tsp.	allspice	1 mL
2 tsp.	ginger	10 mL
⅔ cup	molasses	150 mL
1 cup	boiling water	250 mL

Melt shortening, and allow it to cool. Stir in egg and sugar. Stir together flour, baking soda, cinnamon, cloves, allspice and ginger. Combine molasses and boiling water and stir well. Alternately add dry and liquid ingredients to melted shortening, beating well after each addition. Pour into greased 9″ x 9″ (2.5 L) pan and bake at 350 degrees F (180°C) about 30 minutes, or until toothpick inserted in cake comes out clean.

Horseradish

My first experience with horseradish in its raw, unadorned grated form came a few years ago when my children and I attended a Seder dinner given by a

Gingerbread

friend. The whole meal was presented according to custom, which meant that early on, each of us had to eat raw horseradish until tears came to our eyes. One of the other guests, a well-known gourmand who has a particular fondness for fiery-hot food and has eaten his share of horseradish over the years, said he knew he could eat more than anyone else without crying. Most of us were happy to concede without competing, but my 10-year-old daughter rose to his

challenge. For some reason, she was able to consume an enormous quantity of horseradish with no apparent effect, far outlasting everyone, including the challenger. She has never been able to replicate her success, however, and now, six years later, is only beginning to regain her tolerance for hot foods.

Horseradish is the root of a plant of the mustard family. It is most commonly used in grated form – as a sauce served with roast beef, a flavouring in

Herbs & Spices

Cucumber salad with mint-yogurt dressing

potato or creamy cabbage salad and a spicy seasoning in Bloody Marys. The sauce is available commercially in a variety of strengths and, in some cases, is mixed with beet juice.

Cleaned and peeled, horseradish should be wrapped in plastic, stored in the freezer and grated frozen as needed. Once grated, it must be used as soon as possible because its flavour quickly deteriorates.

You can make your own sauce by grating horseradish and adding a few teaspoons (about 10 to 15 mL) of lemon juice or vinegar. Peel the horseradish thinly, and cut out the tough centre core. Cut the remaining root into strips, and chop in a food processor or grate by hand. But beware. The fumes are very strong, and your eyes will water furiously unless you stand well back from the food processor. Also bear in mind that once cooked, horseradish loses much of its potency, so do not dismiss recipes in which it is cooked for fear that the food will be too hot.

Lovage

Simply put, lovage tastes like celery. Easier to grow than celery, it also possesses certain medicinal qualities, having been used traditionally as a diuretic and to help relieve headaches. Eaten but probably not cultivated by the ancient Greeks and Romans, lovage is native to all of southern Europe as well as to the Isle of Skye.

Use the leaves and stem as you would celery – in salads, soups, sauces and stuffings. The seeds can be dried and used in pickling and dressings. Even the roots are useful: to dry them, wash and slice them, and spread them out in a single layer in a well-ventilated place. Store for use in soups and stews.

Mace

Mace is actually the outer skin of nutmeg, which grows in both the West and East Indies. The East Indies' variety is bright red, while that from the West Indies is golden. All mace should be stored in the refrigerator.

In some places, the spice is available unground in a form called blades of mace, which is the dried skin. The flavour is stronger and more uniform in the blades, but the oily consistency and stringy texture make them difficult to grind, so use only in dishes such as sauces, marinades and soups to which they can be added whole and removed before serving.

Mace is more commonly available in ground form, combined with other spices that stretch its volume. Fortunately, its flavour is strong enough that the other spices do not unduly dilute it. The intense flavour also means that it need be used only in small quantities. It is good in spice mixtures and for pickling, poultry and pies, and it can substitute for nutmeg, although in smaller amounts.

Marjoram

A member of the mint family, marjoram bears a strong resemblance to oregano in both appearance and flavour. Native to the Mediterranean, marjoram has been cultivated as a herb and has had a role in religious rituals at least since ancient Greek times.

Because marjoram is considerably milder-tasting than oregano, make substitutions accordingly. It is generally found in dry form in stores, and both fresh and dry marjoram are commonly used in western European cooking. It is a delicate herb that is best added to a dish near the end of cooking. Dried marjoram is good in stews, stuffings or any dish containing tomatoes. Rub fresh leaves on meat before roasting it.

Mint

Few things smell as much like summer as mint snipped fresh from the garden. Of more than 30 varieties of uniquely scented and flavoured mints – apple, pineapple, lemon, orange, bergamot, Corsican and field mint, to name a few – peppermint and spearmint are the most common.

Primarily a flavouring for candy, peppermint also forms the base for crème de menthe liqueur, and it makes a refreshing contribution to cold drinks and punches. Peppermint also has more medicinal uses than the other mints: it is an excellent aid to digestion, it makes a soothing and relaxing tea, and anyone who has treated a colicky baby with oil of peppermint will testify to its effectiveness.

Spearmint has far more wide-ranging uses in the kitchen, where its presence enhances almost any food. Whole leaves of fresh mint can be added to any tossed green salad, while tabouli, a Middle Eastern salad made with parsley, tomato and cracked wheat, uses chopped mint leaves as its primary seasoning. One of my favourite ways of cooking baby potatoes is to boil them in water with several spearmint leaves, which lend a mild but pleasant flavour. Mint jelly, of course, has long been a condiment for roast lamb, but mint can also be used in marinades, and fresh whole leaves can be rubbed directly onto lamb before it is roasted.

Cucumber Salad

2	large English cucumbers	2
½ tsp.	salt	2 mL
	freshly ground black pepper	
1 cup	low-fat yogurt	250 mL
2 tsp.	lemon juice	10 mL
2 Tbsp.	chopped fresh mint	30 mL
1 Tbsp.	olive oil	15 mL

Cut cucumbers crosswise into ¼-inch-thick slices. Place in a bowl and sprinkle with salt and pepper. In another bowl, combine remaining ingredients, adding oil last. Place cucumbers in a serving dish, pour yogurt mixture over them and toss well.

Serves 4.

Mustard Seed

Mustard has been cultivated and used as a seasoning for as long as humans have been preparing food. The Romans introduced mustard to the French, who rapidly proceeded to make it their own. The town of Dijon was granted the exclusive right to make France's mustard in 1634 and still produces half the world's supply. Today, mustard outsells every other spice, including pepper.

Four kinds of mustard seed exist – black, white, yellow and brown. Black mustard seeds are found only in specialty-food stores, and these and the brown seeds are used in curries. Added before anything else to the hot oil and stirred until they pop and release their flavour into the oil, they create a dramatic visual display and, more important, infuse the curry with a gentle mustard flavour.

White and yellow mustard seeds form the basis of mild commercial mustards and have a place in pickling and some salad dressings; brown mustard seeds are used in Dijon mustards. Dry mustard powder is generally made from a

Herbs & Spices

combination of yellow and brown mustard seeds and is an important ingredient in homemade mayonnaise. (For information on mustard as a condiment, see page 67.)

Nutmeg

Not until the Molucca Islands, formerly known as the Spice Islands, were invaded by the British in the 16th century did the virtues of nutmeg become known. But the spice rapidly became so popular that the control of its trade contributed to a number of disagreements among 17th-century Europeans.

Perhaps its great appeal can be traced to the fact that, taken in large enough quantities, nutmeg can induce euphoria. Even small amounts combined with alcohol heighten the alcohol's effect. Included in both savoury and sweet dishes, nutmeg is often found in pastas, curries, cream sauces, quiches, custards, pastries and, of course, in such festive beverages as hot cider, mulled wine and eggnog.

Although ground nutmeg is readily available, the flavour of the freshly grated spice is far superior. For this, whole nutmeg is needed, as is a special tool called a nutmeg grater, stocked by most kitchenware stores. If you grate more than the recipe calls for, be sure to refrigerate the surplus in an airtight container. Grate only as much as is needed immediately, and keep the remaining whole nutmeg wrapped airtight and stored in the pantry.

Onions

While onions are treated as a vegetable in most kitchens, they are one of the most basic and essential herbaceous seasoning agents. Originally cultivated in the Mediterranean more than 3,000 years ago, onions now grow readily throughout the world and are used in virtually all cuisines.

A wide variety of onion types is available to today's cook. The basic cooking onion – the one that makes us cry when we peel and chop it – is in supermarkets year-round. It is the least expensive onion and can be purchased in quantity and stored for reasonable lengths of time if kept in a dark, dry place with good air circulation.

The cooking onion, as its name suggests, is perfect for cooking, but most people find its flavour too harsh for raw eating. The much larger Spanish onion, on the other hand, has a mild, almost sweet flavour and is delicious finely chopped in salads or thinly sliced on a hamburger. Red onions are also mild enough for use in uncooked dishes, and they contribute colour as well as flavour to salads. Green onions are a separate type entirely: use them raw or in dishes with only a short cooking time, such as Chinese-style stir-fries, or finely chop them for garnishes. The tiny pickling onions, with white, parchmentlike skins, cannot be used successfully for any other purpose. Shallots – close relatives of onions that grow as bulblets attached to a common disc – have a distinctive but mild taste and are often used in French cooking, where they are minced with green herbs and added to sauces and seasoned butters.

Onions are also available in dried form – plain, as salt or as flakes – but these are definitely poor substitutes for the real thing. Since onions are inexpensive, easy to store and universally available year-round, dried onions should be relied on only in emergencies and in special situations – for example, a backpacking trip on which the bulk and weight of fresh onions would be inconvenient.

Oregano

Whether cooked with tomatoes in a pizza or a pasta sauce or simmered in a hearty stew, oregano is synonymous with Italian cooking. A member of the mint family, it has a robust flavour similar to, but stronger than, marjoram's and is a delicious addition to many foods – eggs, cheese, breads and a variety of vegetables and meats. Oregano is also known as wild marjoram, and its flavour varies widely from place to place, increasing in strength in hot, dry climates. Once the plant is mature, the fresh leaves can be snipped from it throughout the summer. Oregano can also be purchased fresh from local markets. I cut my own plants before the first frost, wash and dry them, carefully remove the leaves from the stem and freeze them in plastic bags. All winter, I have access to the richly coloured and fresh-tasting herb.

Paprika

Paprika was first grown by the Spanish in moderate climates. Although it is available in a range of strengths, it still ranks as the mildest spice derived from chili peppers. Fresh paprika should be bright red in colour; to keep it that way, store it, along with other red spices, in the refrigerator. A cool environment is necessary for more than cosmetic reasons, however: paprika contains considerable amounts of vitamin C but will quickly lose its nutritional value as well as its flavour and aroma if not stored properly.

The finest paprika is Hungarian, which can be found in three strengths: sweet, half-sweet and hot. While sweet paprika can be added to dishes for a dash of colour or sprinkled on top as a garnish, it should be enjoyed for its flavour too. Do not be afraid to experiment with the hot varieties. Spanish paprika, which is more readily available, is less delicate in both flavour and texture.

The following recipe for Hungarian chicken paprikash has a pleasant bite but is not unacceptably hot even for those with delicate sensibilities.

Chicken Paprikash

Serve this rich dish over a bed of tender egg noodles to soak up the delicious gravy. The quantity and variety of paprika can be selected to suit individual tastes.

4 Tbsp.	butter	60 mL
2	onions, chopped	2
2	cloves garlic, minced	2
2 Tbsp.	paprika	30 mL
6	chicken breasts, boned & skinned	6
	salt	
3	tomatoes, chopped	3
2 Tbsp.	flour	30 mL
1 cup	sour cream	250 mL

Melt butter in heavy skillet, then add onions and garlic and sauté. Add paprika and cook, stirring, for 2 minutes.

Add chicken, sprinkle with salt and cook for 5 minutes, turning breasts frequently. Add a little water, cover skillet and cook over low heat for 15 to 20 minutes, or until chicken is almost done. Add tomatoes and cook 5 to 10 minutes longer. Sprinkle flour over chicken and stir in. To thicken juices, cook for 2 minutes, stir in sour cream and continue cooking until heated through.

Serves 6.

Parsley

The world's most commonly used herb, parsley is all too often relegated to the role of a garnish discarded at the end of a meal. Few people recognize the versatility of a herb that can serve as the primary ingredient in Middle Eastern tabouli salad or can be battered and deep-fried as a side dish. Parsley also imparts a fresh taste to soup stock and can be added to stuffings or sauces.

Because of its high chlorophyll content, parsley makes an excellent breath freshener when nibbled after a spicy meal. It also contains vitamins A, B, C and E as well as calcium and iron; in

Chicken paprikash

fact, 1 tablespoon (15 mL) of fresh parsley taken three times a day provides the minimum daily requirement of vitamins A and C.

When dried, parsley loses almost all of its flavour, so it is fortunate that fresh parsley is available at a reasonable cost throughout the year. If refrigerated, fresh parsley can be kept for as long as a week. Wash it well, then shake off as much moisture as possible. Wrap it in paper towels and then in plastic.

Peppercorns

We have pepper to thank or curse for the invasion of North America by white Europeans, for it was the search for sea routes to the East for pepper that brought white people to this continent. Pepper has long been one of the most popular spices in the world, and it is no exaggeration to say that the struggle for control of the pepper trade shaped the course of history. It is not difficult to ap-

Herbs & Spices

Chilies rellenos casserole

as stale as dust and has about as much flavour. Pepper grinders offer a range of coarseness, so pepper can be ground to suit anyone's preference.

Green peppercorns are not dried. They are available tinned – most commonly packed in vinegar – or frozen. Their pungent flavour is recognizable in all dishes in which they are cooked, but they are delicious mashed and mixed into softened butter to accompany such strong-tasting food as grilled steak. Be sure to rinse tinned peppercorns before using them, and once opened, they should be refrigerated in a covered container. Their shelf life is short, so discard any whose colour has darkened.

Szechuan, or pink, peppercorns are not really pepper at all but the seeds of the prickly ash tree. Available in specialty-food stores, pink peppercorns add zing to curries and Szechuan dishes. To prepare them for the table, heat the kernels, mix them with salt, and grind them in a food processor or blender.

Peppers, Chili

Chili peppers belong to the genus *Capsicum*, as do the sweet bell peppers, but they are not related to the peppercorn (genus *Piper*) described above. Early Spanish explorers in Latin America thought the *Capsicum* plants were peppers, however, and the name somehow stuck. Native to Latin America, chilies are now cultivated in many parts of the world. More than 100 varieties and many hybrids grow in the Caribbean, South and Central America and Mexico.

The degree of hotness varies wildly, and sometimes the same plant bears chilies of varying strength. Unfortunately, no guidelines exist on how to distinguish hot peppers from sweet ones – the closest I have come is to observe that peppers which are rounded at the bottom are almost always sweet. That rule worked for me for several years, and then a few summers ago, I

preciate pepper's popularity: while I could manage to cook and eat without salt, food without pepper is difficult even to imagine.

The most common kinds of peppercorns found in North American cooking are the black and white varieties. While they both come from the same berry, black peppercorns are stronger in flavour than the white. The former are picked before they are fully ripe and are then allowed to dry, whereupon they shrivel and turn black. The latter are whole, ripened peppercorns from which the outer coating has been removed. For light-coloured dishes, white peppercorns might be preferred, but black and white peppercorns can be substituted for one another, with some allowance for the difference in intensity of flavour.

If you cook with preground pepper, consider making the switch to whole peppercorns. By the time ground pepper finds its way to your table, it is made a salad with a green and, I thought, sweet pepper. As I started to chop it, my hands began to burn. Without thinking, I rubbed my hands on my face and then on my dress. Within seconds, my eyes and hands were burning fiercely. The heat from that pepper was so strong and persistent that, a few days later when I picked up the same dress, my hands began to burn again. While the sweetness of bell peppers is generally assured – although aberrations occur even there – in the world of chili peppers, inconsistencies are much more common.

When buying fresh chilies, even from a familiar grocer, it is impossible to know how hot they will be from batch to batch. Cracking one open and run-

Preservation Strategy

The best of the dryable herbs are the strong-flavoured ones: savory, sage, oregano, rosemary and the killer chili pepper. Moisture, which delays drying and thereby encourages mildew, and sunlight, which bleaches out both colour and flavour, are detrimental to herbs. Loosely bound bundles of plants, cut and tied together by the stems, dry best when hung for several days in a warm, shaded indoor location such as a pantry or summer kitchen.

The leaves of large-leaved varieties, such as sage, are relatively simple to pluck from the stems, but with small-leaved plants, such as oregano and thyme, rub the stems gently between the tips of your fingers.

Store the dry herbs in airtight containers away from light. When adding them to food, always rub the leaves vigorously between the palms of your hands to help release the flavour.

ning your fingers over the seeds will quickly reveal the intensity of that particular lot. A second guide is that the smaller the pepper, the hotter it is likely to be. Refrigerate fresh chilies, but not in plastic. Place them in a loosely closed paper bag in the crisper. When buying chilies fresh, look for plumpness, firmness and a glowing colour.

The heat of chilies comes mostly from their seeds and membranes, so handle these parts with particular care, especially if you have sensitive skin – or wear gloves until your body is accustomed to them. It is also possible to burn your tongue and mouth when eating hot chilies, so caution is recommended to the inexperienced. Some chilies are so intensely hot that only people whose families have eaten the peppers for generations can consume them without discomfort or injury. If you inadvertently purchase chilies that are too hot for your taste, you can weaken their intensity by peeling them, discarding the seeds, then soaking the chilies in salt water for half an hour.

The array of colours and textures in a display of fresh chilies can be almost overwhelming. They range from tiny to huge; some are smooth-skinned, while others are wrinkled; and the colours include several shades of green, as well as red, purple, black and yellow. Some are long, thin and pointed, others are round, and some are quite flat. Asian chili peppers are rarely available in North America, but any from the following list of the more common Latin American varieties can be readily substituted.

Jalapeño Chilies: Very hot, bright green in colour and about two inches (5 cm) long, jalapeños are readily available both fresh and tinned. The degree of hotness is usually indicated on the tin's label. Bear in mind that "mild" by jalapeño standards is quite hot. Jalapeños commonly appear in a number of dishes, such as chilies rellenos, a traditional Mexican dish in which the fresh chilies

are stuffed with a cheese, egg and milk mixture and fried. It can be fairly fussy work, because the peppers are small and hot, but the following recipe blends the same ingredients in a delicious casserole version. Credit for this goes to Sandra Senchuk-Crandall of Santa Rosa, California.

Chilies Rellenos Casserole

16-oz. can	jalapeño chilies, split, seeded & rinsed	455 mL
1 lb.	Monterey Jack cheese, grated	500 g
1 lb.	old Cheddar cheese, grated	500 g
4 Tbsp.	flour	60 mL
2 13-oz. cans	evaporated milk	740 mL
4	large eggs	4

Grease the bottom of a 9″ x 13″ (3.5 L) glass pan. Alternate layers of chilies with the mixed cheeses, beginning and ending with a layer of chilies. Mix flour with a small amount of milk to make a paste, then stir in remaining milk. Beat in eggs. Pour over chilies and bake at 350 degrees F (180°C) for 45 to 50 minutes, or until mixture is somewhat firm. Remove from oven and let stand for 10 minutes before serving.

Serves 10.

Serrano Chilies: As they ripen, these chilies turn from green to orange and finally to red. They are very hot and, like other chilies, intensify in flavour as they cook. I recently made a huge pot of bean chili with serrano chilies that was to be served the next day. By the time people dug in, the food had become so hot that it was almost inedible.

Fresh serrano chilies are not as readily available as jalapeños. They frequently appear tinned whole or in a pickle with other vegetables.

Verde Chilies: Quite large – up to eight inches (20 cm) in length – verde chilies

Herbs & Spices

are available fresh or canned. They are the mildest and sweetest of the varieties in this list and are often simply labelled "green chilies."

Yellow Chilies: Fresh or canned, whole or sliced into rings, these chilies range in strength from mild to very hot. I recommend that you find a brand that suits your taste buds and stick with it; there is no other way to be certain of the pepper's intensity.

Dried Chilies: Available in many supermarkets, much broader selections of dried chilies appear in both Latin American and Asian specialty shops. Again, the range of hotness is wide, and experience is the only reliable guide. Refrigerate or freeze dried chilies if you are keeping them for more than a few weeks, as they deteriorate quickly. Crumbling frozen dried chilies lessens the burning sensation on the fingers and cuts down a bit on the dust that escapes into the air.

Not a pure chili at all, commercial chili powder should not be used in place of dried whole chilies. Other seasonings, such as garlic, oregano and cumin, have been added. If you want pure powdered chili, it is better to grind your own from dried chilies.

Rosemary

One of my favourite herbs, rosemary, with its needlelike texture, takes some getting used to. Originally cultivated in the Mediterranean, it was introduced to the English in the 11th or 12th century, and it was commonly believed to encourage merriment. It is still a mainstay of much Mediterranean cooking but also finds its way into traditional steak and kidney pie. I always rub a leg of lamb with rosemary before roasting it.

Rosemary is available both whole and ground; unless you really cannot tolerate the texture of the whole herb, however, avoid the ground form, as the flavour is less satisfying.

Here is a recipe for what I call "those potatoes," developed accidentally by a friend a few years ago. We eat them as often as our consciences will allow. The combination of rosemary and cumin produces a rich, pungent flavour.

Rosemary Potatoes

In our house, it seems to be impossible to make too much, or even enough, of this dish. The recipe can be followed quite loosely, and it is readily adaptable to any palate and eating capacity.

12	medium-sized potatoes, peeled & sliced into ¼-inch (6 mm) slices	12
½ cup	oil	125 mL
½ cup	melted butter	125 mL
3 Tbsp.	rosemary	45 mL
1 Tbsp.	cumin	15 mL
	salt & pepper	

Boil potato slices until almost cooked. Drain and allow to cool slightly. Pour oil into 9″ x 13″ (3.5 L) baking pan. Place potatoes on top of oil, then pour butter over potatoes, coating them as thoroughly as possible. Sprinkle with rosemary, cumin and salt and pepper.

Bake at 375 degrees F (190°C) for 45 to 60 minutes, turning potatoes several times so that they crisp and brown evenly. Remove from oil and drain briefly before serving.
Serves 8.

Saffron

Sources differ on how many crocus blossoms are needed to make one pound (500 g) of saffron, but estimates range as high as 200,000. While it is possible to grow the right species of flower in North America, not many backyard gardens are spacious enough to produce the necessary yield.

Originating in Greece, saffron quickly became popular in other parts of the world. Spain is now its principal pro-

ducer. It is the most expensive spice you can buy, so be sure to get the real thing. Safflower, sometimes called Mexican saffron, is similar in appearance and will lend the same beautiful colour to food, but it does not have the same flavour. To be sure of getting pure saffron with the richest flavour, buy it in solid form—dried red threads, the once golden stigmas of the crocus. At home, store it in a cool, dark place, or keep it tightly wrapped in the freezer.

Once used as a dye, saffron produces a vibrant yellow-gold colour and adds a pungent, almost musty flavour to any dish. Traditionally, it is found in rice dishes, curry, bouillabaisse and paella, but it can also be added to breads and cakes. Whether using it for colour or flavour, add it sparingly: less than ½ teaspoon (2 mL) will season a sauce or rice dish for six to eight people; any more will leave an unpleasant aftertaste.

Sage

For as long as I can remember, the aroma of sage as it is rubbed from a young, dried branch has made me think of Christmas, probably because sage is the primary herb in poultry stuffings. But its sharp, lemony taste enhances a number of dishes. Freshly cut whole sage leaves are good in salads, and I often toss a few into soup stocks and corn chowder and add some to omelettes and other egg dishes.

Garden sage is the best of the range available, but some of the flavoured varieties, such as pineapple, offer a particular taste that is sometimes desirable.

If you grow your own sage and want to preserve it for winter use, alternate layers of washed sage with salt in a jar and store it in the refrigerator. Pull it out of the jar as you need it, and rinse it. Buy sage dried on the branch whenever possible; as a last resort, purchase dried leaf sage. Avoid using ground sage, because it has virtually no flavour.

Rosemary potatoes

Savory

There are two kinds of savory: summer and winter. Reputed to be an aphrodisiac, summer savory is the milder of the two, while the stronger-tasting winter savory is thought to curb sexual desire. Summer savory has a slightly bitter taste reminiscent of thyme, and it is commonly used to season cream soups and sausages. The stronger taste of winter savory makes it an obvious choice when cooking game. It is also a great addition to many Italian dishes as well as to southern French beans.

Use both kinds of savory sparingly – only about ¼ teaspoon (1 mL) is required to flavour a dish for four people.

Star Anise

The taste of star anise – in a stir-fry or a sweet and sour Chinese dish – is unforgettable. With every bite, the tiny pods burst with the cool flavour of licorice. A member of the magnolia family, it is native to China, where it grows on a small evergreen tree. It is available in North America at most Asian-food stores.

The seeds of star anise come from brown pods, called cloves, or points, clustered in an eight-pointed star. When a recipe calls for this spice, the entire point – pod and seed – is to be included. To crush the pods or separate the seeds

Herbs & Spices

Cream of mushroom soup

from their casings, place them in a cheesecloth bag and break them apart under a rolling pin.

Star anise adds a delicate fragrance and a unique flavour to Chinese food. It also appears in fruit syrups and jams. If none is available, do not substitute the ordinary licorice-flavoured anise in your cooking, because the taste will be overpowering; instead, try five-spice powder, of which star anise is one ingredient.

Tamarind

The fruit of the tamarind tree is a long, bean-shaped pod with a fleshy inner layer that covers the seeds. The sour pulp that surrounds the seeds is used to season Indian-style recipes in the same way that lemon juice is used in North American cuisine. We are familiar with tamarind as one of the main ingredients in Worcestershire sauce.

Tamarind pulp is available mashed in jars, whole in the pod and dried in bricks. The mashed pulp will keep in the refrigerator for about a week. If all the tamarind has not been used in this time, put it in the freezer. I freeze tamarind pulp in an ice cube tray and then bag the tiny blocks in plastic.

The advantage of the whole-pod and dried-brick forms is that they will keep indefinitely on the pantry shelf; they will, however, need to be softened before they are suitable for cooking. To do this, soak the pod or some of the brick in boiling water until it is tender enough to purée in the blender. If tamarind is not available, substitute lemon juice, using two parts lemon juice for every part of tamarind called for in the recipe.

Tarragon

First cultivated in the Himalayas, tarragon later came into use throughout the Orient and, after the 12th century, in Europe. A mainstay of classic French cuisine, it is used in béarnaise sauce, poached fish and specialty vinegars. It has a slightly bitter flavour, so to prevent it from overpowering other herbs and spices, add small quantities late in the cooking process.

Fresh tarragon will keep in the refrigerator wrapped in a damp paper towel and then in plastic. Stored this way, it will remain fresh for up to a week. For indefinite storage, keep washed tarragon in the refrigerator, packed into a jar of vinegar with a tight-fitting lid.

Thyme

Thyme is a truly adaptable herb that blends well with most other herbs and with the ingredients of many recipes. I generally add a pinch of thyme to mayonnaise, and it is the chief herb in my cream of mushroom soup. Originally a decorative plant in the Mediterranean region, where it was first cultivated, thyme is one of the four ingredients in fines herbes; it is also used in bouquets garnis to season many simmering meals and is often added to Cajun and Creole dishes such as jambalaya. Lemon- and oregano-scented thymes add slightly different flavours.

Herb Bread

This nonyeasted herb bread (called a quick bread because you don't have to wait for the dough to rise) can be served with soup or stew

or, for a light lunch, with a salad. If using dried herbs instead of fresh, add only a quarter of the amount specified below.

1½ cups	flour	375 mL
1½ tsp.	baking powder	7 mL
½ tsp.	baking soda	2 mL
2 tsp.	fresh basil	10 mL
2 tsp.	fresh oregano	10 mL
1 tsp.	fresh thyme	5 mL
1 tsp.	fresh dill	5 mL
1	egg	1
2 Tbsp.	honey	30 mL
5 Tbsp.	melted butter	75 mL
¾ cup	yogurt	175 mL

Combine flour, baking powder and soda. Add herbs and mix well. Beat egg, add honey and blend. Add melted butter and yogurt and combine well. Add dry ingredients and stir until just mixed. Place in greased loaf pan (it will still be lumpy) and bake at 400 degrees F (200°C) for 20 minutes or until done.

Cream of Mushroom Soup

This soup will permanently eradicate any desire for canned or dried mushroom soups. It is rich and full of flavour and not particularly difficult to make.

2 lbs.	mushrooms	1 kg
2	onions	2
2	cloves garlic	2
6 Tbsp.	butter	90 mL
6 Tbsp.	flour	90 mL
1 Tbsp.	thyme	15 mL
	pepper	
½ cup	soy sauce	125 mL
2 cups	vegetable or chicken stock	500 mL
4 cups	cream or milk	1 L

Wash and slice mushrooms. Chop onions and garlic. Melt butter in a stockpot, then sauté mushrooms, onions and garlic for approximately 5 minutes—until mushrooms are cooked but not limp. Remove vegetables from pan with a slotted spoon, leaving behind as much butter as possible. If there is no butter

left in the pot, melt another 4 tablespoons (60 mL) of butter before proceeding.

Stir flour into melted butter over medium heat. Add thyme, pepper and soy sauce and cook, stirring, for 3 or 4 minutes. Slowly stir in stock, then cream or milk, cooking until the mixture is somewhat thickened and heated through. Return vegetables to pot, stir to mix thoroughly and serve.

Serves 6 to 8.

Turmeric

Turmeric has been used in India almost since the beginning of time. Not only a dye, it is the spice responsible for the rich golden colour of curry powder, mustard and mustard pickles.

Turmeric is a rhizome, the root of a member of the ginger family. It is available only in its ground form because it is impossible to prepare without industrial equipment: the rhizome must be boiled and dried before it is ground.

In some recipes, turmeric can be substituted for saffron to impart a golden colour (unlike saffron, it is one of the cheapest spices); do not use too much, though, or its musty, floury flavour will overpower the dish.

Taste Test

Generally, 2 teaspoons (10 mL) of a fresh herb equals ½ teaspoon (2 mL) of its much more concentrated dry form. Be careful when cooking in large quantities. A dish can be disastrously overseasoned if you simply multiply the amount of required herbs by the number of servings. Instead, season the recipe to taste. Since dry herbs intensify in flavour as they cook, always simmer the food for 10 to 15 minutes after seasoning, then sample before adding more.

Condiments & Exotica

Chutneys

Chutneys are highly seasoned relishes, but beyond that, they vary widely — they can be cooked or raw, thin or thick, hot or mild, made of fruit or vegetables or a combination thereof. The specific seasoning is a matter of individual taste. Although some of the most popular chutneys are the relatively mild British brands, they are, in fact, originally an East Indian sauce. During their occupation of India, the British adapted the native condiments to suit their palates, and these less authentic versions are the ones with which most of us are familiar. Traditionally, the sauce was used to provide some sweet and spicy relief from the searing hot curries with which it was served.

Storage time depends on the way in which the chutney has been prepared: commercially bottled chutneys will keep for a few months in the refrigerator once opened, cooked homemade chutneys that have been properly preserved have a similar life expectancy, but raw ones will keep only a few days.

Following are two recipes for chutney, one fresh and one cooked.

Fresh Tamarind Chutney

Serve this with any curry, or increase its hotness by adding crushed chili peppers, and serve it with a mild main dish. It should be made the day it is to be eaten. Tamarind can be found in many health-food and Indian grocery stores.

5 Tbsp.	dried tamarind	75 mL
1 cup	boiling water	250 mL
1 tsp.	ground fennel	5 mL
2 tsp.	ground cumin	10 mL
1 Tbsp.	brown sugar	15 mL
½ tsp.	salt	2 mL
1 Tbsp.	grated gingerroot	15 mL
½ tsp.	ground chili peppers	2 mL
	lemon juice	

Soak tamarind in water for 30 minutes. Knead the water into it until the pulp is softened, then press through a sieve, making sure all the pulp gets through and the seeds are left behind. Add remaining ingredients to the pulp and mix well. Makes enough to serve at one dinner.

Major Dynamite's Neotraditionalist Mango Chutney

This recipe comes from a wonderful book, *Putting Up Stuff for the Cold Time*, by Crescent Dragonwagon, which is a product of the back-to-the-land movement of the late 1960s. This is a mild chutney to serve with spicy dishes, and it smells heavenly while cooking.

2	large mangoes, peeled, with the flesh pulled off the pit	2
1	large onion, chopped	1
½ cup	chopped dates	125 mL
1	hot red pepper, fresh or dried, chopped	1
1-2 cups	honey	250-500 mL
1	green pepper, seeded & chopped	1
1½ cups	cider vinegar	375 mL
1½ tsp.	cinnamon	7 mL
1 tsp.	mustard seeds	5 mL
1½ cups	whole raisins	375 mL
1	clove garlic, crushed	1
1	tart apple, diced	1
½ cup	ground raisins	125 mL
½ cup	ground dates	125 mL
½ tsp.	ground cloves	2 mL
½ tsp.	grated ginger	2 mL
½ tsp.	salt	2 mL

Combine all ingredients in a large enamel pot. Bring to a boil, reduce heat and simmer until thick, stirring frequently. Place in clean, hot jars and seal, leaving ¼ inch (6 mm) head space. Makes 2 quarts (2 L).

Miso

Rich in vitamin B, miso is a fermented combination of soy paste and yeast that adds both flavour and nutritive value to soups and stews. A number of flavoured misos are now on the market, and they are usually found in health-food or Asian grocery stores. Refrigerate miso, and use it within several months.

Mushrooms, Dried

Dried mushrooms of many kinds form an important part of Asian cooking. The three types discussed here will keep indefinitely if tightly wrapped. They have distinctive, almost meaty flavours that combine well with a wide variety of seasonings and other foods. Save the soaking water to add to stocks, soups and sauces.

Black Mushrooms: These are expensive, but the flavour is well worth the price. Rinse thoroughly to remove any sand, then soak in hot water for 30 to 90 minutes, depending on the size of the mushrooms. Squeeze, rinse again, and remove the stems before cooking.

Cloud Ears: When dry, cloud ear mushrooms look like black chips, but once soaked, they expand to several times their original size and really do look like a cross between a cloud and an ear. Soak them in boiling water for half an hour, then rinse them thoroughly, and cut off the stems. Chop the cloud ears into bite-sized pieces, and add to soups or stews, or stir-fry with other vegetables and tofu. Their mild, nutty flavour blends nicely in recipes using Chinese oyster sauce.

Shiitake Mushrooms: Japanese mushrooms grown by planting spawn in holes in dead trees, shiitake mushrooms mature quickly. To use them, rinse and then soak them in hot water until they are soft — 10 minutes to an hour, depending on the size of the mushrooms. Squeeze out excess moisture, cut off the woody stems, and use according to the recipe. If wrapped tightly, they can be refrigerated for up to five days once they have been rehydrated.

Chutneys

Mustard

Yellow and white mustard seeds are used to make most North American mustards, including the standard hot-dog variety, the mildest of commercial mustards. Dijon mustard, made with vinegar or wine and black or brown seeds, is much more flavourful. While many types of Dijon take their names from the region of France in which they were once made exclusively, some Di-

jons now originate in other countries.

Coarse-grained, or seed, mustards can vary from mild to very hot. The presence of whole grains in the mustard adds texture. I like to rub it over the skin of ham or pork before roasting and use it to season marinades for boneless breasts or skewered cubes of chicken cooked on the barbecue. Its taste permeates the meat gently, and the crunch of the seeds is very pleasant.

Chinese and English mustards, sinus-

clearing in their intensity, are made from mustard flour and water. English mustard is available dry as well and can be added to food as is or mixed with water and used in sandwiches.

Once wet mustard has been opened, it should be refrigerated and used within a relatively short period. It will not go bad if kept longer, but its flavour will deteriorate. If the mustard develops a dark crust on the surface, simply scrape it off and keep the rest. Since it

Condiments & Exotica

is a good idea to have a variety of mustards in the refrigerator or on the pantry shelf – there are mustards seasoned with herbs, champagne, mixed with honey or garlic and all kinds of other extras – buy only small amounts of the ones you want. Gently stir prepared mustard into the food toward the end of the cooking time to enjoy the full benefit of its flavour.

Sauces

The wide variety of commercially prepared sauces on the market is a great boon to cooks. While most can be made at home, and recipes for some are included, this is one area in which premade is not necessarily bad. By keeping a careful eye on the lists of ingredients, you can almost always find sauces that contain very few artificial elements. That may mean shopping in ethnic groceries and health- and specialty-food stores instead of the supermarket, but the extra trips are worth the effort. Soy sauce, for instance, is available both completely free of artificial additives and entirely in chemical form.

Black Bean Sauce: I use this sauce frequently, and not just in Asian-style cooking; a dash brings a tangy flavour to hamburger patties, meatloafs and marinades. It also combines well with soy sauce and oyster sauce in tofu or vegetable dishes. Steamed broccoli, for example, is delicious when tossed with a few tablespoons of warm black bean sauce. Many brands of black bean sauce are available – look for one that is not laced with salt or chemicals. For texture as well as flavour, fermented black beans can be purchased and worked into a marinade or a sauce. Mash them first if you want the flavour but not the texture of the whole beans. Commercial black bean sauce has a long shelf life and does not require refrigeration – I keep mine on the shelf beside the stove, where it is handy.

Black Bean Sauce Recipe

5 Tbsp.	fermented black beans	75 mL
2½ Tbsp.	oil	37 mL
5 Tbsp.	rice wine	75 mL
10	cloves garlic, crushed	10
5 Tbsp.	minced ginger	75 mL
2 cups	stock	500 mL
2 Tbsp.	mushroom soy sauce	30 mL
3 Tbsp.	light soy sauce	45 mL
3 Tbsp.	oyster sauce	45 mL

Rinse beans well. Combine with oil and mash, then add wine, garlic and ginger. Cook in heavy skillet over low heat for 3 minutes, stirring. Stir in remaining ingredients and simmer until flavours are well blended. If not for immediate use, refrigerate for up to 2 weeks.

Makes 4 cups (1 L).

Chili Sauce: A wide variety of chili sauces is available, ranging from mild to very, very hot. Although we tend to think of chili sauces as having a tomato base, a number are made from other fruits and vegetables, notably apricots and apples. In some, tomatoes are only a minor ingredient, while celery or green peppers may be the base. Many of us have favourite recipes – mine, found below, is for a mild chili sauce that is an excellent accompaniment to roast pork or grilled cheese sandwiches.

Some of the commercial chili sauces are so hot that they are unpalatable to most North Americans. But once one develops a taste for them, there is no turning back. I use Vietnamese hot chili sauce in small amounts in sauces and marinades. Most of these sauces can be found in specialty stores, but if you have access to ethnic shops, buy them there instead, as the price will usually be lower. Chili sauces can be stored indefinitely on the pantry shelf but must be refrigerated once opened.

Chili Sauce Recipe

This mild sauce contains scarcely any chilies—in fact, the ⅛ teaspoon (0.5 mL) of cayenne pepper barely allows it to qualify as a chili sauce. As a sweet sauce, it is wonderful, but if you want something with more bite, add extra pepper along with the cayenne.

6-quart	basket tomatoes	6-L
6 cups	diced celery	1.5 L
4 cups	diced onions	1 L
½ cup	pickling salt	125 mL
5 cups	white sugar	1.25 L
2 cups	cider vinegar	500 mL
1 oz.	mustard seeds	30 g
⅛ tsp.	cayenne	0.5 mL
2	green bell peppers, chopped	2

Chop tomatoes coarsely. Mix with celery and onions, sprinkle with salt and let stand overnight. Drain, and discard liquid, pressing the vegetables thoroughly to remove as much liquid as possible, ensuring a thick sauce. Add remaining ingredients and boil, stirring, until sugar is dissolved. Cook, uncovered, for another 15 minutes or longer until desired consistency is achieved.

Bottle in sterilized Mason jars and process in hot-water bath for 10 minutes. Makes 4 to 6 quarts (4 to 6 L).

Hoisin Sauce: Based on soybeans, this sauce is spiced primarily with chilies. Thick and rich black in colour, its flavour is somehow both sweet and pungent. I use it in sauces and marinades, but it can also be a condiment on its own. Store it in the refrigerator once opened. Hoisin will become very thick if left standing but can be thinned with a little oil if necessary.

Hot-Pepper Sauce: Just as the trade name Xerox has become synonymous with photocopying, so Tabasco has come to mean hot-pepper sauce. In fact, it is only one of many hot sauces on the market, all of which have their particular characteristics. The three main ingredients, however, are constant – hot peppers, vinegar and salt.

The peppers used in hot sauce are from a psychotropic plant, as are psilocybin mushrooms and opium. This does not mean that drinking a full bottle of hot sauce will induce a psychedelic trip, but some people claim that the sauce produces a heightened sense of clarity. A large amount of hot-pepper sauce will definitely jolt the system.

While hot-pepper sauces are sometimes cooked and sometimes not, in all cases, the peppers are fermented for anywhere from one to three years, after which the remaining ingredients are added. Once bottled, the sauce will last indefinitely with or without refrigeration, although keeping it cold prevents discoloration. When cooking with hot sauce, add it at the end of the cooking time to preserve its punch.

Oyster Sauce: One of my favourite sauces for Asian-style cooking, oyster sauce seasons every marinade I make for stir-fried meat and flavours fillings for Chinese dumplings and spring rolls.

Plum Sauce: I do not refer here to the oversweetened plum sauce available in small plastic envelopes in many Chinese restaurants but to the "real thing," which has a consistency and a flavour not unlike those of sweet chutneys. Indeed, plum sauce is made in a similar fashion. Readily available in bottles from Asian grocery stores, it can be kept indefinitely in the refrigerator. It makes a delicious dipping sauce for a number of Chinese finger foods – wontons, egg rolls, dumplings and so on.

Soy Sauce: Many varieties of soy sauce are available – including tamari sauce. The kind one chooses depends largely on personal preference. Avoid the artificial sauces at all costs, since they are laden with unnecessary ingredients and do not taste nearly as good as natural soy sauce. All of the natural types of soy sauce are labelled "naturally brewed"

and are therefore easier to identify.

Soy sauce is made of fermented soybeans, wheat, yeast and salt. It can be light (which is brown in colour), dark or black. The differences in colour are minimal, so if the bottles are not labelled in English, it is best to ask the shopkeeper whether they differ in strength. I generally use light soy sauce in cooking and serve the darker ones as condiments on the table. The flavour of soy sauce intensifies with time and cooking, so it is a good idea to start out with a milder sauce and add to it if necessary. Remember also to limit salt (I use none at all) when cooking with soy sauce, which is itself very salty. Because of the salt content, soy sauce can be stored indefinitely on the pantry shelf, although there is some deterioration in flavour. If you do not use it regularly, buy it in small quantities.

Japanese soy sauces tend to be milder and less salty than the Chinese ones discussed above. If you are preparing tempura and want to make dipping sauce, you are well advised to purchase Japanese soy instead of Chinese.

Tamari sauce is soy sauce made without the wheat. As a result, it is much stronger and saltier. It, too, has a long shelf life.

Worcestershire Sauce: Probably the world's most popular sauce, Worcestershire appears on the table in many restaurants that serve steak and roast beef. Many cooks regularly incorporate it into marinades and sauces, and bartenders add a shot to Bloody Marys. Worcestershire contains a number of ingredients, primarily tamarind, vinegar, onion, garlic and molasses, as well as several spices. After it has been opened, it should be stored in the refrigerator, where it will keep indefinitely.

Shrimp Paste

A common ingredient in Oriental cooking, shrimp paste is very strongly

flavoured. Generally found in dried form in specialty markets, it can be stored for several months in a cool, dark place. Only a small amount is needed to flavour a dish. Its strong odour disappears with cooking. If shrimp paste is unavailable, substitute anchovy paste (see page 70) or other fish pastes, but use only half as much.

Tahini

Tahini is a paste made from ground sesame seeds in much the same way that peanut butter is made from peanuts. Popular in Middle Eastern cooking, it is readily available in shops that specialize in those foods as well as in healthfood stores and some supermarkets. It adds a delicate nutty flavour to sauces and marinades. After opening, it is best to store it in the refrigerator, where it will keep for up to four months.

Felafel With Tahini Sauce

This Middle Eastern patty can be made spicier by adding more garlic, cumin, cayenne and coriander.

1 lb.	uncooked chickpeas	500 g
4	onions, sliced	4
4	cloves garlic	4
½ cup	chopped parsley	125 mL
2 tsp.	cumin	10 mL
2 tsp.	coriander	10 mL
	salt & pepper	
	cayenne	

Cook presoaked chickpeas in water to cover, adding more water, as needed, until just tender but not soft. Grind in a food processor with onions and garlic. Mix in a bowl with remaining ingredients. Chill for 1 hour, form into small balls and fry in oil. Serve in pita bread with bean sprouts and tahini sauce.

For tahini sauce, place in a blender ¾ cup (175 mL) tahini, ½ cup (125 mL) water, juice of 2 lemons and 1 teaspoon (5 mL) honey, and process until creamy and smooth.

Miscellany

Anchovies

Most North Americans think of anchovies as an ingredient in Caesar salad dressing, salade niçoise and Greek salad, but they are not at all restricted to salads. True aficionados eat salty anchovy sandwiches without flinching, and in Italy, anchovies are used in many other ways – batter-dipped and deep-fried as part of an antipasto tray, as a stuffing for fresh artichokes and as an ingredient in a variety of sauces and dips.

Although some specialty-food stores in North America sell unfilleted anchovies packed in salt, the tinned forms are much more common. The flat fillets of anchovy are easily mashed and can be used in sauces, dressings and dips, and the ones that are wrapped around capers can be used directly from the tin to decorate a meal or a platter of hors d'oeuvres. Before using tinned anchovies in a prepared dish, drain the oil from the can and rinse the fish briefly with cold water; otherwise, you may get an unexpected dose of salt.

Unopened tins of anchovies will keep indefinitely on the pantry shelf, but once the tin is open, store the fish in a nonmetal container in the refrigerator for up to three weeks. Although the anchovies will not spoil, the flavour of the fish will deteriorate and become overpowered by the taste of salt.

Because anchovy paste is much easier to work with and there is no difference in flavour, I usually substitute approximately 1 teaspoon (5 mL) of paste for every fillet when recipes, such as those for sauces and dressings, require mashed anchovies. Sold in most supermarkets, anchovy paste will last for several months if kept tightly capped in the refrigerator. To keep it from drying out and to prevent the other food in the refrigerator from acquiring a fishy smell, I usually place the tube in a plastic bag.

Caesar Salad Dressing

This recipe will make enough dressing for a full head of Romaine lettuce. If you like, add garlic croutons and some crisply fried bacon bits to your salad. I often make the salad with lettuce and dressing only.

1	egg	1
2-3	cloves garlic	2-3
1 tsp.	dry mustard	5 mL
1 tsp.	anchovy paste	5 mL
	black pepper	
1 cup	olive oil	250 mL
6-8 Tbsp.	lemon juice	90-120 mL
6 Tbsp.	Parmesan cheese	90 mL

Place the egg in a food processor or a blender. Peel the garlic and add to egg, along with mustard, anchovy paste and a few gratings of pepper. Blend briefly to combine. With the processor running, slowly add oil, then lemon juice. When thoroughly mixed, add cheese and blend for a few more seconds. Taste, adjust seasonings if necessary and toss with fresh Romaine lettuce.

Capers

Grown only in the Mediterranean, capers are expensive to buy in North America. These flower buds are usually sold pickled in vinegar, although specialty stores sometimes sell them loose and salted. Keep loose capers in an airtight container at room temperature for up to four months. Bottled pickled capers should be stored in the refrigerator, where they will keep for months. Drain and add them to salad dressings or to melted butter for pouring over cooked vegetables.

Coffee

Coffee consumption in North America is dropping rapidly and steadily – in 25 years, it has fallen by about 40 percent, mainly because of people's growing concern for their health. Evidence has begun to surface that links high coffee consumption with cancer and a number of other medical problems. While consumption may be declining, those who continue to drink coffee are becoming more and more sophisticated in their tastes. Both at home and in cafés, familiarity with cappuccino, espresso and other specialty coffees is increasing. Many models of specialized coffee makers for domestic use are on the market today. Consumers increasingly patronize coffee stores that offer a variety of blends and grinds, and more and more people are grinding their own coffee at home, fresh for each pot. Those who still drink coffee are now drinking a better-tasting brew.

Originally grown more than 1,000 years ago in northern Africa, coffee spread first to the Middle East, then to central Europe and eventually to Martinique. Great Britain and the Americas were slower to take to coffee, since they already enjoyed a well-established tradition of tea drinking, but eventually, they succumbed as well.

Coffee grows in the Tropics on small trees, one of which produces enough beans in a year for about a pound of the finished product. After they are harvested green and processed, the beans are cured and polished, then shipped to the purchasing country, where they will be roasted and sized. Decaffeination takes place before the beans are roasted.

Two main species of coffee are grown today. *Arabica* is often grown at high altitudes, where the slower rate of growth results in a better-tasting drink. *Robusta* is hardier, cheaper and higher in caffeine.

Coffee must be stored properly, or it will quickly go stale. Vacuum-packed, it stays fresh on the pantry shelf for six months. Whole beans should be tightly wrapped and placed in the freezer, where they will stay fresh for four

Caesar salad

months. Ground coffee stored in the freezer will begin to go stale after only a month. Do not freeze it in the paper bag from the store: wrap it tightly in plastic, or put it in a glass jar with a tight-fitting lid. Besides maintaining freshness, this keeps the aroma of coffee from spreading to other foods.

For coffee that is as fresh as possible when it comes into the house, buy it from a store with a rapid turnover. Although a display of coffee beans in open burlap sacks is an attractive marketing feature, it usually means that the coffee has been around for a while. Instead, buy it from a retailer who keeps it in tightly covered containers.

Knowledgeable makers and drinkers of coffee agree that the drip method of brewing is the best, with water at a temperature just below the boiling point. Likewise, grinding the coffee fresh for each pot results in a much better taste – small electric grinders are inexpensive and easy to operate. Use 2 tablespoons (30 mL) of coffee for each cup. The fabric coffee filters carried by many health-food stores can be quickly rinsed out after each use and are more economical – financially and ecologically – than disposable paper filters. Bring 1 cup (250 mL) of water to a boil for each cup of coffee, but wait until the bubbling has stopped before pouring the water over the coffee in the filter. Coffee will lose its freshly brewed taste if it sits for more than an hour after it is made.

To achieve the flavour of the overpriced spiced blends on the market, add a dash of ground cinnamon or other spice to the coffee grounds, or place a piece of cinnamon stick in a bag of coffee beans.

The coffee substitutes now available neither replicate the taste of coffee nor give the drinker the energy hit that caffeinated coffee does, but they are quite appealing as alternative hot beverages. They should be stored in tightly covered containers and kept dry. Follow package directions for preparation.

Oils

We take cooking oils almost entirely for granted, rarely considering, even in passing, the origin of the oil or the process that brings it to us in its finished state. That attitude might be a mistake, however, because depending on both the source of the oil and the processing method used, different oils have very different nutritional values, health benefits and drawbacks. Flavour must also be taken into account, for in some cases, oil contributes a distinctive taste.

First, some general comments about oil. Cooking oils are pressed from a variety of fruits, nuts and seeds, including olives, sunflower seeds, sesame seeds, peanuts, corn, cottonseed and soybeans. Some of the more delicate oils, such as walnut, are only suitable for raw use – in salad dressings, for example – since their flavours break down when the oil is heated. Most oils are so highly refined that it is virtually impossible to distinguish their flavours. Less refined oils, available in health- and specialty-food stores, take some getting used to, for they taste like the food from which they are pressed.

Oils vary as to the temperature at which they begin to smoke. Olive oil has about the lowest smoking point, followed, in order, by peanut, sesame,

Miscellany

safflower, cottonseed, soybean and corn. When deep-frying, select an oil with a high smoking temperature and use it in combination with ghee (see page 94) to prevent burning. Unrefined oils need to be refrigerated; this will be indicated on the bottle. The oil will become cloudy when it cools, but its flavour will not be affected. Allow it to come to room temperature before using it so that it flows freely. Oils not kept in the refrigerator should be in a lightproof container or a dark cupboard.

While oils can be substituted for hard fats in some recipes, the quantity needs to be cut by 20 percent. Substitution is not always possible, however, since oil is heavier than other fats and will not have the same effect on the texture of the finished product, particularly in the case of delicate pastries and cakes.

Cold-pressed oils retain more of the nutritive value of the food from which they are extracted, but pressing is only workable with seeds that have a high oil content. The seeds are crushed with a slow-turning press, which allows the oils to run out and generates very little nutrient-destroying heat. Very few types are produced this way, though, because it is both expensive and inefficient – too much of the oil is left behind in the seed meal. As a result, various technologies have been developed to remove as much oil as possible from the seeds at a reasonable cost without losing the nutritional value.

For everyday household use, common vegetable oil is often the best option. Inexpensive, light and delicate in flavour, it can be used for myriad purposes – in salad dressings, when sautéing foods and in some baking. Olive oil is another one worth having on hand. Many grades are available, from delicate to very strong in flavour. The less refined are more nutritionally valuable, but the taste for them is an acquired one, and it is necessary to be careful about rancidity. Olive and vegetable oils can often be used together – in mayonnaise, for example – to take advantage of both the flavour of the olive oil and the lightness and lower cost of the vegetable oil.

Olive oils come from Italy, France, Spain, Greece and California, and each has particular qualities, although Italian – the most expensive – is generally considered the most robust yet delicate in flavour. Spanish olive oil, while a little rougher in flavour, is adequate for most uses.

With the highest percentage of unsaturated fats, safflower is the oil of choice for health-conscious consumers. It should be stored in the refrigerator to prevent rancidity. Sunflower oil, surpassed only by safflower, is likewise very light and is readily available for little cost in bulk in health-food stores. Canada and the Soviet Union are the world's primary suppliers.

I use sesame oil for flavouring food rather than for cooking it. I often add a few drops to a stir-fry or a hot pot just before serving: it will bring out the flavour of the dish and contribute a sharp taste of its own. Peanut oil also has a very distinctive taste for which it is prized. An extra advantage is that it absorbs virtually nothing from the foods that are cooked in it, so it can be used over and over again. It is frequently an ingredient in Chinese recipes, and if you can afford it, use it. Do not substitute peanut oil for other oils unless you want the flavour to be altered.

Peanut Butter

For what is purported to be a simple food, peanut butter exists in more forms and varieties than one would imagine, and to complicate matters, there are significant differences in the nutritional values each offers. It is important to be aware of the differences, because peanut butter is a daily staple for many people, one that is presumed to be high in protein and low in salt and sugar. Unless you read the label closely and resist the hard sell of advertising, you may well end up with a highly sweetened, oversalted and oily version of what is a very basic food – ground-up peanuts.

Natural peanut butter (the kind found in health-food stores) contains nothing but peanuts ground to either a crunchy or a smooth texture. It is usually available in bulk containers from which con-

Nut Butters

It may be the best known and best loved of them all, but peanut butter is only one of the nut butters. Almonds, cashews, pecans and walnuts make spreads as delicious as peanut butter.

Nut butters are easy to make in a blender or food processor. Place 1 cup (250 mL) of roasted nuts in the bowl, and pulse the motor until the nuts are ground. If the mixture is too dry, add a little oil.

The following recipe can be made with any one or a combination of nut butters. Serve it over steamed vegetables, rice, tofu or as a sauce for chicken.

Nut Butter Sauce

½ cup	nut butter	125 mL
1	small onion, grated	1
1	clove garlic, crushed	1
¼ cup	instant milk powder	50 mL
½ tsp.	honey	2 mL
2 Tbsp.	lemon juice	30 mL
2 tsp.	soy sauce	10 mL

Blend all ingredients in saucepan over low heat, adding hot water until the mixture has the consistency of heavy cream.

sumers scoop the amount they need. This kind of peanut butter is neither perfectly smooth nor easy to spread, as the oil and solids tend to separate and need some stirring before use. But the effort involved in stirring and spreading is a small price to pay for the purity offered. If natural peanut butter is stored in the refrigerator, there will be less separation, but it can also be kept, tightly covered, on the pantry shelf for four or five months — after this much time, sniff before using to test for rancidity.

Some supermarket peanut butters call themselves "natural" or "old-fashioned," but check the labels carefully: both sugar and salt can be considered natural and old-fashioned. Some people find highly processed peanut butters much more appealing than the rougher-textured natural peanut butter, but with a little patience, anyone can acquire a taste for the healthier, more authentic — and less expensive — natural kinds.

Tea

More and more people are turning to tea as an alternative to coffee. There are teas to suit every palate, and I like to keep a wide selection on hand for guests. Although black tea does contain caffeine, it has only about half as much as coffee, and the tannin in tea slows the release of the caffeine so that it is less of a shock to the nervous system. Certainly, most of us think of having "a cuppa" to relax, whereas we typically drink coffee to pick us up and get us going.

Black tea is still the most popular tea in North America. Of the many varieties, the most common are Ceylon and Lapsang souchong. Oolong tea, similar to black, has not been fermented as long. A common form of oolong is jasmine. Green tea, the most popular tea in Japan, is not fermented at all. There are also many types of blended teas, such as Earl Grey and the breakfast teas, and dozens, if not hundreds, of herbal

Devilled tofu

teas that offer an almost unlimited range of flavours, from cranberry and lemon to orange. Many reputedly help to induce sleep, while others, such as chamomile and cranberry, help to prevent colds or aid with urinary problems.

Tea is available loose or in bags. While loose tea is often fresher, a good guideline is to buy teas from a store with a rapid turnover. There are two ways to make tea with loose leaves: put the tea leaves in a tea ball (a small perforated stainless-steel ball) or in a tea strainer (usually bamboo), and pour the water over them.

Making tea properly is important, although there is often more mystique about the ritual than necessary. The teapot or teacup should be warmed ahead of time — fill it with hot water, and let it sit while the tea water comes to a boil. For a mug of tea, place in the cup 1 bag or 1 teaspoon (5 mL) of loose tea in a ball, then add boiling water. For a pot of tea,

Miscellany

put in 1 or 2 bags (or 1 or 2 teaspoons [5 or 10 mL] in the ball), depending on the desired strength, and fill the pot with boiling water. Let it steep for three to five minutes, according to taste. Make iced tea by adding ice cubes to strongly brewed tea or by soaking tea bags in cold water in a warm place for 12 hours and refrigerating until chilled.

Tofu

Also known as bean curd, tofu is a very inexpensive but rich source of protein. It is made of soybeans that have been soaked, puréed, cooked and solidified into curds by the addition of nigari, a coagulant. Tofu contains all the essential amino acids, making it the only vegetable product that is a complete protein. And because it has little flavour of its own, tofu can be combined with many spices and foods.

People inexperienced with tofu often dislike its texture, which is somewhat rubbery, but when it is prepared properly, that is not a problem. If tofu is new to you, cut it into small pieces or mash it and add it to soups and stews.

Tofu is best when purchased from shops where it is stored in large buckets. Keep it – in water – for only a few days, and change the water after two days. It is available "soft" or "firm." When a recipe calls for tofu that maintains its form, "firm" is the best. Firmness can be increased by pressing it in a sieve under a weight for an hour or two before cooking it. When it is frozen, its texture changes slightly, but only for the better – it firms up and is easier to work with.

I have recently discovered dried tofu and now use it frequently in my cooking. It is available in health-food and Asian grocery stores (where it is considerably cheaper) and generally comes in long, thin, ropelike strands packaged in plastic. It will keep indefinitely. To use dried tofu, break it into chunks and soak it for at least 30 minutes. A couple of hours is even better. Add it to stir-fries, soups and stews.

Devilled Tofu

This tastes remarkably like egg salad and will probably fool tofu haters. It makes a delicious sandwich filling and is also a good dip for raw vegetables or crackers. To avoid runniness, press the tofu thoroughly before beginning.

2	cakes tofu	2
2	stalks celery, minced	2
1	green pepper, minced	1
3	green onions, minced	3
1 cup	mayonnaise (see page 98)	250 mL
¾ tsp.	salt	3 mL
	pepper	
½ tsp.	dry mustard	2 mL
1 tsp.	turmeric	5 mL

Chop pressed tofu into small cubes and mix with celery, green pepper and green onions. Combine mayonnaise with remaining ingredients, stir into the tofu and mix well. Chill.
Makes 2 cups (500 mL).

Tomato Products, Canned

Whole Canned Tomatoes: Look for a brand that does not have added salt and sugar. I prefer canned plum tomatoes because they have more meat to them. When cooking for people who do not like whole tomatoes in their food, I squish the tomatoes as I add them to the pot. This can also be done in a blender or a food processor. Canned tomatoes are on sale frequently, and if you are a big user, it is worthwhile to keep an eye open for sales and buy a case or two.
Stewed Tomatoes: Again, look for brands that do not have sugar and salt. Some have other spices, which is fine if you are looking for those flavours in the completed dish, but it is easy to buy plain stewed tomatoes and add your own seasonings. Stewed tomatoes are handy – there are no whole tomatoes – and the flavour is fuller because of the stewing process.
Tomato Sauce: Although commercial tomato sauces abound, I never buy them. I make my own using canned or frozen tomatoes and tomato paste. I like the flavour and texture better and can be sure of what is in it. For a tomato sauce recipe, see page 104.
Tomato Paste: I keep a good supply of tomato paste in both large and small cans in my pantry. I use it to make tomato sauce for a variety of dishes; I stir it into soup stock for colour and flavour; I put it into marinades for barbecuing meats; and I often add a dollop to gravies. Dishes containing large quantities of tomato paste should be simmered for at least a couple of hours to eliminate the pasty flavour.

Unopened cans of tomato products will keep indefinitely on the pantry shelf (do not buy dented cans, regardless of the price, because of the danger of food poisoning). Once opened, tomato paste will keep in the refrigerator for two weeks in a glass or plastic container.

If a recipe calls for 1 pound (500 g) of fresh tomatoes, substitute 1 cup (250 mL) of canned whole tomatoes or tomato sauce; if it calls for 1 cup (250 mL) of tomato sauce, substitute 6 tablespoons (90 mL) of paste and ½ cup (125 mL) of water.

Vinegars

Probably discovered when a wine maker allowed some wine to ferment too long, vinegar has since become an important item in its own right. A wide variety of vinegars is now commonly available, and while many of the specialty kinds offer unique and desirable flavours, some are overpackaged, overpriced and underflavoured.

White vinegar is the mildest, and it is the vinegar of choice for pickling if a light colour is wanted. Pickling vinegar is white vinegar, but it has a stronger fla-

Roast-pepper salad

until you are sure of the strength you want. Vinegars can be stored indefinitely, although the flavour will begin to dissipate after a few months, even if the bottle is kept tightly capped. If sediment builds up, simply strain the vinegar.

Vinegar is also useful for cleaning. It is effective for polishing glass, and its crisp scent is pleasant in the kitchen.

Roast-Pepper Salad

Make this salad for a special occasion—it is a bit of a luxury because the peppers and vinegar are expensive. The aroma of roasting peppers is mouth-watering.

3	sweet yellow peppers	3
3	sweet red peppers	3
3	sweet orange peppers	3
½ lb.	button mushrooms	250 g
1	red onion	1
	olive oil	
	balsamic vinegar	
⅓ cup	fresh thyme, chopped	75 mL
	salt & pepper	

Roast the peppers: place on cookie sheet on middle oven rack, and cook at 400 degrees F (200 °C) until charred, turning from time to time to char evenly. This will take approximately 45 minutes, but check the peppers frequently after 30 minutes.

Remove from oven and place immediately in a paper bag. Close bag tightly, and let the peppers sit until cool enough to handle. Peel and seed the peppers. The skin should come off easily by hand, but you may need a paring knife for some. If the skin is still tightly fixed, return peppers to the oven and char further. Rinse the peppers and dry thoroughly. Cut into wide julienne strips and place in a salad bowl.

Slice mushrooms and onion, add to peppers and toss. Drizzle with oil and vinegar to coat lightly, then add thyme and salt and pepper. Toss lightly. Set aside to marinate at room temperature for several hours.

Serves 8.

vour than the regular white form does.

Cider and malt vinegars, both with robust flavours, are higher in acetic acid than white. Cider vinegar is made from apple juice or cider and is often used in pickling if a darker colour is acceptable. Malt vinegar derives from fermented barley malt and is traditionally associated with English fish and chips.

Wine vinegars can be made from red or white wines and vary from mild to strong in flavour, depending on the type

of wine and the fermenting process. Balsamic vinegar is made from grapes high in sugar content that are fermented for up to 50 years. As a result, it is relatively expensive, but it offers a delicate, sweet flavour that is welcome in some dishes.

Fresh herbs can be added to any of these vinegars, which are then aged so that the herbs' flavours will steep into the vinegar. Herbed vinegars can be prepared at home quite easily, although it is advisable to make small amounts

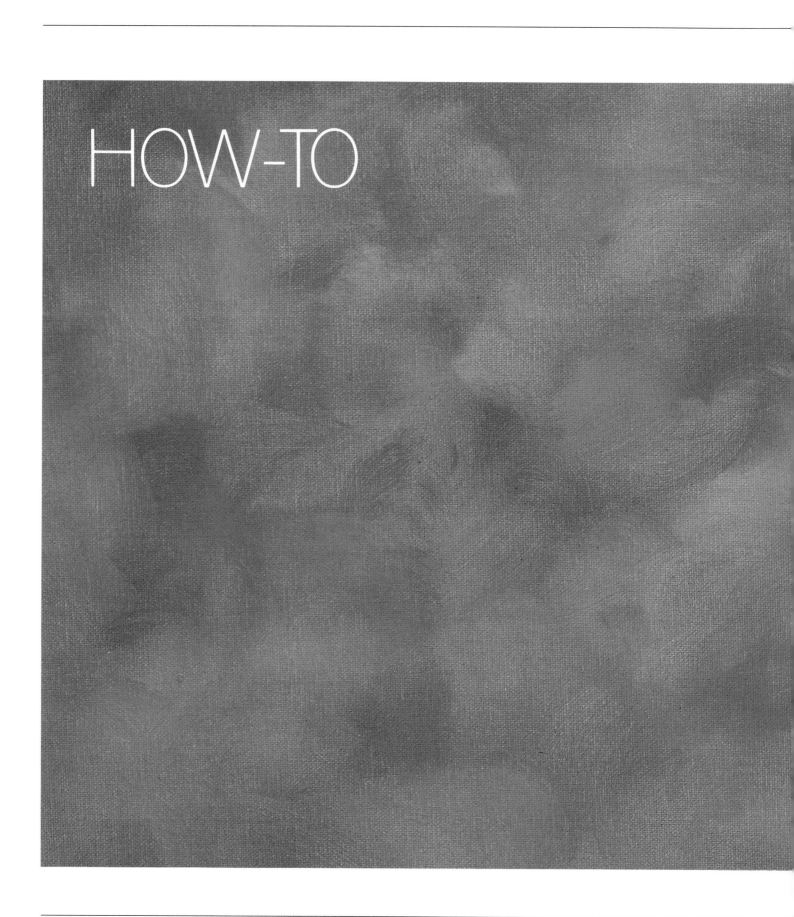

HOW-TO

Homemade linguine, ricotta ravioli

I have a friend who is both an outstanding chef and an inspired teacher. Her straightforward manner of communicating both the technical know-how and the aesthetic subtleties of cooking has a kind of magnetic appeal for people who are interested in food. Consequently, she devotes a great deal of her time to guiding culinary novices through their trials in the kitchen.

A few years ago, the overwhelming demand for her expertise prompted her to compile a small cookbook of her most sought-after recipes. What she thought would be the logical extension of her work as an instructor became, instead, a reminder of the innumerable obstacles encountered by most self-taught cooks. The dry prose of the recipes, compared with the hands-on guidance she was accustomed to providing in the kitchen, seemed like meagre encouragement.

Opening a cookbook can be a daunting experience for anyone, and it is lit-tle wonder that many novices left to fend for themselves in the kitchen are haunted by a feeling of isolation. The spirit of the art that relies on taste, touch and smell cannot be captured in a photograph of an exotic dish. Although it is enticing, that photograph often portrays a standard hopelessly unattainable for a struggling beginner. And there is no doubt that recipe jargon offers cold comfort to anyone trying to bridge the vast expanse between the raw ingredients of flour, cream and eggs and a finished dessert such as a glazed fruit tart.

I recommend that a novice trying to make something like the tart think of it not as one elaborate recipe but as a series of simpler preparations – a custard, a pastry and a glaze. Broken down into its component parts, any recipe will appear less intimidating and more manageable. No matter what the dish, whether it is an intricate dessert, a homemade soup or a pasta dinner, this approach illustrates that all good cooking depends on the accumulation of basic skills. If, for example, you have never made a custard or a pastry crust, what are the chances that you will consider preparing the tart? How likely are you to make homemade soup if you do not know how to prepare a soup stock?

My long-standing claim to "culino-phobic" friends that cooking is very simple has one provision: anyone who has the desire to cook must first be willing to acquire a background in the basics. To do that, beginners must first learn to speak the language of the kitchen. Cooking is a technical art, and not surprisingly, cookbooks are typically written in a technical language with terms that briefly convey specific instructions. Food editors, who are usually experienced cooks, tend to assume that a reader understands what it means to sauté onions or reduce a liquid. To help the novice understand this book and others, the first half of this chapter will attempt to demystify the language of

Shortbread animal cookies

food, providing the whats, whens and hows of recipe terms and techniques.

The second half of the chapter completes the background training. If you are one of those people who slink out of the kitchen when it's time to make the gravy for the holiday turkey, or if you feel your palms grow damp when you are asked to make the salad dressing, then you will come to rely on this section of basic preparations. With neither shortcuts nor gimmicks, these master recipes for such preparations as omelettes, sauces, basic bread dough and muffin mix are the basis of most day-to-day cooking. Memorize, practise, and learn to prepare them without a cookbook, and eventually, you will learn how they can be adapted and improvised in an infinite number of ways. For example, making a good sauce is simple once you have grasped the principles. If you know what a roux is and how it works and can make a basic white sauce, then you can make any of the flour-based sauces – béchamel, béarnaise, cheese, velouté, a cream sauce for moussaka or the cream base for a soup.

Cooking is one form of creative expression that is accessible to anyone. It requires few specialized tools, self-instruction is possible, and every cook is qualified to judge the results of his or her efforts. Once you complete the crash course in this chapter, you can begin to indulge your culinary imagination.

Terms & Techniques

Al Dente

The expression *al dente* quickly formed on every pasta lover's lips in the 1980s as North Americans' rediscovery of pasta inspired a fresh look at its preparation. Literally translated from Italian, *al dente* means "to the teeth" and refers to pasta cooked until it is tender enough to bite through yet still firm.

It takes a watchful eye and a quick hand to rescue a noodle *al dente*. Ready the pasta pot by bringing the water – three times the volume of the pasta – to a rapid boil. Add a tablespoon (15 mL) each of oil and salt to prevent the noodles from sticking to each other or to the pot, and plunge the pasta into the water all at once. Fresh pasta requires very little cooking, so check it after a minute or two. For dry pasta, allow 12 to 20 minutes' boiling time, depending on its thickness, and inspect frequently. (Noodles bound for additional baking – in a lasagna, for example – should be slightly undercooked.) Drain cooked pasta immediately, rinse it briefly but thoroughly under hot water, and toss it lightly with butter or oil and salt and pepper before serving it in a warm dish.

Any pasta to be served with a heavy, cloying sauce is an exception to the *al dente* rule. In this case, cook the pasta until it is completely soft so that it will more readily absorb a sauce. To avoid a sticky texture and a starchy taste, be especially conscientious when rinsing these noodles.

Almosts

A liquid being heated up is "almost boiling" when bubbles begin to form beneath its surface. A sauce has "almost thickened" when it first begins to change consistency and large bubbles slowly rise to the surface and break open with a satisfying plop. While these observations may appear at first to be unenlight-ening, they are important cues to move to the next step of the recipe.

Au Gratin

Au gratin refers to a light topping – bread, cracker or nut crumbs or grated cheese mixed with dots of butter – spread over a casserole or scalloped dish to brown. It enhances dishes made with rich sauces such as vegetable casseroles, macaroni and cheese, scalloped potatoes and shepherd's pie.

An au gratin topping can be sprinkled over a casserole either before it is put in the oven or in the last half-hour of cooking time. In the latter case, brown it in a 350-degree-F (180°C) oven. The topping can also be browned under the broiler, a much faster method (but first,

Roasting Poultry

Since light and dark poultry meat cook at different rates, a few tricks must be relied upon to prepare a large chicken or turkey. There are two basic strategies for minimizing the drying of the breast meat: taking precautions to prevent natural juices from escaping and adding moisture during roasting. An aluminum-foil tent will reflect heat that would otherwise dry the uppermost sections of breast meat. Covering the bird with two or three layers of moistened cheesecloth will also protect it from scorching. A third technique is to baste every 10 minutes after the first half-hour of cooking time with pan drippings or vegetable or sunflower oil, which you can combine with a little soy sauce. This browns the skin nicely and adds a pleasant flavour to the meat. The final method is to place strips of bacon across the breast, which will baste the meat as it cooks.

Before putting the bird in the oven, rinse it thoroughly with water inside and out and pat it dry. Stuff the bird immediately before cooking; salmonella bacteria, which abound in raw poultry, will travel quickly into the dressing if it is left at room temperature for any length of time. (Likewise, leftover stuffing should be removed from the cooked fowl immediately after the meal is over and refrigerated in a separate container.) Allow about ¾ pound (375 g) of stuffing for each pound (500 g) of chicken or turkey.

Whether it is stuffed or not, cook poultry on an oiled rack in a roasting pan, breast side up, with a meat thermometer inserted through the top of the thigh deep into the bird and not resting against a bone. Place the pan in an oven preheated to 450 degrees F (230°C), lower the heat immediately to 325 degrees F (160°C), and roast until the internal temperature climbs to 185 degrees F (85°C). The standard cooking-time calculation for poultry is 20 minutes per pound (40 minutes per kg), with an extra 5 minutes per pound (10 minutes per kg) for a stuffed chicken or turkey. For poultry over 15 pounds (6.8 kg), roast 15 minutes per pound (30 minutes per kg).

Duck and goose require special treatment because of their high fat content. Cook the stuffing separately beforehand to prevent it from soaking up the fat. Fill the cavity with a few apples or potatoes to absorb the fat, discarding them after the bird is cooked. Throughout the roasting time, lightly prick the duck or goose on its lower sides so that the fat can drain away. Place the bird in an oven preheated to 450 degrees F (230°C), immediately lower the temperature to 350 degrees F (180°C), and roast for approximately 20 minutes per pound (40 minutes per kg). Allow all poultry to stand for 15 minutes before carving it.

set the casserole in a pan of hot water to prevent the sauce from separating). Sprinkling the topping with paprika prior to cooking ensures a more richly coloured crust. Once the crust begins to warm, it will brown and then blacken surprisingly quickly, so never abandon the casserole while it is in the oven. Watch it closely when it begins to change colour, and remove it when it appears to be not quite done.

Au Gratin Recipe

½ cup	fine dry bread crumbs	125 mL
½ cup	Parmesan cheese	125 mL
½ tsp.	paprika	2 mL
¼ cup	cold butter, chopped into pieces	50 mL

Combine the dry ingredients. Mix the butter in by hand. Sprinkle over casserole for the final 30 minutes of baking time or broil until browned.

Makes 1 cup (250 mL).

Baste

Basting is a technique for preserving the natural juices in a roast by moistening its surface as it cooks. All roasting meat, except premier cuts that are well marbled (those with a high fat content distributed evenly throughout), requires basting. Melted meat fat is a common basting liquid, but wine, tomato juice, leftover marinades or soy sauce may be used instead of or in addition to the fat for extra flavour. Some cuts of meat will self-baste if you place a solid piece of fat or strips of side bacon on top of them.

Using a pastry brush reserved exclusively for the purpose, brush the roasting pan with fat before placing the meat in it. After the first half-hour of cooking, baste with the liquid and the accumulated pan drippings using a large spoon or basting bulb, repeating every 20 minutes until cooking is complete.

Beat

Beating is a way of mixing ingredients and incorporating air into a mixture to increase its volume. Vigorous strokes with a fork, wooden spoon, wire whisk, hand beater or electric mixer will do the job. Beating the ingredients as thoroughly as directed is important to the success of a dish, so when the recipe instructs you to "beat until creamy" or "beat until thick," do so. Otherwise, a custard will not be dense enough to set, mayonnaise ingredients may separate and so on.

Stewing

After an exhausting day, few meals are as revitalizing as a steaming bowl of homemade stew. Both nourishing and economical, stew is a versatile dish that can include almost any combination of ingredients. In addition to those stews made with whatever is around and some ingenuity, a wide variety of recipes exists for such specialty dishes as goulashes, cassoulets, beef bourguignon, gumbos and ragouts. Stewing is a moist cooking method in which ingredients are simmered in liquid over low heat for an extended period of time to tenderize cuts or types of meat that are less than ideal for roasting or braising—blade, chuck, pot roast, brisket, mutton and stewing chickens all make excellent stew.

Cut the meat into uniform cubes of 1 to 2 inches (2.5 to 5 cm). Dredge them in flour, and brown slowly in hot shortening, a single layer at a time if you have more meat than will fit into the pot. Once the meat is browned, remove it from the pot. Place in the pot finely chopped onion, garlic, green pepper and celery, and sauté them in oil. When the vegetables are done, return the meat to the pot and

There are a few tricks that will help a cook deal with some problematic ingredients. It is difficult to know, for example, when you have achieved fully whipped cream: if underbeaten, it is thin and sloppy; if overbeaten, it turns into butter. Properly whipped cream should be just stiff enough to form soft peaks. Chilling the bowl and beaters in the freezer for 10 or 15 minutes beforehand will help to hold the dairy fat firm throughout the agitation. On hot days, place the mixing bowl in a bed of ice while you beat the cream. Egg yolks, on the other hand, are easier to beat if both eggs and tools are at room temperature.

barely cover with the stewing liquid—water, stock, tomato juice, beer, vegetable cooking juices or any combination of these. Season the stew with salt, pepper, a bay leaf, thyme, marjoram or any of your favourite herbs. Cover the pot with a tightly fitting lid, and heat to a boil. Reduce the heat, and simmer for several hours.

To add large pieces of vegetables to the stew, brown them separately in oil and add them to the pot near the end of the cooking time. Potatoes, onions, carrots and turnips cut into three-quarter-inch (2 cm) cubes will need about 30 minutes to cook thoroughly in the stew; tender vegetables, such as peas, mushrooms and corn, require only 5 minutes.

You may thicken the liquid at any time while the stew is simmering. For every 10 cups (2.5 L) of stew, dissolve 2 tablespoons (30 mL) of cornstarch in an equal amount of cold water. Stir the paste thoroughly, mix it into the centre of the hot stew, then blend it vigorously. Continue heating until the stew thickens. If more thickening is desired, repeat the procedure.

Terms & Techniques

And be careful with egg whites: they will not stiffen properly if even a trace of stray material – a speck of yolk, a chip of shell or a drop of moisture – is in the bowl or on the beaters.

Blanch

Blanching is a technique for loosening the outer skin of raw vegetables and fruit by either plunging them into or covering them with boiling water. Soak almonds, peaches, apricots and tomatoes for approximately two minutes in boiling water, and the skins should slide off easily without scarring the tender tissue. If blanching fails the first time, return the food to the hot bath for an additional few seconds.

Boil

The point at which a liquid changes into a gas is its boiling point. Soft water boils at 212 degrees F (100°C) at sea level, and hard water boils when it is a few degrees hotter. One teaspoon (5 mL) of salt or sugar added to 1 quart (1 L) of water will raise the boiling point slightly. A liquid has reached the boiling point when bubbles form uniformly across the surface; when the bubbles become so vigorous they cannot be stirred down, it is called a rolling, or hard, boil.

Boiling an egg is – despite widespread opinion to the contrary – something of an art. By hard-boiling an egg the correct way, you can avoid the greyish blue ring that sometimes forms around the yolk. Place a room-temperature egg in a saucepan, and cover it with cold water. Heat the water to a boil over medium heat, reduce the heat to low, and cook for 10 to 15 minutes. A smooth, golden, cooked egg yolk will result. When the egg is done, rinse it in cold water, then shatter and remove the shell.

Soft-boiling an egg is a little trickier, and whether you are successful or not is really a matter of individual taste.

Place a room-temperature egg in a saucepan of cold water, covering it by an inch (2.5 cm) or so. Bring the water to a boil over medium heat. Cook the egg for two to three minutes for a runny yolk and a white that is not fully set, or boil it for four minutes for a firm egg. Turn the egg gently as it cooks to distribute the heat evenly.

Braise

Braising is a moist cooking technique that tenderizes tougher cuts of beef such as chucks, shoulders, briskets, short ribs, rolled or standing rump, round steak and pot roast.

Begin by dredging the meat in flour seasoned with salt, pepper, thyme and dry mustard (if marinating, do so first, as described below). In a heavy pot with a tightly fitting lid, heat just enough oil or clarified butter to keep the meat from sticking. Add the meat when the oil or butter is sizzling hot. Turn it often so that it browns evenly on all sides, then add finely diced onion, garlic, carrots and celery. When the meat is brown, pour off all but 2 tablespoons (30 mL) of fat, and add the braising liquid – stock, wine, vegetable water or tomato juice – to a depth of ½ to 1 inch (1.25 to 2.5 cm). Bring the liquid to a boil, then immediately reduce the heat to a simmer. Cover the pot, and continue cooking until the meat is tender, adding liquid periodically if needed.

From this point, the cooking can be done either on the lowest setting on top of the stove or in an oven set at 300 degrees F (150°C). Check from time to time, adding more liquid if needed and turning the meat. Allow at least 30 minutes' cooking time per pound of meat (60 minutes per kg), but don't worry about overcooking.

Particularly tough cuts are tastier if they are marinated – as is sauerbraten – for 24 hours before cooking. For every 4 to 6 pounds (2 to 3 kg) of beef, heat to-

Vegetable Preparations

Vegetables should not all be cooked in the same way. Choose the method— boiling, steaming, stir-frying or baking— to suit the produce. Strongly flavoured, hearty vegetables such as potatoes, turnips, carrots, cabbage and cauliflower are best when boiled. To maintain colour, texture, flavour and nutrition, place them in boiling water, cover pot immediately and cook until tender. The cooking time for potatoes varies, depending on the type: from 5 to 15 minutes if cubed, to half an hour or more for halved or whole potatoes. Cubed turnips require 25 to 30 minutes to cook, while cubed carrots, cabbage and cauliflower take 10 minutes.

Steaming is an excellent method of cooking delicate produce such as peas, beans, broccoli and spinach; the short cooking time results in less damage to the vegetables' tissues. Place sliced or whole vegetables in a steamer over a pot of boiling water. Cover, but test the vegetables frequently. Peas and spinach will steam in as little as 2 minutes, while beans may need 8 to 10 minutes and broccoli (depending on the size of the florets) may require 10 to 12 minutes.

Potatoes, yams and squash are delicious baked in the oven at 350 degrees F (180°C) for about an hour. Before baking a squash, cut it in half, scoop out the seeds, and season it with butter and brown sugar. With a fork, puncture the skins of yams and potatoes that are to be baked whole to prevent them from exploding.

gether 1½ cups (375 mL) of red wine, 1½ cups (375 mL) of water, 2 bay leaves, 1 teaspoon (5 mL) of whole peppercorns and 2 teaspoons (10 mL) of thyme. Pour this over the meat, cover and refrigerate, turning the meat several times. Braise the meat as described, using the marinade as the liquid. At the end of the cooking time, thicken the stock with 2 tablespoons (30 mL) of flour dissolved in an equal amount of water, then stir in 1 cup (250 mL) sour cream or yogurt, and mix well.

To prepare pot roast, brown the meat, then place it on a rack in the pot, and add enough liquid to half fill the pot. Cook as above. Traditionally, diced potatoes, onions and carrots are added during the last half-hour of cooking time.

Caramelize

To caramelize means to change sugar to caramel by melting it and reheating it with water until it becomes a golden brown glaze. In a heavy frying pan, heat the sugar on high, watching it and stirring frequently to prevent it from burning. When the sugar has melted, slowly add ½ cup (125 mL) of very hot water for each cup (250 mL) of sugar, and continue to heat the mixture until it turns a caramel shade. The result is a syrupy glaze that can be used to top crème caramel. The glaze hardens very quickly, so it must be used immediately or stored in the refrigerator in a heat-resistant container and melted later by gently warming the jar in hot water.

Chop

When a recipe calls for ingredients to be chopped, it means to cut them into small pieces of the same size, ranging from fine to coarse, depending on the food. A good sharp knife – one large enough to be held safely at both ends – is the key to successful chopping. Hold the tip of the knife on the board, rocking it in hard, rapid strokes that move across the food. This is a better bet than risking cutting your fingers by pushing the food into the path of the moving blade.

Clarify

To clarify is to remove the sediment from heated butter or to clear soup stock by straining it through cooked egg whites. See aspic and clarified butter on pages 92 and 94, respectively.

Coddle

Cooked ever so lightly, a coddled egg is runny, and its white is just beginning to congeal. Place an unshelled egg at room temperature in a pan of boiling water, cover, remove the pan from the heat,

Roasting Meat

Roasting is a technique of dry cooking in which a whole piece of meat is left uncovered for the entire cooking time. It produces a dry, crisp exterior and a moist interior; the cook's challenge when roasting meat is to prevent it from drying out.

Producing a moist and delicious roast begins with selecting the right cut of meat: only tender cuts will do. Standing rib and rolled rib top the large array of beef roasts, followed by rib-eye and sirloin tip. Tougher cuts require a moist cooking method to enhance their flavour. Lamb cuts from the shoulder or the leg also make delicious roasts. Because of pork's high fat content, all of its cuts can be roasted successfully, but crown and loin roasts are the premier choices.

Remove the roast from the refrigerator two hours ahead of time, and let it warm to room temperature. Season it with garlic, thyme and coarsely ground pepper, and place it on a rack in an open roasting pan with the fat side up so that it will self-baste. Insert a meat thermometer deep into the centre of the roast, making certain that the thermometer tip is not resting against the bone or in fat. Place the roast in an oven preheated to 425 degrees F (220 °C), and immediately lower the heat to 325 degrees F (160 °C). Cook the roast uncovered, but be sure to baste it periodically with cooking juices, stock, wine or marinade to pre-vent it from drying out while cooking.

Rare roast beef should reach an internal temperature of 140 degrees F (60 °C), medium should reach 160 degrees F (71 °C) and well done 170 degrees F (77 °C). The rule of thumb for beef is to cook it approximately 15 minutes per pound (30 minutes per kg) for medium rare, adding 5 minutes per pound (10 minutes per kg) if the roast is rolled. Lamb roasted to medium should cook for 30 minutes per pound (60 minutes per kg) and reach a temperature of 175 degrees F (79 °C); for medium rare, cook for 20 to 25 minutes per pound (40 to 50 minutes per kg) to a temperature of 160 to 165 degrees F (71 °C to 74 °C). Pork, which should always be served well done, must attain an internal temperature of 185 degrees F (85°C)—approximately 35 minutes per pound (70 minutes per kg). Any large piece of meat roasted with a stuffing requires approximately 5 extra minutes per pound (10 minutes per kg).

When the meat thermometer indicates the correct temperature, double-check by pushing it deeper into the meat. If the temperature is sufficiently high in the centre of the roast, remove it from the oven. If not, continue cooking for a few more minutes and check again. Always allow a roast to stand for 15 minutes before carving it.

Terms & Techniques

and let stand for two minutes. Recipes that call for uncooked eggs—such as Caesar salad dressing—are much improved by the addition of a coddled egg.

Cream

Creaming involves combining an oil, such as butter or shortening, with a dry ingredient, often sugar, until the mixture is fully blended, creating a smooth base for a batter mix. "Cream" is an instruction that you will inevitably come across in baking recipes.

Following a few simple steps will guarantee that you master the technique. The first and most important thing is to allow the butter or shortening to warm to room temperature before you start. If you do not do this, the creaming process will be a long, tedious, discouraging battle—never the best start to any activity in the kitchen. Before adding the sugar, cream the butter or shortening on its own by mixing it into a soft, smooth mass with a wooden spoon or a wire whisk. Gradually add the sugar, continuing to cream as you go and for two or three minutes after all the sugar has been incorporated.

Creating the velvety texture of butter and sugar creamed together for a batch of muffins or a cake is a pleasure that makes the task worth doing by hand. But if you have only hard butter and are pressed for time, try one of the following tricks for softening the butter: beat the cold butter in a food processor or mixer until soft; chop the cold butter into small cubes, place in an ovenproof bowl, and heat at 250 degrees F (120°C) for a few minutes, watching vigilantly; or soften the butter using "defrost" on your microwave oven.

Food-Processor Cutting In

Cutting shortening or butter into flour in a food processor is both quick (it takes only a few seconds) and effective (the dough does not become overworked and tough). Place the flour in the bowl of the processor, and using the metal chopping blade, whir the motor briefly. Evenly distribute well-chilled cubes of butter or shortening over the flour, then cut the fat into the flour in two-second pulses, allowing the mixture to fall back from the sides and into the bowl each time before repeating. Continue to pulse until the mixture has a grainy texture or until the fat has just barely disappeared into the flour. One word of caution: do not overfill the bowl of your processor—if you are making a large quantity of pastry, combine the ingredients in smaller batches.

Cube

To cube means just that—to cut food into cubes. Both the proposed use and the kind of ingredient will determine what size the cubes should be. They can range from large, chunky cubes of meat for a stew to more delicate ½-inch (1.25 cm) cubes of vegetables that will be added to casseroles or used in fillings for such pastries as samosas.

Cut In

Cutting in is a term for coarsely blending shortening, lard or butter with flour when making pastry. Place the flour in the bowl, then add uniformly sized cubes of shortening, which must be very cold. Using a pastry cutter or two knives in a crisscrossing motion, cut the fat into the flour until it is in pea-sized grains, being careful not to make the dough creamy. The mealy texture allows the shortening to melt into pockets in the dough, which makes pastry and biscuits flaky.

1. In a deep mixing bowl, distribute well-chilled, evenly cubed butter or shortening (or a combination of the two) over sifted all-purpose flour.

2. Using two knives—drawing the blades in a scissoring motion—quickly cut the butter or shortening into the flour. Be careful not to overwork the mixture.

3. Continue to cut in as the recipe indicates —either until the mixture is the texture of cornmeal or until pea-sized grains of butter or shortening remain.

Deep-Fry

Early in my marriage, my mother-in-law warned me that I should never turn my back on a pot of hot oil. She was right. Deep-frying is just not a safe way to cook if you are distracted by ringing telephones and young children running around the kitchen. Nonetheless, deep-fried foods are delicious, and that cautionary note aside, preparing them at home can be well worth the effort.

A deep, heavy pot and a slotted spoon are the bare essentials for deep-frying; a mesh frying basket is also very handy; and a fat thermometer is useful for monitoring the temperature of the cooking oil. An electric deep fryer, while wonderfully easy to use and infinitely less hazardous, is not essential.

Vegetable oils, peanut oil (which has a particularly high smoking point) and clarified butter (which can be combined with another oil) are all suitable for deep-frying. Pour the oil into the cooking container, filling it halfway, and heat it gradually to evaporate any moisture in the pot. Wait until the oil reaches 365 degrees F (185°C) before putting any food into it so that the food will absorb as little grease as possible. If you are cooking more than one batch of food, allow the pot to reheat between each one. Cooking small amounts of food that can be turned easily in the oil will give the best results.

More essential hints from my mother-in-law: always keep at hand a metal lid and baking soda in case of a fire, and never douse an oil fire with water.

Deglaze

Deglazing is the process of dissolving bits of browned meat and cooking juices from the cooking pan and incorporating them into a flavourful sauce. First, remove the fat from the cooking liquid using one of two methods: tip the pan onto

Step-By-Step: Disjointing Poultry

1. Cut the skin over the joint where the wing meets the body, then press the wing upward until the joint is visible. Insert the tip of a knife and cut through.

2. Slice the skin above the leg, and pull it away from the body. Press down until you can see the joint. Insert the knife tip and gently cut through.

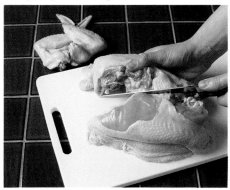

3. Repeat for the other leg, or cut through the skin and press the leg outward and downward until the joint cracks apart. Cut the leg and thigh away from the body.

4. Remove the skin from the breast. Then, using the tip of the knife, score one side of the breast its full length along the line of the breastbone.

5. As the knife blade comes closer to the backbone and ribs, gently pull the breast meat from the bone until it is cleanly cut away. Repeat for the other breast.

6. To separate the thigh from the leg, bend the leg downward from the thigh and cut through the skin until you can see the joint. Insert the knife tip into the joint and cut.

Terms & Techniques

its side, and siphon off the fat with a baster; or pour the hot juices into a heat-proof jar, sit it in cold water, and spoon off the fat that rises to the top. Return the liquid to the cooking pan, and add ½ cup (125 mL) of wine, stock, hot water or a mixture of all three. Heat the liquid, and scrape the sides of the pan clean. Continue to heat, reducing until the sauce is the desired consistency.

Devil

Bland foods, served hot or cold, seasoned with cayenne, paprika and other spicy ingredients and mixed with a dressing of mayonnaise, wine or vinegar are foods we describe as devilled. Eggs are one of the easiest and most delicious devilled treats. Start by hard-boiling the eggs, then shell them, halve them lengthwise, and carefully remove the yolks. Mash the yolks together with enough mayonnaise to moisten them. Season with salt, pepper, hot-pepper sauce and paprika, and spoon or pipe the filling into the hollows of the whites. Garnish with capers or fresh parsley. Store in the refrigerator, and warm to room temperature before serving.

Dice

Diced ingredients are those cut into cubes measuring less than half an inch (1.25 cm). To dice, first cut food in lengthwise strips, then, holding the strips at one end, cut crosswise, moving the handle and resting the tip of the knife on the cutting board for stability.

Dredge

Food dusted with flour, bread crumbs, spices or sometimes sugar is said to be dredged. One of the easiest methods of dredging is to place the coating in a bag, add the food–small quantities at a time–and shake until it is lightly but evenly covered.

Step-By-Step: Filleting Fish

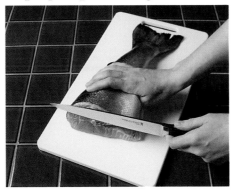

1. Remove the fish head just below the gills, cutting with a sharp chef's knife on a nonporous board. Leave the tail intact to balance the fish during filleting.

2. Using the fish's spine as a guide to keep the knife tip above the skeleton, slit both the dorsal and ventral ridges of the fish from head to tail.

3. Placing the knife next to the spine but just above it, gently cut the fillet away from the skeleton, gradually moving the tip along as you trim the tissue.

4. To prepare the second fillet, turn the fish over–spine against the cutting board–and repeat the above step. Retain the skin, as it helps to hold the fillet together.

Drippings

Drippings consist of bits of meat and secretions of haemoglobin and fat that are lost during roasting. These flavourful bits that collect in the roasting pan can be retrieved by deglazing and adding to an accompanying sauce or gravy or saved for enhancing soups or stews.

Fillet

Filleting is the removal of the bones and fat from meat, chicken or fish. Fillet of beef from the tenderloin produces the choice cuts chateaubriand, tournedos and filet mignon.

Flambé

Flambéing refers to igniting a small amount of brandy or other liqueur that has been poured over food. Both the food and the liquor should be warm. The higher the alcohol content of the liquor, the more readily the dish will catch the flame, and the more alcohol poured on the dish, the longer it will burn. Always light the chafing dish by touching the edge of the pan with the flame of a match. Before guests come for dinner, have a flambé rehearsal, keeping innocent bystanders well back; as an extra precaution, light the dish using long fireplace matches.

Fold

An instruction for combining whipped egg whites with yolks (as in a soufflé) or beaten wet ingredients with dry ingredients in a muffin or cake batter, folding preserves the volume of a whipped mixture, ensuring its leavening effect. It is a very gentle procedure involving a minimum of mixing. The trick is to combine the ingredients gradually by carefully lifting the mixture from the bottom of the bowl with quick strokes. Resist the temptation to blend excessively – if too much air is beaten out of the mixture, the result will be heavy and dense.

Fry

Fried foods are pan-cooked in oil at a high temperature until brown and crisp. Other frying techniques described in this glossary are deep-fry and stir-fry.

Grate

Cheese, citrus peel, vegetables and even chocolate can be grated to a fine, medium or coarse texture. While hand graters are very efficient tools, some food processors have attachments for grating large quantities of food.

Grill

Grilling is the technique of cooking food directly over the source of heat, whether on a barbecue rack or in an open pan. Hamburgers, chicken and fish fillets and thin steaks all grill well and may be basted while cooking to seal in moisture. While soy, lentil, tofu and other meatless burgers can be grilled, they

Step-By-Step: Folding

1. Use a large, deep bowl when folding. Pile the ingredients together in the centre, rather than sprinkling them over the batter, to permit easy distribution throughout.

2. When folding, use a wooden spoon, a rubber spatula, your open hand or any tool with a large surface area that allows you to turn the ingredients efficiently.

3. Move the spoon to the bottom of the mixing bowl with a firm stroke, and lift the batter from underneath using a strong, sweeping action to turn it over completely.

4. Blend the ingredients with as few strokes as possible to avoid removing the air from the batter. Folding is complete once the ingredients are just barely mixed.

will burn and dry out easily because of the absence of fat in them, so watch them closely.

Julienne

An attractive way to cut up food, julienne means to slice into lengthwise slivers such foods as raw and cooked vegetables, fruit, cooked meat and cheese. Obtaining a uniform size can be a challenge, but it becomes less of one if you first cut the food into 2-inch (5 cm) pieces before slicing lengthwise. My children insist that carrots are best

when cut julienne style, cooked lightly so that they are still crunchy and served with a glaze of melted butter combined with mustard seeds, fresh dill and salt and pepper.

Knead

Many doughs, such as those for bread and pasta, require kneading to distribute the leavening agent – yeast, baking powder or eggs – evenly throughout and to activate the gluten that supports the expanding dough by making it elastic. Kneading requires a great deal of

Terms & Techniques

Step-By-Step: Kneading

1. Lightly flour a marble board or smooth countertop surface. Using the palms and heels of your hands, press the dough into the work surface.

2. Fold the dough toward you from the top and in from the sides, and repeat the kneading action. Rotate the dough ball so that all of it is equally worked.

3. It takes 10 to 15 minutes of kneading to activate the gluten in the flour. The process is complete when the dough is smooth and elastic and has a satiny sheen.

strength in both palms and forearms, so make it as easy as possible by working on a surface at a comfortable height.

Mince

Among chopping techniques, mincing produces the smallest pieces, which should be no larger than ⅛ inch (3 mm). A sharp chef's knife is essential for mincing seasonings such as onions, garlic and fresh herbs.

Parblanch

A procedure used to draw salt out of cured ham, tongue and pork and to remove strong flavours from organ meats, parblanching consists of placing the food in cold water, bringing it to a boil uncovered, simmering for a period of time that varies depending on the food, then plunging it quickly into cold water to arrest the cooking process.

Parboil

A technique with a wide variety of applications, parboiling involves placing food in boiling water and then plunging it into cold water. Vegetables and fruits are parboiled before freezing or canning to set the colour and to preserve the nutrients. Parboil such hard vegetables as broccoli, cauliflower and carrots before combining them with the tenderer vegetables in a stir-fry. To ensure that chicken cooks thoroughly on the barbecue, parboil it first. Keep in mind that the boiling time is short, so the food will not be fully cooked.

Peel

Peeling, or paring, is the removal of the skin or outer layer of an ingredient. Use a vegetable peeler rather than a paring knife, and remove only the skin and not the inside as well. One of the hazards of the nearly universal use of chemicals in agriculture is that the outer skins of most foods are loaded with poisons. As a result, commercially grown vegetables and fruits should be peeled whenever possible. If, on the other hand, you have access to organically grown fruits and vegetables, enjoy the skins, because they are both flavourful and packed with nutrients.

Poach

Poaching is a moist-heat method of cooking commonly used for eggs, but fish and chicken can also be poached. To poach an egg, grease the bottom of a small pan, add lightly salted water to fill the pan to twice the depth of an egg and bring to a boil. Break the egg into a small bowl, swirl the water in the pot with a wooden spoon, then drop the egg into the vortex. Reduce the heat to an even simmer, cook uncovered for four minutes, and remove the egg with a slotted spoon. Poached eggs make wonderful fare for an elegant brunch when served on toast and dressed up with Mornay, hollandaise, creole or creamed spinach sauce.

Preheat

To preheat the oven is to set it at the desired temperature ahead of time so that it is fully warm when you use it. The oven must be maintained at a constant temperature for cooking some foods. Baked goods, for example, should be thoroughly heated throughout if they are to be light and fluffy. If started in a cold oven, the heat will be uneven and cakes may fail to rise, pastry will be tough and cookies and squares will be dry. Likewise, high-temperature cooking, such as searing, will not succeed when the oven is not fully prewarmed. Foods cooked for a long period, however, such as casseroles, can warm up gradually with the oven, and preheating is usually not necessary.

Purée

Almost any food can be puréed easily and successfully with an electric blender or food processor. Place only small amounts of food at a time in the machine, adding a little liquid and turning the machine on and off intermittently. A submersible blender is handy for puréeing a small quantity of food right in the pot. Vegetable purées stored in the freezer are handy to have on hand for adding to soups or stews, while puréed frozen fruit makes a great topping for ice cream, yogurt or cereal.

Reduce

A technique for intensifying flavours, reducing involves boiling off much of a liquid in which meat has been cooked to produce sauce, stock or gravy. Reduce liquids over high heat, uncovered, and stir frequently so that solids do not stick to the pot and burn. Reduced liquids can be stored in the refrigerator for several days, if tightly covered, or frozen for months in small portions and later added to soups or stews.

Sauté

To sauté is to cook food rapidly in heated oil or butter until golden brown. As the meaning of the French word *sauter* suggests, ingredients should almost "jump" in the pan. Sauté vegetables and herbs to bring out their subtle flavours before adding them to soups, stews, casseroles or spaghetti sauces.

Scald

To scald a liquid is to bring it gradually, without burning or sticking, almost to the boiling point, the point at which tiny bubbles form around its edge. Recipes for cream soups and sauces, for example, require that scalded milk be added to the hot roux (see page 102) to discourage lumping. Watch carefully as you scald milk, and stir it frequently, reaching down to the bottom of the pan.

Sear

Searing is a technique for quickly browning whole pieces of meat (not poultry) to seal in the natural juices before cooking. In an oven preheated to 400 to 450 degrees F (200 °C to 230 °C), heat just enough oil or meat fat to coat the bottom of a heavy roasting pan. Place the meat in the pan, turning it every few minutes to brown all sides evenly. After 30 minutes, reduce the heat to the normal temperature for roasting, and continue as the recipe indicates. Chunks of meat to be added to a stew can be seared in a similar manner in a frying pan on top of the stove.

Simmer

To simmer is to cook food just below the boiling point, a point at which small bubbles may appear on the surface. Dairy products can be simmered successfully, but if boiled, they will often separate or curdle and will be unusable.

Soup

There are more kinds of soups than there are cooks, but most fall into one of the following categories:

Bisque: a rich, creamy soup made with seafood.

Broth: a clear soup made of a rich stock.

Consommé: a soup made of clarified brown stock (see page 104).

Cream: a soup with a milk or cream base.

Potage: a catchall category that refers to a thick, hearty soup prepared with or without cream and made with any combination of meat, fish or vegetables.

Purée: a soup with puréed vegetables as the thickening agent and made rich

Poaching Chicken and Fish

A moist method of cooking, poaching preserves the natural flavour of eggs, as described on page 88, boneless chicken breasts and whole and filleted fish. Poaching liquids range from water to wine and can be enhanced with fresh herbs. But keep the seasoning delicate: fines herbes or any other combination of herbs that complements the food can be used, and stock seasoned with white wine makes a wonderful poaching liquid for both fish and chicken.

This low-calorie cooking procedure is simple to follow. Wrap fish or chicken in two layers of aluminum foil, and place it in a pot of cold liquid. Do not cover. Bring the liquid to a boil, then reduce the temperature to simmer. Skim the surface, if necessary, and add more liquid as required throughout the cooking time.

Fish fillets cook in approximately 10 minutes, while a chicken breast needs 15 to 20 minutes. Remove the cooked food from the liquid with a slotted spoon, and allow excess liquid to drain away. (The unique texture of poached, chilled fish such as salmon can be preserved by cooling it in the poaching liquid before serving.) Add salt and pepper to the chicken or fish, and serve with a delicate sauce such as hollandaise or béarnaise.

A poaching paper, which covers the surface of the water, contains the heat but allows the steam to escape. To make one, cut a small hole in the centre of a circle of wax paper that will fit inside the pot. To prevent the paper from sticking, grease the underside lightly with butter.

Terms & Techniques

by the addition of butter near the end of simmering.

Velouté: a rich soup based on eggs, cream and velouté sauce (see page 104).

Steam

Steaming is a simple, healthful way of cooking food. Because the food is not immersed in water, the nutrients remain intact instead of leaching into the cooking liquid. Bamboo steamers are available in all sizes, and they can be stacked in layers to cook many different vegetables over one pot of boiling water. Place the vegetables requiring the longest cooking time on the bottom.

Stir-Fry

Sautéing food at a high temperature is a technique originally used only in Asian cooking, but now it has become fully incorporated into North American cuisine. The ideal stir-fry pan is a wok: its rounded bottom distributes heat evenly, and its high sides allow you to toss the contents easily in the pan. Electric woks are not satisfactory because they will not reach a high enough temperature. If carefully used, however, a large, heavy skillet will suffice.

Cooking many different kinds of food in one pot is the goal in stir-frying, so timing is everything. Meat, vegetables and noodles of any variety in any combination make delicious and easy stir-fry meals. For a meat and vegetable stir-fry, start by cutting the meat into strips and marinating it for a short time beforehand so that the flavour of the marinade just penetrates the meat's surface. (A stir-fry is an excellent place to use inexpensive cuts of meat, because they are marinated, thinly cut and cooked at high temperatures to seal in their juices.)

Heat oil in the wok; both ghee and peanut oil work well in stir-fries because of their very high heat thresholds, or smoking points. The wok is ready when the oil has just begun to smoke or when a drop of water sputters and sizzles across the surface of the oil. Toss in the meat, stirring frequently to prevent overcooking. When it is done, remove it and set it aside if you have many raw vegetables to fry. Alternatively, if the vegetables are parboiled, leave the meat in the wok while they cook. Add vegetables in descending order of hardness— carrots first, then celery and so on down to the most tender. Armed with information on how long it takes each type to cook, you can, ideally, time the addition of the vegetables so that they are all nicely cooked at the same time.

A stir-fry can be served as either a side dish or a main-course meal. In the latter case, you can make a sauce by splashing some marinade, soy sauce or wine into the wok and thickening it with a teaspoon (5 mL) of cornstarch dissolved in water. Serve the stir-fry and sauce over rice or noodles.

Broiling Meat

Meat can be broiled in the traditional manner—under a broiler—or it can be pan-broiled—a frying method. New York strip, tenderloin, T-bone, porterhouse and flank are the best cuts of steak for broiling. Remove the meat from the refrigerator an hour before cooking, and tenderize by pounding it with a wooden mallet or the wooden handle of a knife. Before cooking the steak, rub a clove of garlic over it or cut slits in the steak and insert slivers of garlic. Slash the fat around the meat to prevent the edges from curling when exposed to the heat, being careful not to cut through the meat itself. Place the steak on a cold broiling tray, and position it 3 inches (7.5 cm) away from the preheated broiler. A 1-inch-thick (2.5 cm) steak takes 8 to 10 minutes to broil to rare, 12 to 14 minutes for medium and 18 to 20 minutes for well done. For a 1½-inch (4 cm) steak, add approximately 6 minutes to the total cooking time. A ¾-inch (2 cm) hamburger will need 10 minutes to cook to medium. A 1-inch (2.5 cm) lamb chop, which can be prepared for the broiler in the same way as a steak, requires 11 to 13 minutes for medium and 16 to 18 minutes for well done. Season meat with salt at the end of the cooking time, never before.

Brown chicken in a skillet before broiling it. Halve it from top to bottom, brown, then place it skin side down on the broiler tray. Do not use a rack. Brush the chicken with oil, and repeat during broiling as needed. Place the bird 5 to 7 inches (13 to 18 cm) below the heat, and broil for 20 minutes. Turn it over, baste with pan drippings or stock and wine, and cook for 20 minutes more.

Pan-broiling is an effective method for cooking steaks and chops 1 inch (2.5 cm) or less thick. Heat a heavy skillet until water sizzles when flicked on its surface. Rub the pan lightly with a piece of meat fat, add the steak or chop, and sear, uncovered, for 5 minutes on each side. Reduce the heat, and cook for 8 to 10 minutes. Drain excess fat immediately, season with salt and pepper, and serve.

Whether broiled the traditional way or in a pan, meat is delicious when served with garlic butter, herbed butter or béarnaise sauce. Garlic butter can be made quickly and easily by blending together butter and finely chopped garlic; for a mild flavour, use 1 clove garlic to ¼ pound (125 g) of butter. Chill until hard, cut into pats, and place one on each steak before serving. For herb butter, follow the same steps, adding a combination of your favourite fresh herbs.

Stir-Fry Marinade

2	parts soy sauce	2
2	parts oyster sauce	2
1	part black bean sauce	1
2	cloves garlic, crushed	2
	cumin	
	five-spice powder	

Combine soy, oyster and black bean sauces with garlic, add spices to taste and use as a marinade for meat.

Thicken

Sauces, soups and stews all need to be thickened on occasion. Flour, cornstarch, tapioca, arrowroot and even, in some instances, puréed potatoes are excellent thickeners. While I use flour most often, I rely on cornstarch for delicately flavoured sauces and soups.

One tablespoon (15 mL) of thickener for each cup (250 mL) of liquid will make a soup or sauce of medium thickness. Dissolve the thickener in an equal amount of cold water, juice or stock, and mix thoroughly into a paste. Adding a cold thickener to a hot pot will create lumps, so first add ¼ cup (50 mL) of hot stock to the paste to warm it up. Stir the thickening mixture constantly until smooth and thin, pour it into the centre of the soup or stew pot, and stir vigorously. Continue cooking over high heat until the soup comes to a boil and begins to thicken. Reduce heat, but continue to stir frequently until thickening appears to be complete.

But do not panic if a sauce is not the right consistency the first time. It is easy to add liquid to a sauce that is too thick or more thickener to a sauce that is too thin. A sauce will continue to thicken as it cooks, so don't be too quick to repeat the process if it seems too thin. Remember to correct the seasoning to compensate for the flour mixture you have added to the pot.

Barbecuing

Steak and Hamburgers

All kinds of foods, from hamburgers to whole fish, can be easily prepared on the outdoor grill. Even potatoes and corn roasted in a firepit take on a distinctive taste. The simplest and most familiar barbecue dish is steak. Remove the meat from the refrigerator at least an hour ahead of time, and season it with garlic and crushed peppercorns. Use the tenderest cut you can afford—T-bone, sirloin and filet mignon are particularly delicious. Place the steak on a cold, clean rack 3 inches (7.5 cm) above the hot coals. A steak that is 1 inch (2.5 cm) thick will require 8 to 10 minutes total cooking time for rare, 12 to 14 minutes for medium and 18 to 20 minutes for well done. While the meat cooks in about the same amount of time as it does when broiled, it may need to be turned more frequently on a barbecue, because the coals cook less evenly than does a broiler.

For barbecued hamburgers, mix 1 pound (500 g) of meat with 1 beaten egg and 1 cup (250 mL) of fine, dry bread crumbs, adding whatever seasonings you enjoy, chopped cloves of garlic, finely diced onion, salt, pepper, mustard, a bit of soy sauce and Worcestershire sauce. Place the patties on a cold grill over the fire, flipping 3 to 4 times during the 15-to-20-minute cooking time required for medium-rare hamburgers.

Chicken and Spareribs

Parboil chicken pieces for 10 minutes (5 minutes for wings) or spareribs for 10 minutes per rack of ribs before barbecuing. Place the parboiled meat on the barbecue rack 3 to 5 inches (7.5 to 13 cm) above the coals, and grill, basting frequently with barbecue sauce, turning throughout the 15-to-20-minute cooking time. Watch the chicken closely, because the skin burns easily.

Skewer Cooking

Whether done with chicken, beef, pork or lamb, skewer cooking is ideally suited to the barbecue. Cut the meat into 1½-inch (4 cm) cubes, marinate for at least four hours, and wipe dry. For rare shish kebabs, place the meat close together on the skewers; for well-done meat, space it out. Vegetables—onions, green peppers, mushrooms and tomatoes—require less cooking time than the meat, so place them on separate skewers. Rest the skewers on a well-greased grill placed 3 inches (7.5 cm) from the heat source. Cook the meat for 8 to 12 minutes and the vegetables for 5 to 7 minutes, turning frequently and brushing with the marinade if desired.

Barbecue Marinade

1½ cups	red wine	375 mL
½ cup	olive oil	125 mL
3	cloves garlic, diced	3
1	large onion, diced	1
2	bay leaves	2
2 tsp.	coarsely ground pepper	10 mL
1 tsp.	salt	5 mL
1 tsp.	thyme	5 mL
1 tsp.	basil	5 mL
1 tsp.	marjoram	5 mL
1 tsp.	oregano	5 mL

Combine all ingredients. If refrigerated, it will keep for several weeks.

Makes 2 cups (500 mL).

Basics

Aioli

Aioli is a flavourful garlic mayonnaise traditionally served over mounds of steamed vegetables. But it is also a delicious dip for raw vegetables or chilled seafood, a dressing for potato salad or a sauce for baked or poached fish.

Aioli Recipe

½ cup	lemon juice	125 mL
4	cloves garlic, peeled	4
2	eggs	2
2	additional egg yolks	2
2½ cups	olive oil	625 mL

Combine lemon juice, garlic, eggs and yolks in a blender or food processor and mix thoroughly. With machine running on low, gradually drizzle in oil until sauce is thick. Refrigerate immediately.

Aspic

Aspic is a crystal-clear gelatin/stock mixture used to decorate moulded salads, pâtés or cold meats. Made from hot stock mixed with gelatin and chilled until firm, an aspic is simple in composition but time-consuming to prepare. Clarify a reduced stock by adding one slightly beaten egg white and one broken eggshell to each quart (litre). (The flavour of the stock usually matches that of the dish—chicken stock in a moulded chicken salad and so on.) Without stirring, slowly bring the liquid almost to the boiling point—that is, when small bubbles form just beneath the surface. Simmer for 10 minutes, remove it from the heat, and let it stand for one hour. Strain the stock through a piece of moistened cheesecloth, and cool.

For every 2 cups (500 mL) of stock used in the aspic, soften 1 tablespoon (15 mL) of gelatin in a few tablespoons (30 to 45 mL) of cold water, then add a few tablespoons of hot water to dissolve it. Stir the dissolved gelatin into the cooled stock, and chill until it begins to set. If the aspic is used for a mould or salad, add chopped meat or vegetables at this point and pour the mixture into a chilled, moistened mould. Refrigerate until it sets.

For a pâté, pour the liquid aspic over the surface while the pâté is still in the mould, and chill until nearly set. Garnish with parsley or other fresh herbs, and seal with a thin layer of liquid aspic. Continue to chill until it is firm.

Béarnaise Sauce

Béarnaise is a rich, creamy sauce made with egg yolks, wine, shallots and herbs. A classic companion for broiled rare red meat and delicious with fish, béarnaise is easy to make as long as the mixture does not boil after the egg yolks are added. Boiling will make it curdle.

Béarnaise Sauce Recipe

⅓ cup	white wine	75 mL
3 Tbsp.	champagne vinegar	45 mL
2 Tbsp.	chopped shallots	30 mL
3	peppercorns, crushed	3
3-4	sprigs tarragon, crushed	3-4
2	sprigs parsley, chopped	2
4	egg yolks, beaten	4
1 cup	melted butter	250 mL
	salt & pepper	

In the top of a double boiler, combine wine, vinegar, shallots, peppercorns, tarragon and parsley, and cook over direct heat until the mixture is reduced to half its original volume. Allow it to cool, place over hot water and beat steadily, adding yolks and butter alternately in thin streams. Continue to beat until the sauce has thickened, then season to taste with salt and pepper.
Makes 2 cups (500 mL).

Béchamel Sauce

Béchamel sauce, named for its creator, Louis de Béchamel, is a rich white sauce added to fancier creamed dishes, such as moussaka and lasagna, and used as the base for other sauces, such as cheese sauce. Rather time-consuming to prepare and considerably heavier than a basic white sauce, béchamel is not the sauce of choice for a quick macaroni and cheese supper.

Béchamel Sauce Recipe

4 Tbsp.	butter	60 mL
4 Tbsp.	flour	60 mL
	salt & pepper	
	nutmeg	
2 cups	scalded milk	500 mL
1	large onion, studded with 6 cloves	1
1	bay leaf	1

Over low heat, melt the butter in an oven-proof pan, then stir in flour, salt and pepper and nutmeg. Cook, stirring, for 5 minutes, then gradually whisk in milk. Add the onion and bay leaf and continue cooking and stirring until the sauce is thickened and smooth. Bake at 350 degrees F (180° C) for 20 minutes, then remove onion and bay leaf.

Bouquet Garni

The assorted herbs—either fresh or dried—of a bouquet garni impart a wonderful flavour to soups and stews when added for the last 45 minutes of the cooking time. If working with fresh ingredients, tie together four sprigs of parsley, ½ bay leaf, two sprigs of thyme, the white part of a leek and two cloves. If using dried ingredients, place 1 teaspoon (5 mL) each of parsley, thyme and marjoram, ½ bay leaf and ½ teaspoon (2 mL) of chervil in a piece of cheesecloth and tie securely. Remove it from food before serving.

Bread

Every cook should be able to make at least one kind of bread. The following recipe for a basic yeast variety with an even but textured grain is a good one to begin with. Bread books covering the full spectrum of bread types, from coarse dark ryes to light holiday creations, are available for anyone interested in specialty bread making. I have one suggestion: When you are spending the time and effort to make bread, make a few loaves, because a thick slice of homemade bread, hot out of the oven and slathered with butter and jam, is so tempting that one loaf won't last long.

Bread Recipe

A third of the flour for this recipe should be unbleached white, the remainder a blend of whole wheat, rye and buckwheat.

2 cups	milk	500 mL
1 cup	water	250 mL
2½ tsp.	oil	12 mL
3 Tbsp.	honey	45 mL
1 Tbsp.	salt	15 mL
⅓ cup	lukewarm water	75 mL
2 Tbsp.	dry yeast	30 mL
10 cups	flour	2.5 L

Scald the milk, then stir in 1 cup (250 mL) water, oil, honey and salt and set aside. In a separate bowl large enough to hold all of the dough, combine lukewarm water and yeast. Let yeast stand for 5 to 10 minutes, mix well, and stir in milk mixture when it has cooled to lukewarm. With a heavy wooden spoon, stir in flour, 2 cups (500 mL) at a time. Once the consistency is thick and the dough holds together, turn it out onto a floured board and work in any remaining flour by hand. Knead the dough for 10 to 15 minutes, until it is smooth and elastic.

Place dough in a greased bowl, turning once to coat with oil. Cover, and let it rise in a

Aioli

warm place for approximately 1 hour, or until it has doubled in size. Punch it down, and allow it to rise again. Punch it down a second time, shape it into three loaves, and place the loaves in greased loaf pans, which should be about half-full. Cover and let rise until doubled in size, 45 minutes or so.

Preheat the oven to 450 degrees F (230°C), and bake the bread for 10 minutes. Reduce the heat to 350 degrees F (180°C) and bake for 30 minutes more. For a crisp crust, brush with salt water halfway through the baking time; for a golden brown crust, brush with milk near the end of the baking time.

Test each loaf for doneness by tapping the bottom of the pan. If the pan sounds hollow, the bread is done. Remove bread from the pans immediately, and allow the loaves to cool on baking racks. Bag only after the bread is thoroughly cooled.

Makes 3 loaves.

Cake Mix

Basic batter cakes get their volume from baking powder and their lightness from properly creaming the fat before combining it with the dry ingredients. For the best results, all ingredients should be at room temperature or around 70 degrees F (21°C) before mixing.

Cake Mix Recipe

If you enjoy the convenience of ready-to-use commercial cake mixes, the following recipe and storage suggestions allow you to prepare a no-fuss homemade white cake that can be iced or served unfrosted as a lunch-box snack. The quantities listed below make two 9-inch (1.5 L) layers or two 8-by-8-inch (2 L) square cakes, but I suggest that you prepare several individual batches at the same time and store them for use later.

2 cups	flour	500 mL
1½ cups	sugar	375 mL
1 Tbsp.	baking powder	15 mL
½ cup	finely chopped or ground pecans	125 mL
½ cup	finely chopped dried apricots	125 mL
½ tsp.	cinnamon	2 mL
¼ tsp.	nutmeg	1 mL
⅓ cup	milk powder	75 mL

Combine all ingredients well and store in tightly covered container in the refrigerator or freezer. Before preparing cake batter, warm the dry mixture to room temperature.

To make a cake, cream ¾ cup (175 mL) butter, then add 1 egg and 1 teaspoon (5 mL) vanilla. Alternately mix the dry ingredients and ¾ cup (175 mL) water into the butter mixture a third at a time, starting and ending with the dry ingredients. Pour the batter into greased cake pans and bake at 350 degrees F (180°C) for 20 minutes.

Makes two 9" (1.5 L) layers or two 8" x 8" (2 L) square cakes.

Variations:

The above recipe can be adapted to make it more interesting or more appealing to finicky eaters.

● Add ½ cup (125 mL) of cocoa, another ½ cup (125 mL) of sugar and ¼ to ⅓ cup (50 to 75 mL) additional water.

● Vary or omit the fruits and nuts.

Basics

White cake mix

over low heat to allow the oil and milk solids to separate. When fully melted, remove the pan from the heat, and allow it to stand for a few minutes. Skim the foam off the top, and carefully pour the liquid into a container, leaving the solids in the bottom. Ghee can be refrigerated and used later.

Court Bouillon

In essence, court bouillon is a seasoned liquid that can be a marinade, a base for stock or a medium for blanching vegetables and poaching fish. From the simplest variety – water with a splash of wine – to the exotic – bouillon enhanced by diced fresh vegetables and herbs – it can be adapted to complement whatever dish you are preparing. The following is a basic court bouillon that is useful both for cooking hard vegetables, such as cauliflower, carrots, turnips and broccoli, and for marinating them before serving.

Court Bouillon Recipe

3 cups	water	750 mL
4 Tbsp.	olive oil	60 mL
½ cup	lemon juice	125 mL
	salt & pepper	
1	leek, white part only, chopped	1
1	carrot, chopped	1
1	bouquet garni	1

Place all ingredients in heavy stockpot, bring to a boil, reduce heat and simmer, covered, for 20 minutes.

Makes approximately 2 cups (500 mL).

Add vegetables to the court bouillon and cook until done. Let stand for a few minutes to allow them to absorb the flavour.

Cream or White Sauce

The cream, or white, sauce is made according to the same principles as many of the other classic rich sauces, so a fool-

● Spice up the cake with ½ teaspoon (2 mL) each of allspice and cloves.

● To make a heavier snack loaf, add 1 cup (250 mL) of applesauce.

● Add whatever suits your fancy. In general, if the batter is too dry, add a little more liquid, and if it seems too runny, add more flour. The batter should be heavy enough to coat a spoon without running off in a steady stream. For every extra ¾ cup (175 mL) of flour you add, include 1 more teaspoon (5 mL) of baking powder.

Clarified Butter (Ghee)

Also known as drawn butter, or ghee, clarified butter, as its name suggests, is butter with the sediment removed. Delicately flavoured, it is delicious when served with steamed lobster or crab; and as a cooking oil, it has a much higher smoking temperature than regular butter and is therefore good for sautéing meat at a high temperature.

Melt unsalted butter in a saucepan

proof method for preparing such a sauce belongs in every chef's repertoire. By seasoning a white sauce to suit your needs, you can use it to transform leftovers – chicken, turkey or vegetables – into a delicious, main-course casserole that can be served over noodles.

White Sauce Recipe

3 Tbsp.	butter	45 mL
3 Tbsp.	flour	45 mL
	salt & pepper	
2 cups	scalded milk	500 mL

Over medium heat, melt the butter and whisk in flour and salt and pepper. Thoroughly blend, and cook for 2 minutes, until the flour has lost its raw taste. Gradually add scalded milk in a steady stream, whisking constantly to ensure that the sauce does not become lumpy. Continue whisking until smooth and fully thickened. Vary the white sauce by adding grated cheese, white wine or herbs.

Makes 2 cups (500 mL).

Croutons

Croutons are a welcome addition to salads and a great topping for hot vegetables, casseroles and soups. Easy to prepare at home, croutons are a delicious way to use stale bread. I generally keep a supply of stale bread in the freezer and also prepare a selection of variously seasoned croutons that I store in tightly covered jars.

To make croutons, lightly butter both sides of stale bread and sprinkle it with chopped fresh herbs and grated Parmesan cheese. Season croutons with the herbs you like the best and with an eye to their possible use: mixed herbs work well for salad croutons, Caesar salad croutons are good tossed with garlic butter, and dill is a great herb for croutons bound for a bowl of tomato soup.

Cut the bread into cubes, place on a cookie sheet, and bake at 300 degrees F (150 °C) until the cubes are thoroughly dried and crisp; the cooking time will depend on the texture of the bread.

Curry

Curry describes a cooking method, not a single seasoning, so each curry is unique to the cook who prepares it. Cardamom, chilies, coriander, cumin, fenugreek, mace and turmeric are the most common ingredients, and while commercially prepared powders are available, they leave you at the mercy of someone else's cooking chemistry – since there is no prescribed formula for mixing the spices – and are often diluted by the addition of a starch filler.

Rather than falling prey to a commercial product, I suggest that you prepare your own curry, whether it is a powder or a paste. Grinding a fresh powder will provide a strong, pure taste not found in preground blends; a homemade paste not only takes the place of the traditional curry spices but has additional seasonings – garlic, ginger and mustard – already blended in it. Trial and error with the ingredients and with the palates of those at your table will teach you which mixtures are best for you.

Curry Paste Madras Style

Use approximately 1 tablespoon (15 mL) of curry paste for each pound of meat.

1 cup	ground coriander	250 mL
½ cup	ground cumin	125 mL
1 tsp.	black pepper	5 mL
1 Tbsp.	Szechuan pepper	15 mL
1 tsp.	black mustard seeds	5 mL
1 Tbsp.	turmeric	15 mL
1 tsp.	salt	5 mL
4	cloves garlic	4
1''-2''	piece gingerroot	2.5-5 cm
1½ cups	cider vinegar	375 mL
¾ cup	oil	175 mL

Combine the spices and salt. Crush the garlic, peel and grate the ginger, and add both to the spice mixture. Add vinegar and mix into a smooth paste. Heat the oil in a heavy frying pan, reduce heat, and cook the spice mixture, stirring constantly, for 3 to 5 minutes or until the oil separates. Cool and bottle. Curry paste will keep in the refrigerator for 2 months.

Makes approximately 1¾ cups (425 mL).

Curry Powder

This roasted curry powder does not have the powdery taste of most commercial types.

5 Tbsp.	black peppercorns	75 mL
½ cup	coriander seeds	125 mL
1 Tbsp.	whole cloves	15 mL
2 Tbsp.	cumin seeds	30 mL
2 Tbsp.	green cardamom seeds	30 mL
1 Tbsp.	fenugreek seeds	15 mL
2 Tbsp.	turmeric	30 mL
1 tsp.	mace	5 mL
1 tsp.	cinnamon	5 mL
1½ tsp.	ground ginger	7 mL
½ tsp.	cayenne	2 mL

Grind the peppercorns, seeds and cloves coarsely, and place all spices in a heavy skillet or roasting pan. Stirring often, roast until the spices are dark and release an aroma, which takes approximately 5 minutes on top of the stove or 20 minutes in the oven at 375 degrees F (190 °C). When ready, cool and store in a jar with a tight-fitting lid.

Makes approximately 1½ cups (375 mL).

Custard

Custard is a wonderfully versatile dish: it can be served plain, topped with stewed fruit or a syrupy glaze, layered in delicate French pastries or baked in a quiche. With all these alternatives, it is impossible not to satisfy even the confirmed custard hater. Easy to prepare, custards can be cooked on top of the stove, where they become thick and saucelike, or baked to a drier and firmer texture in the oven.

Basics

Stovetop Custard: The cardinal rules of custard making are few but firm:
1. Never let a custard boil; cook stovetop custard in a double boiler. If it appears to be approaching a boil, turn it out into a chilled dish and cool it down by beating quickly.
2. To help prevent curdling, allow the scalded milk to cool a little before adding it to the eggs.

Stovetop Custard Recipe

2 cups	milk	500 mL
4	egg yolks, lightly beaten	4
⅓ cup	sugar	75 mL
1 tsp.	rum	5 mL

Scald the milk in the top of a double boiler. Remove it from the heat to let it cool slightly, then reposition it over hot but not boiling water, and whisk in eggs and sugar. Continue to cook, stirring constantly. When the custard thickens, remove it from the heat, and allow it to cool, beating to release the steam. Stir in rum before chilling.
   Makes 2½ cups (625 mL).

Baked Custard: Ceramic or heavy, ovenproof glass custard cups are the best containers for baked custards. The custard is done when a knife inserted near the edge of the cup pulls out clean. Once the custard is out of the oven, it will thicken in the centre from the heat stored in the cup.

Baked Custard Recipe

3 cups	milk	750 mL
½ cup	sugar	125 mL
5	egg yolks	5
1 tsp.	vanilla	5 mL

Blend together milk, sugar and egg yolks. Beat well, and stir in vanilla. Pour into 6 custard cups, place them in a pan of hot water and bake at 300 degrees F (150 °C) for 20 to 30 minutes.

Crème caramel

Duxelles

Duxelles is a seasoned mushroom flavouring that is used in gravies and stuffings and in cooking meat. It is an excellent way to use mushroom stems.

   Dry mushrooms with a dish towel, squeezing out as much of the natural water as possible before cooking. Finely mince 2 cups (500 mL) of mushrooms and 2 tablespoons (30 mL) of shallots, and sauté in 3 tablespoons (45 mL) of butter over medium-high heat. Cook, stirring frequently, for eight minutes, or until all the liquid has evaporated. Add ¼ cup (50 mL) stock and ¼ cup (50 mL) sherry, and boil the mixture rapidly until the liquid evaporates. Cool and store in a covered container in the refrigerator or freezer. Makes 1 cup (250 mL).

Fines Herbes

Fines herbes is a mix of finely minced fresh green herbs that adds a delicate flavour to many dishes, ranging from soups and sauces to omelettes. The herb oils blend together in a mixture that should be added to a dish only in the final minutes of cooking so that the fresh taste is retained. The most common mixture contains equal parts parsley, chives, chervil and tarragon, but improvisation is allowed. My favourite combination consists of thyme, parsley, oregano and chives.

Ghee

Ghee is another name for drawn, or clarified, butter. For more detail, see clarified butter on page 94.

Glaze

Any shiny coating used to garnish desserts, candies, meats and vegetables is known as a glaze. Dessert glazes are usually sugar-based. A quick cake glaze can be made by dissolving ½ cup (125 mL) of icing sugar in 2 teaspoons (10 mL) of hot milk in a saucepan and adding ¼ teaspoon (1 mL) of vanilla. Pour the mixture over a cooled cake, and decorate it with chopped nuts and candied fruits. For a cake that is still warm, mix together 1 cup (250 mL) of icing sugar, ¼ cup (50 mL) of orange juice and ¾ teaspoon (3 mL) of rum until smooth. Pour the mixture over the warm cake and garnish.

   Fruit tarts can be easily glazed with heated apricot or red currant preserve. Strain ½ cup (125 mL) of either preserve, and heat it over medium heat with 2 tablespoons (30 mL) of white sugar until the glaze is tacky and lightly coats a spoon. While it is still warm, brush it over the tarts.

   Aspics (see page 92) can be used to decorate meat, as can honey glazes (combine ¼ cup [50 mL] honey with ¼ cup [50 mL] soy sauce and 1 teaspoon [5 mL] mustard). And you can make a simple glaze for vegetables by melting butter with a bit of seasoning and a little brown sugar, then stirring the mixture into cooked vegetables.

Gravy

Preparing the gravy for a gigantic turkey dinner was an important contribution to a holiday meal when I was growing up. A great honour, the task was bestowed upon the most experienced cook present. But today, the prestige of the gravy chef does not count for much in my household – a request for a volunteer is guaranteed to clear a crowded kitchen. So for gravyphobes like me, here is the process simplified into three steps: preparing the meat juices, making a thickener and mixing the gravy.

There are two techniques for separating fat from the meat juices. If there is less meat fat than juice, pour the drippings from the pan into a heatproof measuring cup and set it in icy cold water. The fat will rise to the surface and can be easily spooned off. If there is less juice than fat, tip the roasting pan onto its corner, allowing the fat to rise to the top, and siphon out the meat juices with a baster. In both cases, reserve a few tablespoons (45 to 60 mL) of fat for mixing with the thickener.

Gravy Tips

- **For a rich gravy that is tasty on leftovers, quickly whisk in cream or sour cream at the end of the cooking time. Do not overcook; warm through only.**
- **Sauté minced garlic and onion to add to the flour-fat mixture before stirring in the liquid.**
- **Add finely chopped giblets to the finished gravy.**
- **Do not make gravy with the fatty drippings of roast goose or duck. Use butter, oil or fat from another fowl as a base, and flavour the gravy with chicken stock.**

After moving the meat to a platter, use the roasting pan – scraps of browned-on meat and all – for the gravy pot. To make the thickener, return 3 to 4 tablespoons (45 to 60 mL) of fat to the pan, and place it over medium heat. Stir an equal amount of flour into the pan, whisking vigorously to prevent lumps.

Once the paste is smooth, raise the heat to medium-high, and mix the gravy: gradually stir in 2 cups (500 mL) of liquid – the meat juice, plus vegetable stock, water, wine or beer – whisking steadily. When the gravy begins to thicken, reduce the heat to low. Keep warm until fully thickened. Season with salt, pepper, thyme and oregano. Makes 2 cups (500 mL). You can easily extend the gravy by increasing the amounts of flour and liquid proportionately.

Hollandaise Sauce

Hollandaise sauce is one of the richest garnishes for eggs and cooked vegetables, and it is delicious drizzled over chicken or cold rare roast beef. Even though it is dreaded by many new cooks, hollandaise is a guaranteed success if you follow a few simple guidelines:
- When making hollandaise on a humid day, use clarified butter, which will prevent curdling.
- Cook in a double boiler over hot but not boiling water.
- During preparation, stir constantly and scrape solids from the sides and bottom of the pan.
- If the sauce does curdle, immediately beat in 1 to 2 tablespoons (15 to 30 mL) of chilled cream.
- Prepare hollandaise just before use.

Hollandaise Sauce Recipe

¾ cup	butter	175 mL
2 Tbsp.	dry sherry	30 mL
4	large egg yolks	4
6 Tbsp.	boiling water	90 mL
	salt	

Melt butter in a saucepan, set it aside, and keep it warm. In another saucepan, warm the sherry, set it aside, and keep it warm too. Place the egg yolks in the top of a double boiler over hot but not boiling water. Beat until thick, and add 1 tablespoon (15 mL) of boiling water, beating again until eggs thicken once more. Repeat the procedure until all the water—1 tablespoon (15 mL) at a time —is added.

Beat in the warm sherry the same way. Remove the double boiler from the stove, and drizzle in the butter, beating until the sauce is thick. Stir in salt. Serve immediately.

Makes 1½ cups (375 mL).

Madeira Sauce

Made with the fortified wine bearing the same name, Madeira sauce is my favourite of the brown sauces; its rich flavour is a delicious accompaniment to the strong flavours of game, organ meat and beef dishes such as Beef Wellington. When choosing from the several types of Madeira available, unless otherwise specified in the recipe, select a medium-sweet variety, as it will add the best flavour to a cooked sauce.

Madeira Sauce Recipe

2 cups	sauce espagnole (see page 102)	500 mL
¾ cup	Madeira (substitute dry sherry for a lighter flavour)	175 mL
2 Tbsp.	butter	30 mL

Make the sauce espagnole, and reduce it by one-quarter by heating rapidly, stirring constantly to prevent it from burning. Lower the heat, and mix in ½ cup (125 mL) Madeira. Drop butter into the sauce in small dabs, and melt it by swirling the pan in a circular motion. Stir in remaining ¼ cup (50 mL) of Madeira, and heat just until it is warmed through.

Makes 2 cups (500 mL).

How-To

Basics

Mayonnaise

No commercial product even approximates the taste and texture of home-made mayonnaise. Making your own also allows you to ensure that it contains only pure ingredients. The recipe that follows is for a basic mayonnaise. Add various seasonings to it in small quantities to suit the dish being garnished. Dill and curry are two of my favourite seasonings for mayonnaise, especially for serving with toasted tomato and cold chicken sandwiches, respectively.

Mayonnaise Recipe

The amount of garlic used here produces a mild mayonnaise, but more can be added to suit individual preference. Any kind of mild oil is good in this recipe; olive oil has the most flavour, but I generally use half olive and half sunflower.

1	clove garlic	1
1 tsp.	dry mustard	5 mL
	salt & pepper	
2	eggs	2
6 Tbsp.	wine vinegar or lemon juice	90 mL
2 cups	oil	500 mL

Place garlic, mustard, salt and pepper, eggs, vinegar and ½ cup (125 mL) oil in a blender or food processor. Blend to combine. With machine still running, add the remaining oil in a slow, steady stream. Blend until the oil is well mixed in and the mayonnaise is thick and creamy. Store immediately in the refrigerator, where it will keep for about a week.
Makes approximately 3 cups (750 mL).

Meunière Butter

Traditionally, meunière was a term that described a cooking technique for sautéing flour-dredged fish fillets in butter — perhaps the culinary style of the miller's wife, as the literal translation suggests.

Its modern meaning, however, is a reference to the browned and seasoned butter that is used to either sauté or garnish a dish in the meunière style.

Meunière Butter Recipe

¼ cup	clarified butter	50 mL
1 Tbsp.	chopped parsley	15 mL
1 tsp.	lemon juice	5 mL
	salt & pepper	

Heat butter slowly, stirring until golden brown. Add remaining ingredients and stir. Cool and store in the refrigerator for up to 24 hours. For longer periods, store in freezer, divided into individual portions for convenience (1 tablespoon [15 mL] per person).

Mirepoix

Whether spread on roasting meat or used as a bed on which to cook chicken, mirepoix — a blend of diced vegetables — makes a delicious seasoning. After the

Almost Foolproof Mayo

The unique consistency of mayonnaise—a rich, creamy yet gelatinous sauce—is the result of emulsified eggs absorbing oil and holding it in suspension. Each egg yolk will absorb about ¾ cup (175 mL) of oil if it is added gradually, but the fragile balance is destroyed if the quantity of oil exceeds the yolk's capacity to absorb. When the egg becomes saturated, the mayonnaise will separate. Even then, you can rescue a failing batch by stirring in a teaspoon (5 mL) of water. If still curdled, beat another egg yolk and gradually spoon in curdled sauce. If this is unsuccessful, either add it to a salad dressing or mix it into egg, chicken or tuna salad.

meat is cooked, the mirepoix can be used as the base for an accompanying sauce or a soup stock. Prepare the mirepoix only as you need it to preserve the fresh flavours of its ingredients.

Mirepoix Recipe

1	carrot	1
1	onion	1
1	celery heart	1
1 Tbsp.	butter	15 mL
½	bay leaf, crushed	½
1	sprig thyme	1
	sherry	

Dice the vegetables, and sauté them in butter with the herbs. When soft, remove from pan, and deglaze it with sherry. Add the result to the vegetable mixture.

Mornay Sauce

Once you have mastered béchamel sauce, try Mornay sauce, a simple variation of béchamel made by adding cheese and cream. Mornay is delicious when served over poached eggs, steamed broccoli or cauliflower florets or boiled pearl onions or used sparingly as a sauce for roasted veal, baked sole or other broiled white fish.

Mornay Sauce Recipe

2 cups	béchamel sauce (see page 92)	500 mL
2	egg yolks	2
3 Tbsp.	heavy cream	45 mL
5 Tbsp.	grated Swiss or Jarlsberg cheese	75 mL
	salt & pepper	

Warm béchamel sauce over low heat. Beat together egg yolks and cream, and warm the mixture with a bit of the sauce. Now add it to the sauce and heat through. Stir in cheese and salt and pepper and continue cooking and stirring until cheese melts and sauce thickens.
Makes approximately 2½ cups (625 mL).

Muffins with whipped butter and comb honey

Muffin Mix

Loaded with protein and vitamin B, this basic dry mix is easily stored in a tightly covered container for handy homemade muffins. Store it in the refrigerator for two months or in the freezer for six; allow it to reach room temperature before using. Chopped dried fruit, nuts, chocolate chips, poppy seeds, grated carrot, apple, zucchini, cheese and mashed banana are all suitable additions.

Muffin Mix Recipe

10 cups	white flour	2.5 L
10 cups	whole wheat flour	2.5 L
1 cup	good-tasting yeast	250 mL
1 cup	wheat germ	250 mL
1 cup	baking powder	250 mL
4 cups	instant milk powder	1 L
2 Tbsp.	salt	30 mL
½ cup	brown or white sugar	125 mL
4 cups	shortening	1 L

Combine the dry ingredients, mix well, and cut in the shortening until the consistency of cornmeal. Makes 8 pounds (3.5 kg) of dry mix.

To make a dozen muffins, mix together 1 beaten egg, 1 cup (250 mL) milk and 2 tablespoons (30 mL) sugar. Add 3 cups (750 mL) dry mix to the wet ingredients, mixing them together in a few quick strokes, being careful not to overbeat.

Spoon the batter into greased muffin tins until two-thirds full and bake at 425 degrees F (220 °C) for 20 minutes.

How-To

Basics

Omelette

Because it has one main ingredient and is cooked in a single pan, an omelette is one of the easiest dishes to prepare. A frittata is an omelette in which chopped vegetables, meat or cheese are mixed with the eggs before cooking. Both the American-style fluffy omelette and the classic flat French omelette are filled after the eggs are cooked.

To prepare a French omelette for one person, mix 3 room-temperature eggs in a bowl. In a hot 7-inch (18 cm) nonstick skillet, melt 1 tablespoon (15 mL) of clarified butter, swirling the pan to coat the sides and bottom. When the pan is hot, pour in the eggs to a depth of no more than ¼ inch (6 mm), swirling them in the pan to coat it evenly. Cook uncovered until the eggs are just firm. (Eggs toughen if exposed to prolonged heat, so try to cook the omelette quickly. If there is a risk of burning, however, remove the pan from the heat and let the pan's warmth complete the process.)

Fill the omelette once the eggs are cooked. About ¾ cup (175 mL) of filling is enough for a 3-egg omelette. Creamed mushrooms, grated cheese, sautéed vegetables and chopped meat are all delicious for the purpose. Place about a third of the filling on top of the cooked eggs, then fold the omelette into thirds, slide onto a warm serving dish, and spoon the remaining filling over the top. Serve at once.

Pancake Mix

Laced with fresh blueberries or chopped peaches, dusted with icing sugar or slathered with butter and pure maple syrup, hot pancakes are a satisfying breakfast treat. For a light pancake, mix the wet and dry ingredients together minimally, leaving any lumps that form. For a fluffy pancake, allow enough time to chill the batter for at least an hour before cooking so that the flour particles can expand.

While many cooks find that, for making pancakes, a nonstick frying pan is unmatched for its convenience, others swear by the well-seasoned cast-iron frying pan for its ability to conduct heat and distribute it evenly. Obtaining a golden brown colour and a smooth surface on a pancake is simple if you possess the willpower to turn each cake only once, letting the formation of holes on top of the raw side be your clue as to when to turn it over; the second side will cook in about half the time of the first.

Pancake Mix Recipe

For quick batches of hassle-free breakfast pancakes or waffles, a large quantity of the dry ingredients can be mixed in advance and kept in the refrigerator for two months or in the freezer for six. But be sure to let it warm to room temperature before using.

10 cups	white flour	2.5 L
10 cups	whole wheat flour	2.5 L
1 cup	baking powder	250 mL
4 cups	instant milk powder	1 L
2 Tbsp.	salt	30 mL
½ cup	sugar	125 mL
4 cups	shortening	1 L

Combine dry ingredients, mix well, and cut in shortening until it is the consistency of cornmeal. Store tightly covered in the refrigerator. Makes 10 pounds (4.5 kg) of dry mix.

To prepare the batter, beat together 1 cup (250 mL) milk and 1 egg. Stir in 1½ cups (375 mL) dry mix, ½ teaspoon (2 mL) cinnamon and ¼ teaspoon (1 mL) cloves. Make peach or blueberry pancakes by mixing the fruit right into the batter. Cook the pancakes in a greased frying pan.

For a lighter pancake or a waffle, separate the egg yolk from the egg white. Beat the yolk with the milk, but whip the egg white until it is stiff, and fold it into the batter just before cooking.

Serves 4.

Pasta

Whether pasta is plain, whole wheat, tomato, spinach or mixed-vegetable, whether it is cut into spaghetti, lasagna or fettuccine shapes, the possibilities for this homemade treat are deliciously endless. The dough can be mixed by hand or in a food processor; in both cases, it requires kneading. It can be cut by hand or by machine. Most hand-operated pasta makers have attachments for cutting a variety of flat noodles. Fresh pasta can be cut by hand, but it takes Herculean strength to roll the dough out into sufficiently thin sheets. Once the dough is cut, use either a commercial pasta dryer or a broomstick supported on the backs of two chairs to dry the pasta thoroughly—about 12 hours —before packaging. Bag tightly and store in a cool place.

Basic Pasta Dough

2 cups	flour	500 mL
3	eggs	3
2 tsp.	oil	10 mL
2 Tbsp.	water	30 mL

By hand: Place flour in a mound on the work surface, and make a well in the centre. Combine eggs, oil and water, and pour the mixture into the well. Using a fork at first and then working by hand, mix ingredients together. Knead the dough for 5 minutes or until smooth and elastic. Cover and let stand for 10 minutes. Roll out to desired thickness. Cut by hand or in a pasta cutter.

In food processor: Place all the ingredients in the bowl of the machine and mix until they form a ball. Knead 2 to 4 minutes, or until the dough is smooth and elastic. Cover and let stand for 5 minutes. Roll out to desired thickness. Cut pasta by hand or in a pasta cutter.
Variations:
• Vegetables—Cook vegetables until tender and purée, leaving some tiny pieces to give the pasta texture. For the above recipe, mix

Ground beef, red pepper, ripe olive pizza

½ cup (125 mL) puréed vegetables into the dough and reduce the recipe by 1 egg.

• Herbs—Wash, dry and finely chop 4 tablespoons (60 mL) of herbs. Mix into the flour before making the pasta.

• Other flours—Make whole wheat pasta using 1½ cups (375 mL) whole wheat flour with ½ cup (125 mL) unbleached white flour. Semolina, buckwheat and triticale flours are also good in place of and in the same proportions as whole wheat.

Pastry

Discovering a reliable and delicious basic pastry dough (one that serves equally well for both main-course and dessert dishes) makes it easier to tackle more elaborate pie and tart recipes. Every pastry shell you make will be light and tender if you remember one trick: when blending the ingredients together,

handle the dough as delicately – and as little – as possible. One of the easiest ways to mix pastry dough is with the sharp, fast chopping blade of a food processor, which will quickly cut the butter into the flour without creaming it.

Pastry Recipe

This recipe for a double-crust pie calls for butter rather than shortening, which results in a tender, flaky pastry. See page 84 for information on cutting in.

3½ cups	unbleached white flour	875 mL
12 oz.	butter, cubed	375 g
10 Tbsp.	ice-cold water	150 mL

By hand: Place the flour in a chilled bowl, and using two chilled knives or a pastry cutter, cut in the butter until the mixture is the con-

sistency of cornmeal. Gradually add water, mixing with a wooden spoon, until the dough clings together. Chill for 1 hour.

In food processor: Place the flour in the bowl of the machine, and add the butter in chunks. Using a chilled metal cutting blade, whir the motor in 2-second pulses until the dough is the consistency of cornmeal. Then, with the processor running, add the water a few tablespoons (45 mL) at a time, blending until the dough holds together but is not wet. Chill for 1 hour.

After following either procedure, roll the dough out to desired thickness on a chilled, floured marble or glass pastry board using a chilled rolling pin. Roll the crust a little larger in circumference than the baking dish, and trim it to fit the plate later.

Makes dough for a 9″ (1 L) 2-crust pie.

Pizza Dough

No pizza will ever taste better than one you prepare yourself. Piled thick with favourite toppings, pizza is a delicious, healthful supper that is entertaining for families and friends to create together. Simple enough for a child to make, the following recipe for dough takes a little over an hour from start to finish.

Pizza Dough Recipe

2 Tbsp.	yeast	30 mL
1 tsp.	honey	5 mL
1¼ cups	warm water	300 mL
¼ cup	olive oil	50 mL
3½ cups	unbleached white flour	875 mL

Dissolve the yeast and honey in water. Add the oil and flour and mix well. Turn the dough onto a floured surface, and knead it until it is smooth and elastic, about 3 to 5 minutes. Cover, and let rise in a warm place for 1 hour or until doubled in size. Punch down, knead again briefly, divide into three equal pieces, and roll to fit baking pans.

Makes enough dough for three 10-inch (25 cm) pizzas.

How-To

Basics

Clam chowder

Rice

Rice is unforgiving when cooked improperly; after years of eating both pasty and gravelly results, I have developed a foolproof method for preparing fluffy rice, whether it is white, brown, short- or long-grain.

Begin by thoroughly rinsing 2 cups (500 mL) of rice in a strainer and allowing it to drain well. On a medium-high setting, heat 4 tablespoons (60 mL) of oil or ghee in a heavy pot, add the rice, and cook until it absorbs the oil – three to four minutes – stirring constantly. Pour in 4 cups (1 L) of cold water, cover the pot and, without peeking under the lid, listen for the water to boil. When it does, turn the heat off. Let stand for 5 minutes, then bring to a boil again. Reduce the heat, and cook at a very low boil. After cooking white rice for 10 minutes

and brown rice for 20, turn the heat off once more. Let stand, covered, for another 5 minutes, remove the lid, fluff the rice with a fork and serve.

Roux

A roux is a mixture of equal parts melted butter and flour heated together and used as the base for many classic French sauces. (While cholesterol-free vegetable oils can be used in a roux, many purists believe there is no substitute for the velvety texture and rich taste of butter.) Melt the butter in a pan, and stir in the flour. The butter and flour should be thoroughly blended and the mixture heated evenly to ensure absorbency for thickening sauces. The roux should also be cooked long enough (approximately two to three minutes at medium-high heat) to eliminate the taste of raw flour.

A roux can be cooked very lightly for a white sauce, such as béchamel, or browned slightly for a darker sauce, such as sauce espagnole.

Salad Dressings

Homemade salad dressings are flavourful, healthy and considerably less expensive than their commercial counterparts. For mayonnaise-based dressings, blend plain mayonnaise in a food processor with dill or blue cheese for a rich and tangy dressing. For oil-and-vinegar dressings, follow the basic rule of 2 parts oil to 1 part vinegar. For different flavours, add herbs – chives, parsley or tarragon – to taste; use different kinds of vinegar – red wine, balsamic or tarragon – or lemon or lime juice; or add a little honey or grated onion. A quick creamy dressing can be made with yogurt, lemon juice and herbs. Mashed tofu can be used instead of yogurt for anyone sensitive to dairy products.

Sauce Espagnole

Also known as brown sauce, sauce espagnole is the base for Madeira sauce. Although it takes several hours to make, it is well worth the effort and can be frozen and used to flavour soup stocks, gravies and other sauces.

Sauce Espagnole Recipe

¾ cup	meat drippings	175 mL
1½ cups	mirepoix	375 mL
	(see page 98)	
¾ cup	flour	175 mL
8	peppercorns	8
2 cups	chopped tomatoes	500 mL
¾ cup	chopped parsley	175 mL
10 cups	beef stock	2.5 L

Combine the drippings and mirepoix in a heavy pot and cook until the mixture begins to turn a golden colour. Stir in the flour and cook until it is brown. Add remaining ingre-

dients, bring the sauce to a boil, then reduce the heat and simmer, uncovered, for approximately 3 hours, or until the sauce is reduced by half. Stir the sauce occasionally while cooking, skimming off any fat that rises to the top. Strain. Store in the refrigerator or freezer.

Makes approximately 8 cups (2 L).

Scalloping

The procedure of layering solid food with a cream sauce is known as scalloping. It is most commonly done with potatoes, but such firm vegetables as turnip make a delicious scallop, as do fish fillets and chicken breasts. The following is a recipe for a dressed-up scalloped potato casserole that cooks in its own cream sauce.

Scalloped Potatoes

6	large potatoes	6
2	onions	2
10 Tbsp.	flour	150 mL
10 Tbsp.	butter	150 mL
	salt & pepper	
2 cups	grated Swiss cheese	500 mL
3 cups	milk or cream	750 mL
	Parmesan cheese	

Wash, peel, and thinly slice potatoes and onions. In a greased casserole dish, make a layer using one-third of the potatoes topped with one-third of the onions. Sprinkle over it 3 tablespoons (45 mL) of flour, 3 tablespoons (45 mL) of butter divided into small dabs, salt and pepper and a third of the Swiss cheese. Repeat the procedure twice more, and cover the top layer with the extra butter and flour. Pour milk evenly over the top, then sprinkle with Parmesan cheese. Cover and bake at 375 degrees F (190 °C) for 45 minutes, then uncover and bake for another 30 minutes.

Serves 6.

Sprouts

In winter, when fresh domestic produce is hard to find, homegrown sprouts are a wonderful addition to salads and sandwiches. Many kinds of beans and seeds – generally available at health-food stores – can be sprouted at home. Mung beans and alfalfa seeds are most commonly used for mild sprouts, while radish and mustard seeds make delicious spicy sprouts.

Soak 4 tablespoons (60 mL) of seeds in warm water overnight. In the morning, pour out the water, rinse the seeds and place them in a 1-quart (1 L) Mason jar. Stretch two or three layers of cheesecloth over the top, and secure them with an elastic band. Place the jar in a warm spot out of direct sunlight.

Two or three times a day, rinse the seeds in warm water by filling the jar, swirling the water around and draining it out through the cloth. Small seeds will sprout fully in two to four days, and large seeds will take slightly longer. To intensify the colour, place the jar of nearly ready sprouts in the sun for a few hours. When they are a satisfactory colour, place the sprouts in an airtight plastic container and store them in the refrigerator, where they will retain their peak flavour and nutritional value for a few days.

Stock

Every good cook needs to know how to make stock, not only as a base for soups but as the cooking liquid for rice, vegetables and meat and as a delicious addition to any sauce. Make it whenever you can, and keep a supply on hand in the refrigerator or freezer. If it is frozen, it will store for several months.

Chicken Stock

1	chicken carcass	1
2	carrots, peeled & cut into chunks	2
1	celery stalk, including leaves, cut into chunks	1
3	onions, peeled & quartered	3
	salt	
12	peppercorns	12

Place all ingredients in a stockpot and cover with cold water. Bring water to a boil, reduce heat, cover and simmer for 3 to 4 hours, periodically skimming foam from the top. Cool slightly and strain out solids. Cool completely in the refrigerator, then skim fat from the surface. Store in an airtight container in the refrigerator or freezer.

Vegetable Stock

	scrubbed potato peels	
4	carrots, peeled & cut into chunks	4
2	celery stalks, including leaves, cut into chunks	2
3	onions, peeled & quartered	3
3-4	tomatoes, quartered	3-4
	salt	
8	peppercorns	8

Combine all the ingredients in a stockpot and cover with cold water. Bring to a boil, reduce the heat, cover and simmer for 40 minutes. After cooling slightly, strain, and then store the stock in an airtight container in the refrigerator or freezer.

Fish Stock

2 lbs.	fish bones	1 kg
1	onion, quartered	1
1	carrot, peeled & chopped	1
2	stalks celery, chopped	2
	bouquet garni	
8	peppercorns	8
2	whole cloves	2

Place all ingredients in a stockpot, cover with cold water and bring to a boil. Reduce the heat, cover and let simmer for 30 minutes,

How-To

Basics

Using Soup Stock

Stock is perhaps the single most important liquid for a cook to have on hand. It is a delicious ingredient in gravies, stews and marinades, and it can be used plain or seasoned with herbs or wine as a poaching and braising liquid. Sauces prepared with stock, while not as rich as those made with cream or milk, are more delicately flavoured.

My primary use for stock, however, is as a base for homemade soups, both cream and clear. Match the stock to what you are putting in the soup: beef stock in beef or hearty vegetable soup, fish stock for fish soup only, and chicken stock for chicken or vegetable soup. Stocks can be livened up with tomato juice —for a beef-vegetable soup, for instance—or with herbs that complement the other soup ingredients. Begin by cooking the vegetables or meat in the stock, then add milk or cream. Once the broth is hot, thicken it by stirring in a few tablespoons (30 to 45 mL) of flour or cornstarch dissolved in an equal amount of water.

A delicious chicken soup can be made quickly if you have chicken stock on hand. Heat the stock to a boil, and in a separate pot, prepare egg noodles, draining and rinsing them thoroughly once they are cooked. Sauté diced onion, garlic, celery and carrots in a frying pan, and add them to the stock, cooking until the carrots are just tender. Season the broth with salt, pepper, marjoram and thyme, then add the noodles. (Leftover cooked chicken is also a delicious addition.) Heat thoroughly, and serve with biscuits.

periodically skimming off foam. Remove from heat, cool slightly and strain. Allow to cool completely and store in an airtight container in the refrigerator or freezer.

Brown Stock

Brown stock is a rich, hearty stock that is used as the base for other heavy sauces such as espagnole and Madeira. When using brown stock for a beef soup base, dilute its intense flavour first.

5 lbs.	lean beef bones	2.25 kg
5 Tbsp.	oil or butter	75 mL
10	peppercorns	10
2	bay leaves	2
2	sprigs thyme	2
5	stalks celery, chopped	5
2	carrots, peeled & chopped	2
2	onions, quartered	2
1 quart	tomatoes	1 L

In a stockpot, brown the beef bones in oil or butter. Cover with 12 cups (3 L) water and bring to a boil. Reduce the heat and simmer, uncovered, for 20 minutes, then skim. Add remaining ingredients, cover and cook for 4 to 5 hours. Cool slightly and strain. Refrigerate, and then remove fat from the surface. Store in the refrigerator or freezer in an airtight container.

Tomato Sauce

Homemade tomato sauce can be used in its pure form on pizza, or it can be the base for a pasta topping to which you can add browned meat or vegetables. If you want a thicker sauce, add more tomato paste.

Tomato Sauce Recipe

5 Tbsp.	olive oil	75 mL
4	onions, chopped	4
5	cloves garlic, minced	5
1	green pepper, minced	1
2	bay leaves	2
1½ tsp.	basil	7 mL
1 tsp.	oregano	5 mL
1 tsp.	thyme	5 mL
	salt & pepper	
3 28-oz. cans	Italian plum tomatoes, crushed	2.4 L
6½-oz. can	tomato paste	185 mL

Heat the olive oil in a heavy pot. Add the onions and garlic and sauté over high heat, stirring until golden. Reduce heat to medium, and add the green pepper, herbs and salt and pepper. Cook for 5 to 7 minutes, stirring frequently. Add tomatoes, increase the heat to high and bring to a boil. Stir in the tomato paste, and reduce the heat to simmer, cooking the sauce uncovered for at least 1 hour.
Makes approximately 8 cups (2 L).

Velouté Sauce

While milk or cream is added to béchamel and white sauces, chicken, vegetable, veal or fish stock is used in the preparation of velouté sauce, resulting in a light and velvety concoction that is suitable as the base for many cream soup recipes.

Velouté Sauce Recipe

3 Tbsp.	butter	45 mL
3 Tbsp.	flour	45 mL
3 cups	stock	750 mL
	salt & pepper	

Melt butter, stir in flour and cook, stirring, until golden brown. Slowly add stock and cook over medium-high heat until thickened. Season with salt and pepper.

Yogurt

Yogurt, both delicious and easy to make at home, is a healthy snack topped with fruit or granola and a suitable substitute for sour cream in dips and dressings and on baked potatoes.

With an electric yogurt maker or incubator: Scald 1 quart (1 L) of milk and

Strawberry frozen yogurt

tasting yeast, and mix in a blender or food processor set on high. Serve over ice in a tall glass.

Frozen Yogurt

4 cups	fresh or frozen berries (raspberries, strawberries or blueberries)	1 L
2	bananas	2
¼ cup	sugar	50 mL
½ cup	frozen unsweetened juice concentrate (orange or berry)	125 mL
1 tsp.	vanilla	5 mL
2 cups	yogurt	500 mL

In a food processor or blender, purée berries until smooth and set aside. Purée banana in the food processor, add berry purée, brown sugar, juice concentrate and vanilla, then blend. Add yogurt and blend briefly. Serve immediately or freeze in a tightly covered plastic container for up to 4 days. If the yogurt has frozen solid, allow to soften in the refrigerator for 30 minutes before serving or whip briefly in food processor until smooth.
    Serves 8 to 10.

Zest

Zest is the colourful grated rind of citrus fruit used as a seasoning. Its piquant taste enhances the natural flavour of many foods and beverages, including icings, sauces, cakes, muffins, soups and meats. To prepare zest, thoroughly scrub the fruit to remove any agricultural sprays, and using the finest cut on a cheese grater, shave the surface layer of peel; do not include the bitter white pith. (Zest peelers that remove the skin in larger pieces are available.) Zest should be used sparingly. The high concentration of oil in the peel gives it a much more intense flavour than the juice has – 1 teaspoon (5 mL) of freshly grated zest is the equivalent of 2 tablespoons (30 mL) of freshly squeezed juice.

cool to 105 degrees F (41 °C). Heat a 1-quart (1 L) Mason jar with warm water. Pour in milk, then add a starter – 2 tablespoons (30 mL) of yogurt – and cover. Be sure to use fresh, natural yogurt. Some commercial yogurts are made with gelatin rather than bacteria, and if you use one for a starter, your yogurt will not turn out. Old yogurt will not provide the necessary impetus to start a new batch. Incubate at 105 degrees F (41 °C) for four hours, remove from the incubator when thickened and chill for at least 12 hours before eating.

Without an electric yogurt maker: With a little more vigilance, you can make your own yogurt without the appliance. Follow the directions above, but incubate in this manner: Place the jar in a large pot, and add water at a temperature of 115 degrees F (46 °C) to the pot, filling to a depth that reaches half-way up the sides of the jar. Incubate for four hours, using a thermometer to check the temperature frequently and adding more warm water as needed to maintain a temperature between 105 and 110 degrees F (41 °C to 43 °C) for the incubation period.

Two tips: Instead of a pot, use a plastic picnic cooler as an incubator, which will reduce the amount of monitoring needed. You can also place the pot (but not the cooler) in the oven to keep it warm, maintaining a close watch on the oven temperature.

Yogurt can be enjoyed as is, mixed with fresh fruit, made into frozen desserts or incorporated into many blender drinks: Combine 2 cups (500 mL) plain yogurt with 1 cup (250 mL) of fruit, a tablespoon (15 mL) of honey or maple syrup, a teaspoon (5 mL) of vanilla and a few teaspoons (5 to 15 mL) of good-

TOOLS & EQUIPMENT

Any discussion of cooking tools and equipment must be prefaced by a consideration of the room in which they will be used. For people who enjoy preparing food as much as consuming it, the kitchen can be the most important room in the house. My own preference lies with a big, warm, comfortable room that can be enjoyed simultaneously by noncooks and chefs without their tripping over one another. Others prefer a sleek, streamlined room where one cook can speedily and efficiently whip up meals to be presented as if by magic to appreciative guests. Whatever our ideals, however, most of us have to be content with kitchens that fall far short of our dreams.

Even without renovation, a lot can be done with an unsatisfactory kitchen. The one I have cooked in for the past five years (in which I have tested many of the recipes for the third volume of *The Harrowsmith Cookbook*, prepared meals for my family and for large groups of people and conducted a successful catering business) has only a two-foot-long counter on one side of the single sink and a one-foot-long counter on the other. It is also located at the rear of the house, which makes it so dark that the overhead light has to be on even during summer days.

On the other hand, it is a huge room and has a little room opening off it. I painted everything white, put a high-wattage bulb in the outlet, stuck an overstuffed armchair in one corner and turned the buffet and kitchen table into counters. The freezer went into the adjoining room, along with hanging baskets I use for storing potatoes and onions and a lot of wall-mounted shelves for plastic storage containers, serving trays and dishes.

Cupboard space was also at a premium, so I converted a hutch into a dried-goods cupboard and built shelves everywhere. The kitchen is now a place where two or even three people can

Built-in cabinets maximize limited space

work at the same time with relative ease and where guests are always welcome to join the cook in conversation and a glass of wine while the finishing touches are put on a meal. My kitchen "renovation" cost almost nothing – a couple of cans of paint and some used lumber to build shelves. Four children, as well as a minimum of two adults, live in the house, and we all feel that, for the most part, the kitchen meets our needs.

My point is that a space need not be professionally designed, but it can be made pleasantly functional with a little imagination and effort. While being able to place food from the refrigerator directly on a nearby surface may be very convenient, it is not impossible to carry the food 10 feet to the sink or counter. For me, it is far more important to organize the space so that socializing and food preparation can go on at the same time. This is, obviously, a matter of personal preference – a close friend, who is one of the best cooks I know, likes cooking to be a solitary experience. Because his kitchen flows into the main part of the house, he rises early – at 4 or 5 a.m.

every day – so that he can do his cooking in privacy.

The Perfect Kitchen

After 15 years of adapting myself to inadequate kitchens and adapting inadequate kitchens to suit me, I must admit, however, that I am ready for "the perfect kitchen," even though I know that no such thing exists. For one thing, everyone's style of cooking changes from time to time, which results in different needs in the kitchen; for another, no matter how much one knows about cooking and kitchens, it is only after using one regularly that its flaws and strengths become apparent. Because we have recently begun to design a new house, I have had a series of late-night rendezvous with a stack of kitchen books and magazines as I struggle to bring the dreamy part of planning into line with the hard reality of construction.

I need to design a kitchen that is affordable (we are building this house without the benefit of a mortgage), relatively simple to construct (we are doing most of the work ourselves), functional as a family kitchen that will serve, on average, 10 to 12 people a day and that will be used by more than one cook at a time (we are planning a community house rather than a nuclear-family dwelling). As well, it must meet local health regulations so that I can continue my catering business and also have enough options to be useful as a test kitchen for *Harrowsmith* projects.

Some of the elements I dream of may be included right away, depending on time, energy and financial resources; others will be added over the next several years. Among my favourites are a separate small sink for hand washing; cupboards that go beyond the functional to the truly wonderful – sliding in and out, turning and performing all kinds of other tricks; and a suspended-from-the-ceiling saucepan rack. Naturally, every-

Open layout integrates food-preparation and living areas

one's lists of fantasy and necessary items will be different, reflecting individual preferences and needs.

First, of course, come the constants. No matter where I relocate the sink and appliances, I will always leave a large space for an armchair and enough room to add one or two other straight-backed chairs for extra visitors. A triple sink, which will never be sacrificed for any reason, will make it possible to stack and even wash and rinse dishes while food is being prepared. Adjacent to the kitchen is a pantry that will hold at least the freezer and storage shelves, and later on, it will become a mudroom complete with shower. And lots of windows will face south and west; in our minds, we have moved all the other rooms several times, but the kitchen always remains in the southwest corner. I also want a kitchen that can be adapted relatively easily as time goes by, for there is no way of knowing for certain how well it will work until it has been tested through every season. Cooking needs change according to the weather, the produce from the garden, the amount of time people spend indoors and other variables.

Less Is More

After much contemplation, discussion and reworking, I divided this chapter into two basic sections that I believe are self-explanatory: Essentials and Nonessentials. Many of the nonessentials are wonderful items I would be hard-pressed to do without. And readers will have their own ideas on which of these are indispensable. The beauty of cooking is that it is a highly individual pursuit with few set rules. While I have included a wide variety of tools in this chapter, whether I use them myself or not (I drew the line at electric hot-dog makers), it inevitably reflects my own experience and interests.

Let me issue a caveat: Cooking has become one of our culture's most commercialized pastimes in recent years. In some cases, that has resulted in the development of very good tools (the submersible blender comes to mind), but far more often, people inexperienced in cooking are lured into buying ridiculously expensive, useless toys. While it is sometimes true that a high price reflects high quality (kitchen knives, for instance), more often than not, expensive kitchen gadgets are created in response to food trends, the primary goal being profit to the manufacturer rather than service to the consumer. (At the height of the homemade-pasta craze several years ago, I bought a pasta dryer that now gathers dust in the back of a cupboard. Before spotting it in a kitchen store, I had been drying my noodles quite successfully on a broom handle supported on the backs of two chairs, a system I soon returned to.)

I can offer only a few rules about buy-

Side counter and stools transform small space into an eat-in kitchen

ing kitchen tools. Use common sense. If you have never felt the lack of a particular gizmo until you saw it advertised or displayed in a store, you probably do not need it. If it catches your fancy, go home and think about it for a few days. Prepare the food that the thing is supposed to make easier or faster or better. Would it really help you? Where would you keep it? Appliances that must be stored away because they take up too much counter space are often soon for-

gotten. If you still feel you could use it, find out what the options, features and, of course, prices are on different manufacturers' versions of the same item.

Consider the history of food preparation: What tools are as much in use today as they were 200 years ago? The simple answer is bowls, pots, spoons and knives. If you seem to need one or two of everything else on the market, remind yourself that great chefs existed long before electric carving knives.

Another general rule about buying kitchen tools is that you can often buy high-quality items in hardware stores considerably less expensively than in specialty stores. This applies to basics ranging from wooden spoons (which you should always buy individually so that you can bang them on the back of your hand a few times to make sure they will not break the first time you stir a stiff dough) through measuring cups to food processors. More specialized items are more readily found in kitchen stores. I never buy anything for my kitchen at discount outlets. At these places, you truly do get what you pay for—usually not much. When purchasing larger, more expensive items, patronize a store with a good reputation for service. I recently had to "make do" for a full month without the use of an oven when the stove broke down and the store I bought it from had stopped servicing its products. I won't let myself get caught like that again.

Finally, buy two good-quality wooden spoons of different sizes rather than six or seven cheaper ones. Buy one set of stainless-steel measuring spoons, not two sets of plastic ones. Many books will try to convince you to buy several of everything to "save on dishwashing." Well, those six wooden spoons all have to be washed eventually. The two I own, rinsed off while I am preparing a meal, are often used for more than one thing. But I have two good spoons that work very well and will never break, and when I am finished cooking, there are only two of them to wash.

Of course, only you can determine what you need. My goals in cooking—and I hope they will become yours if they aren't already—are to be as self-sufficient as possible and to be able to prepare wholesome, tasty meals, with lots of room for experimentation and, from time to time, gourmet extravagance. I hope this chapter shows you that sometimes less is more.

Beyond the Triangle

Despite the revolution in kitchen technology, the underlying principle for functional kitchen design remains the work triangle: as a means of maximizing the efficiency of the kitchen, the major appliances—refrigerator, stove and sink—are positioned in a triangular configuration. Ideally, the total length of the triangle's three sides should be between 12 and 22 feet. The sink-to-stove side should be 4 to 6 feet, the sink-to-refrigerator side 4 to 7 feet, and the stove-to-refrigerator side 4 to 9 feet.

When first devised, the work triangle catered to the most common kitchen floor plans of the era—the single wall, the galley, the U and the L—and encouraged the creation of "work centres" within each. Modern kitchens, however, are conforming less and less strictly to these models. With one major appliance positioned at each angle of the triangle, even the once preferred U-shaped plan has given way to open-ended designs given definition not by solid walls but by unusual kinds of work surfaces, appliances and unkitchenlike furnishings such as desks, computers and stereos.

Regardless of how informal or contemporary your design may be, you should remember that your kitchen's primary function is still food preparation. Its layout should facilitate productivity in a way that suits the habits (and quirks) of your household. The following is a list of a few commonsense ideas to keep in mind when planning your kitchen.

● Drawings on paper alone cannot tell you what will work most effectively. Visit kitchen design showrooms, and spend time in friends' kitchens with a critical eye open for pros and cons.

● Do not blithely surrender the details of your kitchen to the advice of a contractor. Lighting, ventilation, room dimensions, windows, clearances, countertop widths, lengths and heights, position and number of electrical outlets, cabinet design, height and accessibility, and even the placement of doorways, are individual decisions.

● Eliminate room doors that open against the front of an appliance. Mount the doors to open to the outside of the room, or use folding, or pocket, doors.

● Position the work triangle away from the general-traffic pathway.

● Try not to have cabinet or appliance doors opening into a traffic pathway. When this is unavoidable, make the traffic corridor wide enough for people to pass even when the doors are open.

● Never underestimate the amount of work surface you need. Don't forget how much you can lose if you store appliances and tools on the countertop.

● Allow space on either side of the stove as a buffer zone for hot pot handles, and consider adding a heat-resistant countertop where you can place hot pots, pans and baking dishes.

● Leave yourself lots of room on either side of the sink.

● Position the refrigerator so that it is adjacent to counter space.

● While the dishwasher and sink need to be side by side, avoid positioning them at right angles to each other. Likewise, do not position the dishwasher facing the oven or refrigerator, since all the open doors could block traffic. If possible, locate the dishwasher near storage cupboards.

● Avoid placing the oven or dishwasher next to the refrigerator. If this is not possible, insulate between them.

● Install a built-in oven at counter height.

Essentials

Stoves

The stove is probably the most important tool in the kitchen. While there are many ways to "make do" to keep foods cool, a reliable and sensitive source of heat is much more difficult to improvise.

Wood, electric and gas are the three main kinds of stoves. My preference lies with gas, but each has its advantages and disadvantages and each is better suited to different kinds of cooking.

A gas stovetop burner can be adjusted to provide any amount of heat, from very high to extremely low. As well, you can turn gas on and off instantly; with an electric burner, fine heat control can often be managed only by removing a pot from the burner and replacing it later. Another major advantage of a gas stove is that pans without flat bottoms (woks, for instance) can be heated evenly with the open flame. The heat in a gas oven is drier than that in an electric oven (dry heat is better for baking yeast doughs); and although the heat in an electric oven is distributed more evenly than in a gas appliance, it only takes a little experimentation to discover the distribution pattern in a particular gas oven. Once that has been determined, it is possible to cook different foods at slightly different temperatures simultaneously.

Electric stoves nevertheless offer a number of benefits: They are relatively inexpensive. The risk of fire is slightly lower with an electric stove than with a gas range, although I do not think this should be the determining factor when selecting a stove – gas explosions certainly occur, but they are very rare, and electrical wiring can also short-circuit or otherwise malfunction and cause a fire. Electric stoves are easy to use, especially for cooks who are leery of the open flame. I must reiterate, however, that it is impossible to get the precise heat control with electric burners that one

Stainless-steel countertops provide the ultimate work surface

can with gas, and that alone is why I prefer gas.

While personal needs and cooking habits will influence the selection of a stove, a few general considerations should be kept in mind that apply to both types: Look for a stove with as few dirt traps as possible and one that has elements that either lift out or are easily manipulated to allow the drip trays to be cleaned thoroughly. The control knobs should be simple in design and removable for cleaning. The floor of the oven should also be easy to remove. The extra cost of a self-cleaning oven is not, in my opinion, worthwhile. If an oven is used properly and you put drip trays in place whenever spills are anticipated,

it is not very difficult to clean. Nothing stronger than baking soda, dish detergent, a good scrub pad and a bit of elbow grease need be applied, whereas self-cleaning ovens require huge amounts of energy.

Also, your stove should be on casters so that you can move it easily to clean the floor around and under it. Look for an oven with a door that opens down (by far the most common) rather than to the side to facilitate removing hot pots and pans. If buying a secondhand appliance, be sure that the door has a window in it and the oven an interior light so that you can supervise cooking foods without having to open the door repeatedly.

When positioning a stove in the kitchen, allow at least one inch (2.5 cm) of space on each side for air circulation. Avoid, if possible, placing the stove and refrigerator next to each other. If they must be placed side by side, put an insulating shield between them.

I have left wood cookstoves until last. Aesthetically, a woodstove is hard to beat, and it has a number of practical advantages as well. It allows you to keep a pot of soup or stew simmering for days; it has a compartment just for keeping things warm; if a large pan of water is kept on a back burner, it helps humidify the house; it provides heat for the kitchen; and next to a brick oven, it bakes the best bread.

On the other hand, it is more difficult to control the temperature precisely on a woodstove than on electric or gas ranges, and keeping it fed with fuel requires regular, devoted attention. Perhaps its biggest disadvantage arises from its secondary purpose: to provide heat. Using a woodstove in the summer is almost unbearable. In the past, woodstoves were moved out of the house to the summer kitchen, where they were used for pickling, jam making and other summertime cooking, thus protecting everyone but the cook from the heat. I am not sure that I would be so quick to subject the cook to this form of torture, and it is not practical for most of us to move an item as large as a stove twice a year. In a large kitchen, however, a woodstove can have two useful roles: cooking in winter and storage and counter space in summer.

Refrigerators

Over the past 20 or 30 years, we have come to "need" enormous refrigerators. While it is certainly convenient to have an appliance that will hold everything we want it to, large size is far from essential. Many fruits and vegetables can be kept adequately cool in a root cellar.

Half walls lend a spacious air to an otherwise confining kitchen

While dairy products, meats and some opened processed foods require refrigeration, the amount of space they take up can be kept to a minimum by judicious and frequent shopping. I grew up believing that grocery shopping ought to be done in a once-a-week blitz, but I have reformed. I now shop every couple of days, going to the market, the health-food store, the butcher and the supermarket in separate expeditions. As a result, my refrigerator is never bulging or empty (it always seemed to be one or the other when I shopped once a week), and I can shop on foot or bicycle without becoming overburdened.

If the refrigerator is for an existing kitchen, buy a model that opens onto the room's main work space so that you can move food directly from the refrigerator to a table or counter. A refrigerator with a small freezer at the top, with a separate outside door, is a good idea even if you have a large freestanding freezer. The space is handy for storing herbs and spices, frozen juices and small bits of food—it is much easier to find little things here than in a large freezer.

The separate door makes it more energy-efficient. Adjustable shelves and at least one or two closed drawers are important features, and shelves in the door make effective use of space. A butter compartment and egg trays are handy but not essential. Temperature-controlled butter compartments and gizmos that spew out ice cubes or cold water automatically use extra energy, increase the initial cost of the appliance and often break down. I am a lot more interested in interior and exterior surfaces that wipe clean easily.

The two most important characteristics of a refrigerator, however, are good insulation and a tightly sealed door. It is possible to find out how much insulation new models have, but that is difficult to determine with secondhand refrigerators. Find a reliable dealer, and check out any claims made about insulation before buying.

Finally, automatic defrosting: as with cleaning an oven, manual defrosting does not require a great effort. If it is done on a regular basis, the operation of the refrigerator will not be impeded

Essentials

and you save on both initial cost and energy use.

Knives

Knives are quite simply the most important tools a cook can have. So my advice is to spend money on them. Buy good-quality knives, and get several for different purposes. The handles should be riveted to the blades; any other kind of fastening will sooner or later (probably sooner) loosen. Also, the handles should be made of wood – if possible, wood that has been sealed with plastic – and the blade should run the full length of the handle. Forged knife blades are stronger than moulded, and high-carbon stainless steel is better than carbon steel or stainless steel for a number of reasons: it cuts all food well, does not rust and keeps a sharp edge. And while high-carbon stainless steel is the most expensive, a good knife will last a lifetime or longer if cared for properly. Carbon steel corrodes easily and discolours highly acidic foods, and stainless steel dulls readily and is difficult to sharpen.

The few knives that every cook needs include an all-purpose chef's knife, two small paring knives, a serrated fruit knife, a chicken-boning knife, a bread knife and a cleaver. You will also need a sharpening steel. Over time, you may want to add a carving knife, a filleting knife and additional paring knives to your collection.

To protect what can amount to a significant investment, take good care of your knives. Storing them loose in a drawer will not only dull the blades but will inevitably lead to an accident when someone reaches into the drawer for something else. Keep them in a wooden block, or design knife slots into the back of a counter. Sharpen your knives on a sharpening steel every time they are used. Wash them one at a time – don't dump them all into a sink full of sudsy water, or you may lose your fingers –

and clean them thoroughly in soapy water before rinsing and drying.

Cookware

Pots, pans, casserole dishes and cookie sheets come in an array of choices almost too great to contemplate. Some are necessary only for specific kinds of cooking, many are wonderful to have, and a very few are essential to every kitchen. As with many tools, a higher initial investment in cookware will result in longer use, less frustration and better food.

The most common materials for pots and pans are aluminum and stainless steel. I always recommend stainless steel. Although it is very expensive, buy it if you can possibly afford it, selecting the pieces individually; you will have no regrets. Stainless steel conducts heat evenly and well, it cleans easily, it is sturdy enough to stand up to heavy use, food sticks to it less than to aluminum, and it never affects the flavour of the food. Also, it requires minimal maintenance: just wash in warm, soapy water and rinse well. No seasoning of the cookware is necessary. Be sure to buy only heavy stainless steel – the thinner types do not produce good results.

Aluminum has acquired a bad name in recent years because its consumption is suspected of being related to Alzheimer's disease. Although the relationship has not been proved or disproved, it is clearly a factor that should be taken into account. Aluminum generally conducts heat easily and is considerably less expensive than stainless steel. It is also easy to care for and does not need to be seasoned. On the other hand, it reacts with acidic and alkaline foods and may leave them with a metallic taste. The thin metal also warps with use.

Cast-iron cookware is no longer used as widely as it once was. An excellent conductor of heat, it also holds heat well and is therefore ideal for casserole

dishes and frying pans. But cast-iron cookware is very heavy and tends to rust if not dried thoroughly after washing. Cast iron should be seasoned before use – lightly oil the new pot or pan, place in the oven or on a burner, heat it to the point of smoking at a moderately high temperature, then remove it from the heat and let it cool. Oil the pot or pan lightly after each use. Often, cast-iron cookware can be adequately cleaned by simply wiping out and reoiling. It can be washed, but don't scour it.

Copper cookware has become very popular in recent years. There is no question that it is good – it conducts heat evenly and does not rust. It is, however, very expensive and requires considerable maintenance to keep it attractive. The inside can never be scrubbed, or the lining will wear away, and the outside must be polished with a commercial cleaner or vinegar and salt.

Cookware coated with nonstick materials is handy for some cooking. Nonstick frying pans are great for frying eggs and other foods that tend to stick even to well-greased surfaces.

Glass makes a good bakeware material: it conducts heat evenly, does not discolour or flavour food and has the added attraction of being inexpensive. If purchasing glassware, be sure that it is labelled flameproof (for the stovetop) or ovenproof.

Basic Cookware and Bakeware

• One Dutch oven – a large, heavy pot to use for soups and stews or for casseroles or roasting in the oven. It should have a lid and handles suitable for oven use.

• One small saucepan with a lid (1 quart/1 litre) for boiling water and eggs and cooking small quantities of food.

• One large cast-iron frying pan, preferably with a lid, for frying bacon, eggs, hamburgers and grilled cheese sandwiches. It can also serve as a wok.

• One small skillet for frying and sautéing small items.

• One 9-by-13-inch (3.5 L) cake pan – a cake made in this pan can be halved and served as a layer cake; it can also be used for lasagna and other casseroles.

• One deep-dish pie plate – the shallow ones are not worthwhile if you like to make hearty, filling pies.

• Two loaf pans – who makes only one loaf of bread? These are also good for meatloaf, pâté, terrine and cake.

• One muffin tray – made of the heaviest material you can find; if it is properly greased, muffin papers are not necessary.

• One cookie sheet – again, made of the heaviest possible material. A cookie sheet can serve as a pizza pan as well.

Everything Else

To furnish a basic kitchen inexpensively but adequately requires only a few more implements:

• Mixing bowls – one large enough for bread dough or cake or muffin batter, and one small enough for beating a couple of egg yolks without losing them. I prefer stainless-steel bowls to glass, largely because they are unbreakable but also because they are ovenproof and can be easily chilled.

• Spoons – two heavy wooden spoons of different sizes, and a soup ladle, a slotted spoon and an unslotted spoon made of stainless steel.

• A hard rubber spatula and a metal spatula/scraper.

• A medium-weight whisk for everything from beating eggs to stirring cream sauces.

• A manual eggbeater.

• A 2-cup (500 mL) measuring cup that is made of heat-resistant glass and marked with both dry and liquid measurements.

• One chopping board is adequate, but two are better. Use a washable plastic

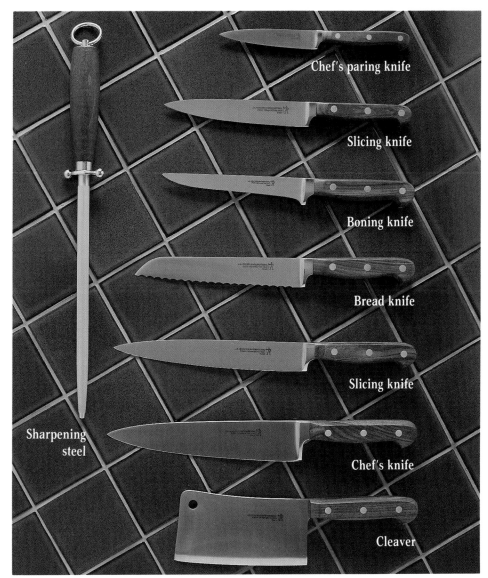

The cutting edge: high-carbon stainless-steel knives

one for meat and fish and a wooden one for everything else, restricting onion, garlic and ginger to one side.

• A set of metal measuring spoons.

• A sieve – a large one, particularly if you do not have a colander.

• A heavy rolling pin, preferably marble.

• A manual can opener and a bottle opener.

• A cheese grater – the kind that stands on the counter and offers several grating sizes.

• Storage containers – for keeping food in the refrigerator, nothing is better (or cheaper) than used plastic yogurt or cottage cheese containers. They come in a variety of sizes, are sturdily made and have tightly fitting lids. As well, begin to accumulate a selection of lidded wide-mouthed jars for storing dried goods so that you can easily see what you have and can measure directly from the jar.

• A fire extinguisher.

Nonessentials

The kitchen I have described thus far is functional and equipped to allow a competent cook to prepare a variety of foods. But a lot of fun can be had by adding to the basic list.

While decisions about what extras to buy will be based largely on personal preference and cooking style, some basic criteria do apply. When considering the purchase of something new for the kitchen – something that costs more than a vegetable peeler – spend some time thinking about how you cook and eat. If you like to be able to get a meal on the table as quickly as possible, time-saving devices may rank high on your list of priorities. Once a new gadget has caught your fancy, ask yourself why you think you need or want it. It is useful to recognize that wanting something is not the same as actually needing it. How often will you use it? How will it help you in your cooking? How long will it take to recoup the investment? Do you have an appropriate place to store it? Don't buy kitchen equipment just because your friend has one or it looks irresistible in a magazine advertisement.

Obviously, no two cooks will ever come up with the same list of kitchen equipment. The one that follows reflects my own cooking interests, but I hope it is not too biased. I have canvassed a number of people who represent the gamut of cooking styles, and I have scoured cookbooks and kitchen shops for ideas. Whether an item is essential or nonessential, you want it to last, so pay attention to quality. Unfortunately, the trendier a tool becomes, the poorer its quality is likely to be. A wary consumer will shop around before making any decisions. Do not be fooled by fancy packaging and promotional campaigns. And make impulse buying a rare event.

As did the list of essentials, the list of nonessentials begins with large items – first, those that warm foods, then those that keep foods cold.

Illuminated island on T-frame base serves as workspace or informal eating area

Microwave Ovens

Five years ago, I swore that microwave ovens were the worst thing ever invented, but although I still don't use one, I have modified my position somewhat. Their convenience cannot be denied, and they consume much less electricity than conventional stoves. And I have to admit there have been times – when I have wanted to soften butter in a hurry or thaw something for dinner – that I have fleetingly wished for one.

My biggest concern (in addition to not being convinced that they really are safe although all the experts tell us they are) is that reliance upon microwaves will create lazy cooks who pick up a frozen meal on the way home from work, stick it in the microwave and bypass the pleasures of preparing a meal from scratch. The other problem, and one most of us have already experienced, is that restaurants often heat up precooked food in microwave ovens and serve it as though it were prepared just for us. There is no requirement that restaurants indicate on their menus whether they prepare their own food or they buy it already cooked, so it is imperative for consumers who care to ask. I do care, mostly because if I am going to spend money to eat out, I want to be sure that I am not getting something that I could buy – much more cheaply – in the frozen-foods section of the grocery store.

If you are contemplating a microwave, think about how often you will use it, given your family's life style; if it is only going to be used once or twice a week, it will take up a lot of counter space that could be put to better use, although space-saving models that can be fitted under a cupboard are now available. Shop around, and be sure that the model you buy is well insulated, that the door is well sealed and that it meets the Canadian Safety Association's standards. Then examine your approach to cooking, and try not to let it make you lazy.

Microwaves have proved a godsend for people who would otherwise have to rely on others to prepare their food. I have a friend who is a quadriplegic. His kitchen is equipped with a microwave, a stovetop, a freezer and a refrigerator, which allow him to enjoy delicious meals independently. His friends make extra of whatever they cook, package it in individual freezer/microwave containers and plunk a supply in his freezer. He keeps a running list of what he has (and it is indeed a wide variety of food), and each morning, his attendant removes the evening's meal from the freezer and puts it in the microwave. At suppertime, all he has to do is heat up his food. Whether dining alone or entertaining, he is much more self-sufficient than he would be otherwise.

A number of other kitchen tools fit into this category—not necessary for those of us with fully able bodies but immeasurably helpful for those who are not so fortunate. Most health units, senior citizens' councils and agencies for the disabled provide information on setting up a special-needs kitchen.

Toaster Ovens

Not as controversial as microwaves, toaster ovens can be quite handy. The one in our house is used extensively at breakfast, when four children are all eating at separate times, each one wanting something different. A toaster oven consumes much less energy than does a full-sized oven, so it is especially useful for heating a single muffin, making a single melted-cheese sandwich or baking two or three potatoes. Although I would not want to make a habit of it, I recently made biscuits, muffins and even a quick bread in the toaster oven when the stove was out of commission. Look for a toaster oven that will bake, broil and toast. Some come complete with a rotisserie, which may be useful (although it strikes me as being just something else that can break). Choose one with easy-to-remove and easy-to-clean trays and control switches. And remember, as I did not, that it is a real oven, only smaller, so anything left on

Space savers: built-in appliances and utensil drawers are located in preparation area

top of it while it is operating will melt. Also, insist that those who use it clean it, because it is so small that dirt and grease build up quickly.

Freezers

Without exaggeration, I could not cook or live the way I do without a freezer. It allows me to keep a good supply of home-frozen vegetables and fruits on hand to eat throughout the year. I can cook in bulk and have meals ready at the drop of a hat because of the range of basic stocks, doughs and sauces that require minimal additional work before serving. It also allows me to take advantage of sales on freezable foods.

A chest freezer is more energy-efficient than an upright freezer. When it is opened, less cold air escapes and less warm air enters. An upright freezer, however, can be more convenient because everything can be seen at a glance. To use a chest freezer effectively, you need to be organized. Store things in an orderly fashion, list everything in the freezer on a piece of paper attached to the lid, and remember to cross things off the list as you remove them. I start out this way every spring, certain that this year I will keep the freezer tidy, but inevitably, the system breaks down about three months later. I always blame it on the other people who use the freezer, but of course, I am as guilty as anyone.

Tools & Equipment

Nonessentials

Wall-mounted power bar and integrated appliance centre offer extra convenience

Plan to clean out your freezer once a year. Spring is ideal, because the freezer is probably emptier then than at any other time. Unplug it, and take everything out. Check the food for spoilage, make sure that everything going back into the freezer is still tightly packaged and clearly labelled, and wash off any spillage. Throw out anything that is unidentifiable. Rinse out the defrosted freezer with baking soda dissolved in warm water, dry thoroughly, and plug

it in. Leave a fresh box of baking soda in an out-of-the-way spot, and refill the freezer, organizing things in a sensible fashion and updating the list.

There are a few basic guidelines to follow when shopping for a freezer. If you want a chest freezer, make sure the lid will stay open when you want it to. Both chest and upright freezers should have interior lights. I find I do not need a quick-freeze option on my chest freezer because the refrigerator freezer does a

fine job of fast freezing. Secondhand freezers, when they can be found, are often a good buy. Check the seal around the opening; it may be possible to replace a defective one if necessary, but be sure you know what you are buying. Once you buy a chest freezer, you can cover the lid with laminate of some sort so that it can do double duty as extra work space.

Food Processors

One kitchen appliance that has received a vast amount of attention in the past decade is the food processor. I could not live without mine, but I know scores of people who bought one in a fit of excitement and now store it in a dusty cupboard, hauling it out once a month for a minimal workout.

For some, however, a food processor is indispensable. Making coleslaw once a month for three or four people does not justify a processor, but shredding cabbage for many people on a regular basis, making bread crumbs frequently, puréeing soups, making pie dough and grating large quantities of cheese do. I use my food processor almost every day, and there is no question that it saves time and effort.

I seldom use it for slicing or grating vegetables because that is a job I enjoy doing by hand, but if I am cooking for a crowd, it does save time. I always make pastry dough in the food processor — it is quick, keeps the butter and dough from absorbing body heat and grease and helps produce a light, flaky crust, even though it is a nuisance to wash afterward. I grate cheese in the machine only when I need a lot of it (and use it only for hard cheeses — grating soft cheeses such as mozzarella can damage the machine). But I always make bread crumbs in the food processor, and it is also useful for making mayonnaise and whipping up puréed soups and sauces quickly.

Look for a food processor with a good solid motor, for it makes the difference between a reliable machine and one that breaks down quickly. I prefer a model with a bowl to one with a spout that transfers the processed food to a bowl set beneath it. You cannot make mayonnaise or purée in a spout model. If you do not intend to use the machine for slicing, look for a model that does not provide this option. Above all, find a food processor that is easy to clean. This means avoiding models with intricate feeding tubes – they are impossible to clean adequately and become breeding grounds for bacteria. There is little point in using a food processor to save time if the extra time is spent in cleaning the machine.

So many types of food processors are on the market now that it is possible to find almost anything you want. It is worth shopping around to find a machine that suits your needs – no more and no less. If the food processor you favour has a heavy-duty motor, you cannot go too far wrong. Be sure to buy from a store that provides good service.

Once you have purchased a food processor, read the instructions carefully. Find out everything about it before you use it; take it apart and put it back together a few times. Find a place on the counter where you can store it – out of the way when not needed but accessible when it is. If you have to haul it out from the back of a cupboard every time you use it, it will soon fall into oblivion.

Blenders

A blender is a very useful kitchen tool and one that can frequently replace a food processor. It is perfectly adequate for making mayonnaise, can be used to purée foods (admittedly in smaller amounts than in a food processor), makes wonderful whipped drinks and even chops vegetables (place a small quantity of vegetables in the blender, cover with water, chop, then drain). Of course, there are a number of functions that a blender does not perform, but these may be tasks you will never carry out. As with a food processor, look for a solid motor. A glass container is preferable to plastic. Some blenders come with two or three small containers as well as the standard one, also very convenient. Be on the lookout for an easy-to-clean control panel. Again, make sure you have storage space on the counter if you plan to use the blender frequently.

The submersible blenders that have appeared on the market over the past few years are convenient. I have the most basic model and use it for whipping cream, puréeing soups in the pot, puréeing tomatoes and other soft vegetables and making yogurt drinks. The complex models have optional attachments that will beat dough, among other things. The submersible blender is definitely not a must-have item, but it is handy. Fairly easy to clean, it comes with a wall rack, making it easily accessible without tying up counter space.

Electric Mixers

In my mother's day, the table-model electric mixer was considered an essential kitchen tool, but I don't think this is the case any longer. I had one that never left its cupboard. A food processor, blender and hand-held mixer allow me a wider variety of options than would a table mixer alone and are better targets for financial resources.

A hand-held mixer should be sturdy and easy to clean and have several speeds. If you decide to buy the table model, let the quality of the motor be the determining factor rather than how many gizmos the machine has attached to it. Be sure that its base is sturdy – my mixer met a sudden death several years ago when it was knocked to the floor and the motor separated from every-thing else. It had been held together by a cheap, hard plastic casing that shattered on impact. Look for beaters that come in and out of the machine easily and for a machine that is simple to clean. As with food processors, it is probably wise to pay for high quality.

Ice-Cream Makers

I own an ice-cream maker and find it a wonderful tool. If you have children or are an ice-cream addict in your own right, this is something you will use year-round. With your own ice-cream machine, you can whip up tasty desserts incorporating fruit frozen the previous summer.

Pasta Makers

The difference in flavour between fresh and dried pasta is indescribable. Consequently, I use a hand-operated pasta maker frequently. It can make any kind of flat noodle, but to make tube pasta, an electric extrusion model is required. I have worked with these machines and found that, for me, they are not worth the investment, nor do I feel seriously limited by only being able to produce flat noodles. Making pasta provides an engaging social focus to meal preparation.

Coffee Grinders

An electric coffee grinder is handy in the kitchen, and not just for coffee, although it does provide wonderful freshly ground coffee beans at the drop of a hat. I do not drink coffee but use mine for grinding herbs and spices. Do not use the same grinder for both coffee and herbs, though, or the flavour of coffee will appear in the most unexpected dishes.

Mortars and Pestles

I would not give up my mortar and pestle for love nor money. They let me

Nonessentials

crush spices as I need them, and the results are fragrant and flavourful. Buy a large porcelain or clay set rather than a tiny one. A pepper mill can be used for spices in the kitchen and at the table. Look for a model that offers a variety of grinds from fine to coarse and is easy to refill.

Meat Grinders

A manually operated meat grinder is handy, not just for grinding meat but for cracking nuts and roughly crushing other hard foods as well. Probably the best way to acquire one is at a lawn sale or auction, where you may find a model of predetermined quality.

Waffle Irons

A waffle iron is a lovely luxury – some models come with a reversible surface so that the same machine can also function as a small grill. Again, you will probably be happier in the long run if you look around for an old iron. You may have to replace the electrical cord, but when you do, you will have a perfect machine that may indeed outlast and outperform any new model.

Garlic Presses

A garlic press is an item some cooks would not work without. I prefer to crush and then chop garlic with a knife. If you want a garlic press, look for one made of heavy plastic rather than aluminum and choose a model that is easy to clean. Inexpensive garlic presses fail to work with frustrating regularity and end up gathering dust in the back of a drawer.

Pastry Boards

A pastry board is important for the cook who makes pastries with any regularity. A slab of marble, which can sometimes

China cabinets are conveniently positioned near dishwasher with bar sink for rinsing

be found at a wrecker's yard, is perfect for keeping dough chilled while it is being rolled out.

Scales

Although few kitchens possess them, a set of scales can be invaluable. Some recipes provide quantities by weight only, and second-guess translations into liquid measurements – millilitres, cups or teaspoons – are not accurate. Also, if anyone in your house follows a restricted diet, being able to weigh foods is very convenient. Shop around for a sturdy (not lightweight) set of scales marked in both metric and imperial measures. Store it in a cupboard where

it will not be jostled, and check the setting each time you use it.

Pressure Cookers

Once popular kitchen gadgetry across North America, pressure cookers have, regrettably, been sent out to appliance pasture over the past 20 years. Although primitive compared with the powerful microwave, the pressure cooker still holds its own as a time-efficient device for preparing food. Air is forced out of the pot so that pressure builds up in the cooking chamber, allowing the temperature to climb as high as 250 degrees F (120 °C). Taking just a third of the time needed to boil or bake, the cooker also preserves moisture and nutritive value. Dried beans and legumes need not be soaked for hours before cooking, and fish and vegetables retain more of their original texture: the exception is meat, which tends to toughen.

Generic instructions for using a pressure cooker are hard to outline, since each model operates differently. Carefully read the instructions accompanying your cooker and follow them rigorously. Considerable pressure builds up inside the chamber, so handle the cooker carefully to avoid injury.

Everything Else

In addition to the basic pots, pans and bakeware previously described, a cook can make good use of the following:
- One 2-quart (2 L) saucepan with lid.
- One large, heavy stockpot with lid.
- One double boiler.
- One large nonstick skillet.
- One wok – a heavy stainless-steel one: the light, inexpensive models will burn foods long before they reach a temperature high enough for stir-frying.
- One roasting pan.
- One more muffin tray.
- One more cookie sheet.
- One or two springform pans – I use mine for cheesecakes and quiches. The quiche is deep, and the sides of the pan can be snapped off for an attractive presentation.
- One nonstick bundt pan.
- Two more loaf pans.
- Two 9-by-9-inch (2.5 L) square cake pans.
- Two round cake pans.
- One more deep-dish pie plate.
- Four pizza pans.
- One or two more 9-by-13-inch (3.5 L) cake pans.
- An assortment of deep, round casserole dishes with lids.
- Two more whisks – one light, one heavy.
- Two or three more wooden spoons.

The serious cook's kitchen

- Two or three pastry brushes – use different brushes for pastry, greasing pans and brushing marinade on meats.
- Rubber spatulas.
- Two or three glass measuring cups of 1- to 4-cup (250 mL to 1 L) capacity.
- One set of stacking plastic or metal measuring cups for dry measures.
- One more set of metal measuring spoons.
- More mixing bowls, including a glass one.
- Oven thermometer.
- Meat thermometer.
- Candy thermometer.
- Flour sifter – although a sieve used for nothing else works just as well.
- Pastry scraper – a square piece of metal with a wooden handle for scraping the pastry board clean after use.
- Large colander.
- Cookie cutters – it is worth buying decent ones, as they will last forever. Store in a box in a drawer or cupboard so that they will not get crushed or lost.
- Icing bags and nozzles – buy these individually rather than in a set to ensure better quality. Again, store so that they do not get dirty, crushed or lost.
- Four cooling racks.
- Vegetable steamer, preferably a bamboo one.
- Tongs.
- Corkscrew.
- Juice squeezer.

This is not a complete list, but it is enough to allow the first-time cook to set up a kitchen and to interest other cooks in experimenting with some new equipment. Temper the guidelines in this chapter with your own desires and instincts, and you will equip yourself with a kitchen that will meet your particular needs and challenges.

CHARTS & TABLES

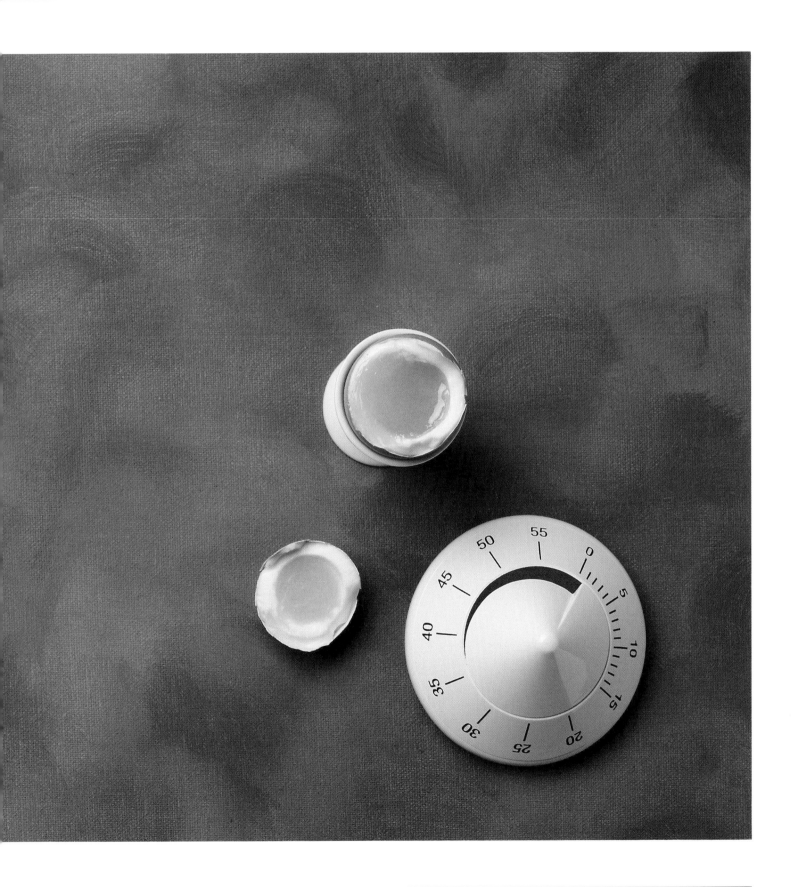

Cooking Dry Pasta

Name	Description	Al Dente Cooking Time	Uses
Bucatini	thick, spaghetti-length tubes	12 minutes	serve with rich tomato or cream sauces
Cannelloni	straight cut, plain large tubes	stuff uncooked noodles, and bake in sauce according to recipe	stuff with cooked meat, alone or in combination with cheese—ricotta, cottage or mozzarella—and chopped spinach or other leafy greens
Cappelletti	pasta stuffed with spinach and cheese	8 minutes	serve with tomato sauce
Capelli d'Angelo	fine strands, somewhat shorter than spaghetti	2 minutes	serve shaped into nests and filled with light vegetable or cream sauces
Conchiglie	large, ridged shells	10 minutes	serve with heavy sauce containing vegetable or meat chunks
Conchigliette	small, ridged shells	8 minutes	in soups, salads and with a light sauce
Farfalle	butterfly-shaped	10 minutes	toss with vinaigrette and summer vegetables
Fettuccine	¼"-wide pasta ribbons made of white durum, whole wheat or spinach flours	6 minutes	serve with seafood, heavy cream or vegetable sauces such as tomato or pesto
Fusilli	fine spiral strands	10 minutes	serve with a tomato or cream sauce, smooth or with vegetables
Lasagna	wide ribbons, fluted or plain-edged; made of white durum, spinach, whole wheat or vegetables	5 minutes (plus baking time)	bake in layered casseroles such as lasagna
Linguine	long, flattened ribbons made of white durum, egg, whole wheat or spinach	6 minutes	serve with hearty vegetable, tomato or cream sauces
Macaroni	1"-long, thick-walled, elbow-shaped tubes	8 minutes	bake in casseroles with heavy cream or cheese sauces
Manicotti	large, diagonally cut tubes with ridged exterior	stuff uncooked noodles, and bake in sauce according to recipe	stuff with cooked meat, alone or in combination with cheese—ricotta, cottage or mozzarella—and chopped spinach or other leafy greens
Orzo	rice-shaped grains	7 minutes	baked casseroles, salads and soups
Penne Rigate	2"-long, diagonally cut ridged tubes	10 minutes	serve with light tomato or vegetable sauces

Name	Description	Al Dente Cooking Time	Uses
Ravioli	meat, cheese or vegetable stuffed squares	7 minutes	top with tomato sauce and grated cheese
Rigatoni	2″-long ribbed tubes	10 minutes	great with light or chunky vegetable, meat or cream sauces
Rotini	large, spiral strands, usually white durum	8 minutes	one of the best pasta shapes for cold salad
Ruote de Carro	spoked wheels	8 minutes	serve with hearty meat and vegetable sauces or in soups and salads
Spaghetti	long, thin, round strands made of white durum, whole wheat, spinach or vegetables	10 minutes	serve with hearty meat or vegetable sauces
Spaghettini	finest of traditional spaghetti strands made of white durum, spinach or whole wheat	8 minutes	serve with garlic oil or butter and other light sauces
Tortellini	twisted crescents filled with meat, cheese or vegetables	10 minutes	serve with spicy tomato sauce
Vermicelli	very thin strands, white durum and rice flour pasta	4 minutes	toss with butter or vegetables in a light vinaigrette, add to soups, or stir-fry as crispy side dish
Ziti	long tubes	10 minutes	serve with a rich, creamy cheese sauce

Bean Cookery

Beans	Soaking Time	Simmer Time	Pressure Cooker (after soaking)	Best Use
Adzuki Beans	4 hours	1 hour	15 minutes	in Asian cuisine or cooked alone and served with rice
Black Beans (Turtle Beans)	4 hours	2 hours	15 minutes	use hot in Mexican and Latin American soups and stews or chilled in marinated vegetable salads
Black-Eyed Peas		1½ hours		with rice, in breads or mixed with steamed greens
Cannellini Beans (White Kidney Beans)	4 hours	1½ hours	15 minutes	in Italian stews made with tomatoes, herbs and chunks of spicy sausage
Chili Beans (Pink Beans)	4 hours	1 hour	20 minutes	use in refritos or in other recipes in place of pinto beans
Fava Beans (Broad Beans)	12 hours (then remove tough skins)	3 hours	40 minutes	in casseroles or baked beans, puréed or marinated and tossed in a salad
Garbanzo Beans (Chickpeas)	4 hours	2½ hours	25 minutes	purée for hummus tahini dip, add to soups and stews, chill and toss in leafy green salads, or serve alone with sweet red pepper and a vinaigrette
Great Northern Beans	4 hours	1 hour	20 minutes	use plain, in baked bean casseroles or in French cassoulet
Kidney Beans	4 hours	2 hours	20 minutes	in hearty tomato soups or stews such as chili
Lentils		½ hour		delicious in a hearty tomato-lentil soup made with pan-fried onions or added to stews made with spicy Italian sausage
Mung Beans	4 hours	1 hour		toss into vegetable or meat stir-fry dishes
Navy Beans	4 hours	2 hours	25 minutes	most common use is in baked bean casseroles; also good in soups and stews or chilled and marinated and added to salads
Pinto Beans	4 hours	1½ hours	20 minutes	used in Mexican cooking as refritos or as filling for bean enchiladas
Soybeans	12 hours	3 hours	30 minutes	used in stews
Split Peas		½ hour		used in pea soup

Grain Cookery

Grains	Description	Cooking Time	Uses
Barley	whole grains, polished barley	boil 1 part barley in 2 parts water for 45 minutes, or until soft	add to vegetable and meat soups; mix with vegetables as a side dish.
Bulgur	crushed kernels of whole wheat	cover in warm water, and soak until soft, usually a few hours	mixed with herbs and scallions as a side dish; main ingredient in tabouli salad
Cornmeal	ground corn kernels, soft yellow colour	for baking, add dry to other ingredients unless otherwise specified; for cereal, simmer 1 part cornmeal in 4 parts lightly salted water	corn bread and polenta
Millet	small tan-coloured kernels	simmer 1 part millet in 2 parts lightly salted water for 30 minutes	add to soup, serve as side dish, or chill and toss with salad greens
Oatmeal	flattened flakes of whole oat grain	use uncooked in recipe unless otherwise specified; for hot cereal, simmer 1 part oatmeal in 2 parts lightly salted water, according to time instructions on package	use in cookies, muffins, granola and porridge
Wheat Bran	tan-coloured flakes that are the outer coating of the wheat seed	need not be cooked; store in pantry	use in muffins, cookies or granola, or sprinkle on commercial cereals
Wheat Germ	embryo of the wheat kernel	can be used without cooking, but should be refrigerated	add to muffins, cookies or granola, or sprinkle over cereal or yogurt topped with fruit

Vegetable Cookery

Vegetable	Preparation	Cooking
Artichokes	Wash and trim stems; cut 1″ (2.5 cm) off top, and remove loose outer leaves, snipping any remaining leaf barbs; use lemon juice to seal cut edges.	Steam 30 to 40 minutes over boiling water, or simmer 20 to 30 minutes, or until leaves are tender and can be easily pulled from flower.
Asparagus	Thoroughly rinse with cold water to remove sand, and cut off woody portion of stem where it breaks easily; then trim spears to uniform length.	Gently tie spears together with butcher's string, and stand in a few inches of boiling water. The cooking time varies with the size of the asparagus spear. Pencil-thin spears take only a few minutes, while heavy stalks may take up to 15 minutes. Steam or sauté cut pieces for 5 to 10 minutes.
Beans, Green and Yellow	Wash and snap off ends to remove stems and strings. Cook whole or cut.	Cook only until tender but crisp. Steam or simmer for 20 minutes, or sauté 5 to 10 minutes.
Beets	Cut off root, and trim stem to 1″ (2.5 cm). Wash, but for whole beets, do not remove skin until after cooking.	Simmer whole beets 35 to 50 minutes, cool, and slip beets from skins. Sliced or diced beets should be peeled first, then simmered for 15 to 20 minutes.
Broccoli	Wash by soaking in cold, salted water for 20 to 30 minutes. Trim outer leaves and woody portion of stalks. Cook whole stalks, or break apart at stem joints into small florets.	Steam over boiling water for about 20 minutes. Simmer whole stalks in water for 10 to 15 minutes, or sauté or stir-fry florets for 5 minutes. Cook until tender but crisp.
Brussels Sprouts	Trim stems, and remove any withered leaves. Cut an X in the base of the stem to speed up cooking.	Steam whole sprouts over boiling water for 20 minutes, or simmer in water for 10 to 15 minutes, then sauté in butter.
Carrots	Wash, trim and peel. Slice large carrots into medallions, or cut into julienne strips; cook baby carrots whole.	Simmer in water 5 to 10 minutes, or steam over boiling water for 10 to 20 minutes. Sauté or stir-fry only 5 minutes. Cook until tender but still crisp.
Cauliflower	Wash by soaking in cold, salted water for 20 minutes. Remove leaves and trim woody stem. Cook whole, or divide into small florets.	Steam whole cauliflower over boiling water for 20 to 30 minutes. Steam florets for 8 to 10 minutes, or sauté or stir-fry for 5 to 7 minutes. Cook until just tender and still slightly crisp.
Corn on the Cob	Remove corn husks and silk.	Simmer in boiling water for 6 to 10 minutes, or butter, wrap in aluminum foil, and roast on the barbecue for 10 minutes.
Eggplant	Wash and trim stem ends. Slice or cut lengthwise into boats for roasting.	Rub eggplant boats with olive oil, and bake in covered pan for 30 to 50 minutes at 350 degrees F (180 °C), or until the inner membrane and skin are completely soft. Pan-fry slices in olive oil approximately 2 to 3 minutes per side.
Mushrooms	Wipe clean with a damp cloth, then dry.	Sauté whole, sliced or chopped mushrooms in melted butter for 5 to 10 minutes, or until soft.

Vegetable	Preparation	Cooking
Onions	Before cleaning, place onions in the freezer for 10 minutes. Peel skins, and remove stem ends. Cook small onions whole, and slice large ones.	Steam whole onions over boiling water for 25 to 30 minutes until completely soft. Sauté slices in oil or butter until brown, 5 to 10 minutes.
Parsnips	Wash, peel and slice into medallions or julienne strips.	Steam or simmer in boiling water for 20 to 30 minutes.
Peas	Shell and rinse peas.	Simmer 5 minutes in boiling water, or steam until just tender. Sauté in butter for 5 minutes, or add to a stir-fry for the last minute of cooking time.
Snow Peas	Remove stem and string, and rinse in cold water.	Steam over boiling water until tender but crisp, or add to a stir-fry for final minute of cooking time.
Potatoes	Peel potatoes, and if frying or boiling, remove eyes, and slice, quarter or cube. Thoroughly scrub skin before baking, and puncture.	Cook in boiling water until tender—25 to 40 minutes if whole or large pieces, 15 to 20 minutes if quartered or cubed. Bake whole at 400 degrees F (200 °C) for 50 to 60 minutes.
Sweet Potatoes or Yams	Thoroughly scrub skins before baking, trimming off any woody stems or eyes. Peel for use in casseroles or stews.	Bake at 400 degrees F (200 °C) for 50 to 70 minutes. Simmer in stew until soft.
Spinach	Trim coarse stems, and bathe leaves in sink full of warm water. Rinse a second time.	Place in large pot, and steam for 5 minutes using only the water trapped on the washed leaves. Or gently sauté in pan for 5 minutes.
Squash (Acorn, Buttercup, Butternut, Hubbard)	Wash skin, cut in half, remove seeds and membrane, and rub with butter. For boiling, peel and cube.	Bake squash halves, cut side down, in a baking pan with ½ inch (1.25 cm) of water for 45 to 75 minutes, or until tender. Steam pieces over boiling water for 35 minutes, or boil for 10 to 15 minutes, or until they are soft.
Tomatoes	Wash skin, trim stem off, and remove core.	Place whole tomatoes in baking pan with ¼ inch (6 mm) of water, and place under broiler for 5 to 10 minutes, or until soft.
Turnips	Quarter turnip, peel pieces, then cube or slice.	Cook until tender in boiling water for 15 to 20 minutes, or steam for 25 to 30 minutes.
Zucchini	Wash skins, trim stem off, and slice.	Sauté in butter for 3 to 5 minutes, or until tender but firm.

Not all vegetables are created equal, and justice will be served only by finding the right cooking method for each variety. Minimum cooking time is perhaps the only rule of thumb, resulting in tender but not overcooked vegetables that still retain both flavour and nutrients. The size and shape of vegetables before preparation will determine the total cooking time, so keep in mind that these are only suggestions and periodically check the vegetables as they cook.

Making Use of Herbs & Spices

Name	Uses	Name	Uses
Allspice	From sweet baked goods to savoury pickles and chutneys, any dish that needs a mildly spicy flavour will benefit from allspice. Delicious in spice cakes and cookies, fruit pies, barbecue and chili sauces or a simmering beef brisket.	**Cayenne**	Add ground cayenne to any egg dish or cheese dip. A must for shrimps fried in olive oil with garlic and scallions.
Anise	Add fresh anise leaves to vegetable and fruit salads. Bake ground anise seeds in cookies, breads and cakes, sauté the seeds with scallops, or add them to a herb mix for a pizza topping.	**Celery Seed**	Add whole dry celery seeds to sauces, salad dressings, mixed vegetable salads and cold, creamy salads such as potato, cole slaw and marinated red cabbage. A pinch of ground celery seed or a few whole ones can also be added to most stocks, soups and court bouillons.
Basil	Dried or fresh, basil can be added to olive oil and red-wine vinegar salad dressings or to melted butter sauces used to dress baked fish, and it is a must in every Italian recipe made with a tomato sauce. Pesto for hot buttered pasta or boiled new potatoes is traditionally made using fresh, ground basil leaves.	**Chervil**	Add chopped, fresh chervil leaves to green salads and to melted butter for steamed vegetables or grilled steak, or sprinkle over glazed baby carrots or broiled tomatoes. Combine it with other herbs in egg dishes such as quiche or in herbed cheese spreads.
Bay	Add a fresh or dry bay leaf to almost any cooking liquid: poaching water for fish, marinades, vegetables, poultry, meat stews and soups. Cooked custards and rice puddings will also absorb the faint cinnamon flavour of the bay leaf.	**Chives**	Add chopped, fresh chives to cream sauces and soups, spreads and dips made with yogurt or cheese, herbed butter, eggs, potatoes, bulgur or any leafy green salad.
Bergamot	Add fresh, chopped bergamot to leafy green and fresh fruit salads, mint and pepper jellies, curries and uncooked tomato salsas.	**Cilantro**	See Coriander.
		Cinnamon	Add ground cinnamon to desserts, cakes, pastries and cookies and to anything made with apples. Simmer in Middle Eastern lamb casseroles, add to chicken stewed with tomatoes and onions, or simply sprinkle on top of baked sweet potatoes, squash and cooked carrots.
Borage	Only fresh borage leaves should be used in cooking, in green and fruit salads, as a seasoning in white sauces for chicken or fish and in pea and bean soups. Young borage leaves can be steamed and cooked as a vegetable side dish.		
Caraway	Fresh caraway root can be boiled, buttered and eaten as a vegetable, and the leaves can be added to soups and stews. Season cheese spreads, bread, cabbage salad and sauerbraten with caraway seeds, or crush them and toss with hot, buttery potatoes, shredded and steamed white cabbage, sliced beets or carrots and mashed turnip.	**Cloves**	Season ham by decorating the rind with whole cloves during baking; add to curries, marinades or chutneys. Use ground cloves in gingerbread, ginger snaps, spice cakes, cookies and pumpkin pies and to season boiled and mashed root vegetables, such as carrots or sweet potatoes.
Cardamom	Use freshly crushed cardamom seeds in spice cakes, fruit bread and pumpkin and apple pie. Put some in curries, or blend them with mashed sweet potatoes.	**Coriander**	Use the whole seeds in marinades and pickles. Add finely ground coriander seeds to curries, and use in baking. The fresh leaves are known as cilantro and are a staple seasoning in Mexican, Asian and South American cuisine. Add chopped cilantro to salsa, guacamole or the shredded lettuce used to garnish a taco or fajita, or include in a marinated onion salad that accompanies a spicy curry.

Name	Uses	Name	Uses
Cumin	Ground cumin is an important addition to Mexican salsa, chili, refritos and seasoned ground beef for tacos, enchiladas and burritos. Most Indian vegetable dishes, such as cauliflower, and potato and meat curries require cumin, and it is a surprisingly delicious addition to spicy yogurt dips for raw vegetables.	Garlic	If you enjoy garlic, you probably know instinctively when to add it to a dish. But for those who still do not know the pleasures that fresh crushed garlic can bring, here is a list of its uses, both raw and cooked: Add chopped raw garlic to vinaigrettes and marinades, to yogurt-and-cucumber tzatsiki, to mayonnaise for a raw vegetable dip, to cold potato purée, to parsleyed butter for seafood, or mix it with butter, spread on bread and broil. Roasted garlic can be spread on crusty white bread, and sautéed garlic can be added to almost any Italian tomato sauce, Mexican dish, Indian curry, Mediterranean stew or Chinese stir-fry.
Dandelion	Make a tossed salad from dandelion leaves, add them to green salads, or sauté with butter.		
Dill	Use dill seed for pickles, seasoned vinegars and salad dressing. It is also a delicious flavouring for poached white fish, creamy vegetable soups and cheese sauce. Add fresh dill leaves to mayonnaise accompanying chilled fish, to yogurt dressing for a creamy cucumber or potato salad or to a herb mixture in a cream cheese spread. Sprinkle chopped, fresh dill over boiled and buttered new potatoes or carrots. Fresh dill leaves also make a great alternative to basil in pesto sauce.	Ginger	Use dry, ground ginger in spice cakes and cookies, in meat and chicken marinades and as a seasoning in Chinese stir-fries. Peeled, sliced gingerroot can be rubbed over a breast of chicken or a fillet of white fish before broiling. Also, try stirring slivers of crystallized ginger in with melon balls, or chill the balls for a few hours in a marinade of ginger and lemon juice.
Fennel	Fennel leaves lose their flavour in the drying process, so use only the fresh form in cooking. Add it to the poaching water for fish, or place it directly in the cleaned middle section of a whole baking fish. Mince the leaves into green salads, and add to butter sauces used to dress cooked vegetables, especially boiled new potatoes, and meat. Fennel seeds are also good in any tomato-based pizza and pasta sauces.	**Horseradish**	Use horseradish sauce as a condiment for grilled steak or roast beef, or mix it with tomato paste and serve with a grilled-cheese sandwich. Add it to the dressing for a pasta or potato salad, or mix it with sliced red radishes for a side salad. Try flavouring a Bloody Mary with only lemon juice and horseradish instead of the traditional mixture of Worcestershire sauce, hot pepper and celery salt.
Fenugreek	Add dry, crushed seeds of fenugreek to curry powder or paste. Roast the seeds slightly before you crush them.	Lovage	Use lovage leaves as a celery substitute in vegetable soups, salads and meat stews, but add it sparingly. The stalks can be steamed and eaten as a vegetable.
Five-Spice Powder	Add five-spice powder to marinades for tofu, chicken and meat used in stir-fries. It gives a subtle spicy flavour to Asian-style dressings, such as hot peanut sauce, that are used in meat dishes, steamed greens and stir-fried vegetables.	**Mace**	Add ground mace when cooking such fruit fillings as plum, peach and apple. It is also good in spice cakes and cookies.
Garam Masala	Garam masala, with its exotic taste and aroma, is most commonly found in Indian curries, but try combining it with olive oil for a fragrant sauce for both marinating and barbecuing boneless chicken breasts.	**Marjoram**	Fresh sweet marjoram has a perfumy aroma that is delicious in homemade sausages, meatloaf and rice-and-meat fillings for green peppers or zucchini stewed in tomato juice. Use marjoram in poultry stuffing and in herb mixtures.

Making Use of Herbs & Spices

Name	Uses	Name	Uses
Mint	Add fresh mint leaves to fruit salads and desserts. Use chopped leaves in soups and leafy green or grain salads. Grind fresh mint leaves with a splash of tarragon vinegar to serve as a chutney with grilled or roasted lamb.	**Saffron**	Add the whole dry thread of saffron to creamy seafood recipes, paella, couscous and, for both flavour and colour, to white rice.
Mustard	Roast and crush mustard seeds, and use in sauces for dressing pork roasts or grilled chops, or add to a bit of seasoned vinegar to make a thick, spicy marinade for a chicken brochette. Whole mustard seeds are often added to pickling brine, and a few tossed into a pan of frying potatoes make a delicious treat.	**Sage**	Sage can be the main flavouring in bread stuffing for pork and poultry, but also rub the dried herb on pork, or stuff a duckling with whole fresh leaves before roasting. Use the fresh leaves sparingly in salads, sprinkle on meat stews and soups, and chop them for cream cheese dips.
Nutmeg	Add ground nutmeg to custards, eggnog and cream sauces. It enhances spinach, broccoli or cauliflower soups and mushrooms sautéed with garlic and a splash of sherry.	**Savory**	Nearly all meat and fish stews, eggs, bean soups and casseroles, especially green pea and lentil, benefit from the addition of savory. Add fresh, minced leaves to summer salads made from garden-fresh yellow and green beans, and toss in a light vinaigrette. Dry savory is an excellent substitute for oregano and basil in rich pizza, pasta and cheese sauces.
Oregano	An essential herb in Italian, Greek and Mexican cooking, oregano can flavour poached fish and is good sprinkled on broiling chicken breasts with a little lemon juice or mixed with ground beef destined for hamburger patties, meatloaf or chili. Add oregano to salad dressings and any kind of cooked tomato—whether in a sauce or quickly heated under the broiler.	**Star Anise**	For both fragrance and flavour, add star anise to meat or vegetable stir-fries.
		Tamarind	Add small amounts of tamarind pulp to stews and soups for a sour citrus flavour.
Paprika	Use paprika in raw-vegetable dips and in creamy dressings for potato, cabbage or pasta salads. It is a key ingredient in goulash, paprikash and other spicy stews and hearty soups. Sprinkle a little over devilled eggs.	**Tarragon**	Make a delicious vinaigrette for a summer tomato salad with red-wine vinegar and tarragon as the principal herb. Add fresh leaves to butter sauces for such steamed vegetables as artichokes, broccoli, cauliflower, new potatoes and green beans. Tarragon is good in yogurt sauces for a creamy chicken-tarragon casserole or a yogurt-mayonnaise dressing for summer salads. Rub fresh tarragon leaves on pork or chicken before roasting.
Parsley	Add minced fresh parsley leaves to all leafy green salads, coleslaws, potato salads, homemade soups and cream sauces. Parsley combined with melted butter is a delicious topping for most hard vegetables, such as carrots or potatoes, and a must for seafood. It is wonderful battered and deep-fried, is a key ingredient in tabouli and is good in pesto.	**Thyme**	A classic addition to poultry stuffing and bouquets garnis for soups and stews and a companion herb for basil and oregano.
Rosemary	Use fresh or dry with grilled lamb or chicken. Sautéed mushrooms, fried potatoes and poultry stuffing all benefit from this aromatic herb.	**Turmeric**	Dry, ground turmeric is an essential ingredient in mustard pickles, savoury relishes and Indian curry powders and pastes.

Substitutions

Ingredient	Amount	Substitutions
Baking Chocolate	1 oz. or 1 square (30 g)	• 3 Tbsp. (45 mL) cocoa powder plus 1 Tbsp. (15 mL) butter or margarine • 3 Tbsp. (45 mL) carob powder plus 2 Tbsp. (30 mL) water
Baking Powder (single-acting)	1 tsp. (5 mL)	• ⅓ tsp. (2 mL) baking soda plus ½ tsp. (2 mL) cream of tartar • ¼ tsp. (1 mL) baking soda plus ½ cup (125 mL) buttermilk or yogurt
Baking Powder (double-acting)	1 tsp. (5 mL)	• 1½ tsp. (7 mL) phosphate or tartrate
Butter	1 cup (250 mL)	• 1 cup (250 mL) margarine • ¾ cup (175 mL) chicken fat, clarified • ⅞ cup (225 mL) vegetable (nut, cottonseed, corn) oil
Corn Syrup	1 cup (250 mL)	• 1 cup (250 mL) granulated sugar plus ¼ cup (50 mL) liquid
Cream, Sour	1 cup (250 mL)	• 3 Tbsp. (45 mL) butter plus ⅞ cup (225 mL) sour milk • 1 cup (250 mL) plain yogurt
Cream, Whipping	1 cup (250 mL)	• ¾ cup (175 mL) milk plus ⅓ cup (75 mL) butter
Honey	1 cup (250 mL)	• 1¼ cups (300 mL) granulated sugar plus ¼ cup (50 mL) liquid
Lemon Juice	1 tsp. (5 mL)	• ½ tsp. (2 mL) vinegar
Sugar, Brown	1 cup (250 mL)	• ½ cup (125 mL) granulated sugar plus 2 Tbsp. (30 mL) molasses
Sugar, Granulated	1 cup (250 mL)	• 2 cups (500 mL) sifted powdered sugar • 1 cup (250 mL) packed brown sugar • ¾ cup (175 mL) honey, and reduce liquid by ¼ cup (50 mL) • 1¼ cups (300 mL) molasses, and reduce liquid by ¼ cup (50 mL)
Yeast	1 package active dry yeast	• 1 cake compressed yeast
Yogurt	1 cup (250 mL)	• 1 cup (250 mL) buttermilk

Food Storage

Pantry

Times apply to unopened packages, unless otherwise specified.

Cereal Grains
Store in airtight containers away from heat and light.

Bread crumbs, dry	3 months
Cereals, ready-to-eat	8 months
Cornmeal	6-8 months
Flour, white	2 years
Flour, whole wheat	6 weeks
Granola	6 months
Oats, rolled	6-10 months
Pasta	several years
Rice	several years

Dry Foods
Store in airtight containers away from heat and light.

Baking powder	1 year
Baking soda	1 year
Beans, dry	1 year
Chocolate, baking	7 months
Cocoa	10-12 months
Coffee, ground	1 month
Fruit, dried	1 year
Skim milk powder	1 year
opened	1 month
Sugar, all types	several years
Tea bags	1 year

Miscellaneous Foods

Honey	18 months
Jams, jellies (once opened, store covered in refrigerator)	1 year
Nuts	1 month
Peanut butter	6 months
opened	2 months
Salad dressings	8 months
opened (store covered in refrigerator)	1½-2 months
Syrups: maple, corn, table (once opened, store covered in refrigerator)	1 year
Vegetable oils (once opened, store covered in refrigerator)	1 year
Yeast, baking (dry)	1 year

Refrigerator (39°F, 4°C)

Cover all foods unless otherwise specified.

Dairy Products and Fats

Butter	
unopened	2 weeks
opened	1 week
Cheese	
cottage	
unopened	check "best before" date
opened	3 days
firm	several months
processed	
unopened	several months
opened	3-4 weeks
Margarine	
unopened	8 months
opened	1 month
Milk, cream, yogurt	
unopened	check "best before" date
opened	3 days

Fish and Shellfish

Fish, cleaned	
raw	3-4 days
cooked	1-2 days
Crab, clams, lobster, mussels (live)	12-24 hours
Oysters (live)	several weeks
Scallops, shrimp (fresh)	1-2 days
Shellfish, cooked	1-2 days

Meat, Poultry, Eggs
Uncooked:

Eggs	3 weeks
Ground meat	1-2 days
Poultry	2-3 days
Roasts	3-4 days
Steaks and chops	2-3 days

Cooked:

All meats and poultry	3-4 days
Casseroles, meat pies	2-3 days

Miscellaneous Foods

Coffee, ground	2 months
Flour, whole wheat	3 months
Nuts	4 months

Freezer (-4°F, -18°C)

Use freezer wrapping or airtight containers.

Dairy Products and Fats

Butter	
salted	1 year
unsalted	3 months
Cheese, firm and processed	3 months
Margarine	6 months
Milk	6 weeks

Fish and Shellfish

Fish, fat species: salmon, mackerel, lake trout	2 months
Fish, lean species: cod, haddock, pike, smelt	6 months
Shellfish	2-4 months

Fruits and Vegetables — 1 year

Meat, Poultry, Eggs
Uncooked:

Beef roasts and steaks	10-12 months
Chicken and turkey	
cut up	6 months
whole	1 year
Duck, goose	3 months
Ground meat	2-3 months
Lamb and pork	8-10 months
Sausages, wieners	2-3 months
Veal, chops and roasts	4-5 months

Cooked:

All meat	2-3 months
All poultry	1-3 months
Casseroles, meat pies	3 months

Miscellaneous Foods

Breads, yeast, baked or unbaked	1 month
Cakes, cookies, baked	4 months
Herbs	1 year
Pastries, quick breads, baked	1 month
Pastry, unbaked	2 months
Pie, fruit, unbaked	6 months
Soups, stock or cream	4 months

Adapted from the Ministry of Agriculture and Food's Food Handler's Storage Guide.

Bakeware Glossary

Bakeware	Imperial Dimensions	Imperial Volume	Metric Dimensions	Metric Volume
Baking Dishes	11 x 7 x 1½ inches	8 cups	12 x 18 x 4 cm	2 L
	12 x 8 x 1¾ inches	12 cups	30 x 20 x 4.5 cm	3 L
	13 x 9 x 2 inches	14 cups	33 x 23 x 5 cm	3.5 L
Bundt Pan	10 x 3¾ inches	12 cups	25 x 9.5 cm	3L
Cake Pans, Round Layer	8 x 1½ inches	5 cups	20 x 4 cm	1.2 L
	9 x 1³/₈ inches	6 cups	22 x 3.5 cm	1.5 L
Cake Pans, Square	8 x 8 x 2 inches	8 cups	20 x 20 x 5 cm	2 L
	9 x 9 x 1¾ inches	10 cups	23 x 23 x 4.5 cm	2.5 L
Flan Pans	8 x 1½ inches	3 cups	20 x 4 cm	750 mL
	9 x 1½ inches	4 cups	23 x 4 cm	1 L
	10 x 1¾ inches	6 cups	25 x 4.5 cm	1.5 L
Fruitcake Pans, Square	6 x 6 x 3 inches	8 cups	15 x 15 x 8 cm	2 L
	7 x 7 x 3 inches	10 cups	18 x 18 x 8 cm	2.5 L
	8 x 8 x 3 inches	12 cups	20 x 20 x 8 cm	3 L
Jelly-Roll Pans	15½ x 10½ x ¾ inches	8 cups	39 x 27 x 2 cm	2 L
	17½ x 11½ x ¾ inches	12 cups	45 x 29 x 2 cm	3 L
Loaf Pans	8½ x 4½ x 2½ inches	6 cups	22 x 11 x 6 cm	1.5 L
	9 x 5 x 2½ inches	8 cups	23 x 13 x 6 cm	2 L
Muffin Cups	2¾ x 1 inches	⅓ cup	7 x 2.5 cm	75 mL
	2¾ x 1¼ inches	½ cup	7 x 3.2 cm	125 mL
Pie Plates	8 x 1½ inches	3 cups	20 x 4 cm	750 mL
	9 x 1½ inches	4 cups	23 x 4 cm	1 L
	10 x 1¾ inches	6 cups	25 x 4.5 cm	1.5 L
Ring Moulds	8½ x 1¾ inches	4 cups	22 x 4.5 cm	1 L
	9½ x 2 inches	6 cups	24 x 5 cm	1.5 L
Soufflé Dishes	7 x 3 inches	6 cups	18 x 8 cm	1.5 L
	8 x 3¾ inches	10 cups	20 x 9.5 cm	2.5 L
Springform Pans	8 x 2½ inches	8 cups	20 x 6 cm	2 L
	9 x 2½ inches	10 cups	23 x 6 cm	2.5 L
	10 x 2½ inches	12 cups	25 x 6 cm	3 L
Tube Pans	9 x 4 inches	12 cups	23 x 10 cm	3 L
	10 x 4½ inches	16 cups	25 x 11 cm	4L

Index

Index

Index

Credits

Photographs

All photographs by Ernie Sparks, with the exception of those listed below.

P.108 Brian Vanden Brink; Designer, Robert Currie. P.109 Karen Bussolini; Designer, Signature Kitchen and Bath. P.110 Brian Vanden Brink; Architects, Steven Foote, Perry Dean Rogers and Partners. P.112 Brian Vanden Brink; Architect, Phil Kelley. P.113 Brian Vanden Brink; Architects, Reed & Barba. P.116 Karen Bussolini; Architect, Andrew Robinson. P.117 Brian Vanden Brink; Architect, Jack Silverio. P.118 Brian Vanden Brink; Architects, Reed & Barba; Designer, Daniel Roux. P.120 Brian Vanden Brink; Designer, Lou Eckus. P.121 Brian Vanden Brink; Designers, Early New England Restorations.

Props

The success of the photographs in this book is due in large part to the generosity of the craftspeople and local merchants who loaned us props.

P.11 colander: Staples, Newburgh, Ont.; p.17 canisters and spice jars: Kitchen Cargo, Kingston, Ont.; p.26 all pottery: Andrea Pillar, Oakville, Ont.; p.32 plates: Wilton Pottery, Wilton, Ont.; p.38 cake plate: Anna Elmberg Wright, Landfall Studio, Bath, Ont.; p.41 glass plate: Mary Alton, Toronto, Ont.; p.42 plates: Wilton Pottery, Wilton, Ont.; p.44 all glassware: Cactus Trading Company, Kingston, Ont.; p.48 wooden bowl: Don Stinson, Tamworth, Ont.; p.63 casserole: Anna Elmberg Wright, Landfall Studio, Bath, Ont.; p.67 glassware: Mollieglass, Battersea, Ont. and Cornerstone, Kingston, Ont.; p.71 wooden bowls: Don Stinson, Tamworth, Ont.; p.84 & 87 mixing bowl: Wilton Pottery, Wilton, Ont.; p.93 bowls: Wilton Pottery, Wilton, Ont.; p.94 cake plate: Anna Elmberg Wright, Landfall Studio, Bath, Ont.; p.115 knives: Junors – The Kitchen Collection, Kingston, Ont.; p.123 timer: Junors – The Kitchen Collection, Kingston, Ont.

Thank You

We wish to express our thanks to the following for their assistance:

Sam Anderson, Susan Dickinson, Anne Fisher, Pat Garrod, Wayne Grady, Maya Jagger, Andrew McLachlan, Shirley Menyes and Marta Scythes, as well as the Block and Cleaver Ltd., Murphy's Seafood, Health and Welfare Canada, Ontario Egg Producers Marketing Board and the Ontario Ministry of Agriculture and Food.